Moral

Instruction

and

Fiction

✳   ✳   ✳   ✳

for

Children,

1749–1820

The

University

of Georgia

Press

*

Athens

and

London

Samuel F. Pickering, Jr.

Moral

Instruction

and

Fiction

for

hildren,

1749–1820

© 1993 by the University
of Georgia Press
Athens, Georgia 30602
Designed by Richard Hendel
Set in 10/14 Linotype Walbaum
by Tseng Information Systems
Printed and bound by
Thomson-Shore Inc.
The paper in this book meets the
guidelines for permanence and
durability of the Committee on
Production Guidelines for Book
Longevity of the Council on Library
Resources.
Printed in the United States of
America
97 96 95 94 93   C   5 4 3 2 1

The author and publisher gratefully
acknowledge the following
publications in which portions of
this book first appeared: *AB
Bookman's Weekly*, *Journal of
Narrative Technique*, and *Psychiatry
and the Humanities*.

Library of Congress Cataloging in
Publication Data
Pickering, Samuel F., 1941–
    Moral instruction and fiction for
children, 1749–1820 / Samuel F.
Pickering, Jr.
    p. cm.
    Includes bibliographical
references (p.) and index. k
    ISBN 0-8203-1463-3 (alk. paper)
    1. Children's stories, English—
History and criticism.
2. Children—England—Books and
reading—History—18th century.
3. Children—England—Books and
reading—History—19th century.
4. English fiction—18th century—
History and criticism. 5. English
fiction—19th century—History and
criticism. 6. Didactic fiction,
English—History and criticism.
7. Children—England—Conduct of
life—History. 8. Ethics in
literature. I. Title.
PR858.C513P5 1993
823'.6099282—dc20 92-6567
                                    CIP
British Library Cataloging in
Publication Data available

Contents

✻   ✻   ✻   ✻

Preface

❋   ❋   ❋   ❋   ❋

 ehind this book lies my earlier study *John Locke and Children's Books in Eighteenth-Century England* (1981). Locke was the century's man for most educational ideas, providing it with a basis for the science of human development and an explanation of the formative influence of childhood education. More than those of any other philosopher Locke's ideas influenced early children's books. In this work, I assume the importance and presence of Locke and read children's fiction almost as educational texts.

Early children's fiction was rigorously instructive. Although the narratives were often wonderfully entertaining and imaginative, they rarely presented complex views of human nature. Written to influence behavior, and to sell, the books avoided confusing complexity. Choosing between good and evil was simple, and although characters erred for the sake of story, tales were not liable to lead readers astray. For the critic eager to discover subtlety, the books present a problem: how to write about simple stories and not appear simpleminded. For many straightforward texts, critics have created artistic interpretations. Such a thing could be done for early children's fiction. I, however, have not done it. Instead, I give lengthy excerpts from the books themselves. Readers, I hope, will turn from this study, not marveling at a Jamesian figure hidden in the carpet of children's books, but with a knowledge of the carpet itself, its texture and colors, perhaps even a sense of its place in the House of Fiction.

Although writers in the eighteenth century were certain childhood reading influenced development, I suspect claims about the effects of reading. If literature does influence behavior and shape the future adult, it does so in mysterious ways. Despite authors' intentions, most books have the potential for bundles of messages, and what an individual child took away from even the simplest tale, if anything lasting, is probably unknowable. For my part I suspect that each child decoded or fashioned a message or group of messages particular to his or her own mood, experience, or even the time of day the story was read. In any case certainty about the effects of reading almost inevitably leads to moral or political judgments and is often the enemy of thought and enjoyment. Consequently I have concluded little about fiction's effects upon young readers. Instead I have focused on the clearer matter of the book and have tried to reach conclusions about narrative practice and authorial intention.

Children's literature is often divided into books which teach lessons and which appeal to the imagination. "But we possess at least two complementary, and potentially conflicting, ways of knowing," Geoffrey Summerfield wrote in *Fantasy and Reason: Children's Literature in the Eighteenth Century*; "one is the poetic, metaphorical, animistic, even magical—the 'useless'—way. The other is the empirical, scientific—the 'useful'—way." [1] Aligned on one side, that which embodies, as Dickens labeled it, the wisdom of the heart, are Wordsworth, fairy tales, and Dickens himself. On the other side, the wisdom of the head, lurk lesser figures like Sarah Trimmer and Hannah More. While the wisdom of the head, so the argument usually runs, smothers the imagination and mutilates the natural, the wisdom of the heart nurtures and heals.

The problem with this division is that it is too simple. Although much early fiction warned children against the dangers of the imagination, it did so in imaginative stories. In the wanderings of their plots, these stories often led children across marvelously drawn landscapes, woods and meadows which may have delighted readers as much as or more than fairyland.

What follows in this study is, I suppose, a covert celebration of imaginative instruction. Seven chapters compose the book. In the first I discuss allegory and the eastern tale. For a while allegory was widespread. Associated with evangelical Christianity and the other world, its popularity declined at the end of the century. The devices of allegorical tales did not vanish, however. They were used as vehicles of instruction in both eastern tales and school stories. In the second chapter I focus on school stories. The third and fifth chapters discuss *Robinson Crusoe* and *Pamela*, adaptations of which were popular in children's books. In the fourth chapter I examine the foundling, showing how disadvantages were often seen as advantages. My sixth chapter focuses on servants. Throughout the study I discuss lessons which appeared in fiction for children. In the last chapter I concentrate on honesty. Finally the book includes an appendix in which I discuss the use children's fiction made of traditional Christian emblems.

Most early American children's books were reprints of British books and did not alter the lessons conveyed. Thus while Master Friendly was "a Parliament-Man" in Newbery and Carnan's *Nurse Truelove's Christmas-Box* (c. 1770), in Isaiah Thomas's version, published in Worcester, Massachusetts, in 1789, he became a "Congress man."[2] Because British and American editions were so similar, I have used them interchangeably, noting the publication date of the edition used in parentheses. I begin my study in 1749, the year Sarah Fielding's *The Governess* was published. I end it in 1820 although I occasionally stretch this last date to accommodate particularly winning quotations. By confining myself to writing before 1820 I try to give the study focus.

Lastly, reading for this book was fun. Pruy Savoury was so "gluttonous," the author of *The Juvenile Story-Teller* (1805) wrote, that her nose "was ever in the cupboard, and her finger as constantly in the sugar-bowl." One day Mrs. Savoury gave a dinner party to which she invited a company picked for "elegance of manners and propriety of behaviour." Beforehand she prepared a magnificent dessert, "consisting of a variety of the choicest sweetmeats, and of fruits of the richest flavour to the taste, and of the greatest beauty to the eye." When Mrs. Savoury finished the dessert, the butler put it in his pantry. Unfortunately he forgot to lock the pantry door, and "this occasioned a temptation to Miss Pruy which her voracity could not surmount. Here went her fingers into one dish, pop went they straight into another, ice-creams, currant-jellies, cheese-cakes, gooseberry tarts, all went hickeldy-pickeldy into the devouring tomb of her stomach, and left behind them such havoc and devastation as have never been witnessed since the creation of confectioner's shops."[3]

Taste varies. For those who find my penchant for sweets unappealing, the library door remains unlocked, the books choice and unspoiled. I hope that after closing this study, students will rummage the shelves for fiber and bone, gristle and sinew.

1

❋ ❋ ❋ ❋ ❋

Allegory and

Eastern Tale

n 1800 Mary Burges lamented the declin-
ing popularity of John Bunyan's *Pilgrim's
Progress* (1678). "The pilgrim CHRISTIAN,"
she wrote, "was the companion of our
childhood, till the refinements of modern
education banished him from our nurseries." As prosperity enlarged the middle classes in the eighteenth century, parents,
nurtured on Locke's ideas, envisioned both secular and religious
futures for children. As a result, books which fostered moral and
worldly success became popular while godly books lost much of
their appeal. Although middle-class parents still saw children as
pilgrims who needed close guidance, the notion of a progress
had been secularized. In *The Lilliputian Auction* (1802), Charly
Chatter sold "one of the most curious Things ever invented,"
a watch which "instead of twenty four hours gives twenty four

Rules for the Conduct of human Life." Each rule was associated with a letter of the alphabet and proferred moral or practical advice. Thus, *D* urged "Diligently pass the Day" while *P* taught "Praise the merit of a Foe." The watch was bought by Master Paul Pilgrim, not Bunyan's Christian laboring toward the Celestial City, but a child of this world who in making his progress toward becoming an adult learned to live both morally and intelligently.

Most successful characters in eighteenth-century fiction for children were virtuous and educated. In *The Twelfth-Day Gift* (1767) members of the Bettering Society purchased ledgers in which they kept two accounts, the first being "a moral Reckoning, or an Account of their Good and bad Actions, which tend to make them good Citizens; and the other a Cash Account, or a Diary of their Expenses, which tend to make them good Oeconomists." Not simply the members of the Bettering Society but all children could purchase the helpful ledgers. Sometime after 1765 John Newbery published *The Important Pocket Book*, an account book in diary form in which children could detail their daily activities. While the left-hand page provided space for entries referring to money matters, the right, labeled "The Moral Account," had columns headed "Good" and "Bad." [1]

Although the emphasis placed upon success in this life undermined the popularity of *The Pilgrim's Progress*, allegory itself was a staple of early children's books. In *The Lounger* (1785) Henry MacKenzie discussed the danger of reading novels. Particularly dangerous to youth, he warned, was "that character of mingled virtue and vice which is to be found in some of the best of our Novels." It was dangerous, MacKenzie wrote, "to bring us into the society of Vice, though introduced or accompanied by Virtue. In the application to ourselves, in which the moral tendency of all imaginary characters must be supposed to consist, this nourishes and supports a very common kind of self-deception, by which men are apt to balance their faults by the consideration of their good qualities." Although children's books often depicted the reformation of bad children and the corruption of good children, few rounded characters of "mingled virtue and vice" appeared. The overwhelming majority of characters were flat allegorical representations of either virtue or vice. In *The History of Tommy Playlove and Jacky Lovebook* (1793), for example, among Tommy's bad companions were Bobby Wilful, Bobby Scapegrace, and Ned Slippery while Peter Pippin's friends in *The History of Little King Pippin* (1814) included Billy Meanwell, Sammy Sober, Bobby Bright, and Tommy Telltruth.[2]

In children's books allegory was used in different ways. Often it provided the structure for a simple moral tale. In *The Caterpillars and the Gooseberry Bush* (1802), Samuel's father, "a venerable clergyman," explained to his son that the caterpillars eating the bush were "*figures* of those more terrible caterpillars, which may devour you"—"your own *bad passions, corrupt tempers* and *inclinations.*" Worried that his son would not only be led astray by but be satisfied with the surface of worldly existence, Samuel's father urged him to "see with better eyes," preaching that "when you behold either animals or plants, or any other parts of the visible creation, you will not be content with only looking on their outward forms." Instead Samuel should, his father said, "consider, diligently and attentively, what they are *within*, and what their outward forms thus speak to you in the *language of figure.*" So long as this figurative language was clear, there was little criticism of it. The danger, however, was that children would be so attracted by the surface of allegory that they would miss the lessons conveyed. Thus, although the compiler of *A New Hieroglyphic Bible* (c. 1796) declared that his object was "to imprint on the memory of Youth, by lively and sensible images, the sacred and important truths of Holy Writ," Sarah Trimmer attacked the work in the *Guardian of Education* (1802). Using pictures in place of words, the book, she wrote, was "too *abstruse* and too *mysterious* for children to comprehend."[3]

Unlike the emblems in *A New Hieroglyphic Bible*, most allegory in early children's fiction was clear and clearly instructive. In *The Selector: Being a New and Chaste Collection of Visions, Tales, and Allegories* (1797) appeared "The Mount of Fortune," a story which began like *The Pilgrim's Progress* with the narrator falling asleep and dreaming. In the dream the narrator found himself atop a flowery green hill called the Mount of Fortune. Obscured by "a vast desert of cloudiness" the world stretched down the slope beneath him. From under the cloud a thousand roads climbed up toward the summit, their ways "intricate and mazy." "A mixed multitude of both sexes, and of all ages and conditions" poured out of the roads and hurried to Mend-all Market built on a plain at the center of the mount. The market resembled a fair with trumpeters, jugglers, ropedancers, merry-andrews, opera makers, and "tumult makers" confusing people and making their heads ache. At the center of the market was a "kind of may-pole"; heaped about it were piles of commodities to be bartered. Like Christian at the cross, people who attended the market "were allowed the happy privilege" of laying down their burdens and taking up "lighter in the room of them." In front of each pile stood an alabaster pillar; on it hung a picture "filled with figures, all in motion, representing whatever was most tempting and desirable in the merchandise it recommended." Before each pillar was an ebony chair, on both sides of which stood beautiful women, "dressed like muses and graces; some inviting passengers to take possession of the empty seat; others pointing up to a compartment on the top of it, where were to be read, in golden letters, the name and quality of the merchandise." Unfortunately, as soon as a person sat down, the appealing scene was transformed, and the picture on the alabaster pole became "horrible" while the muses and graces turned into serpents and satyrs that hissed and grinned.[4]

The narrator and his companion Miss Frolic stopped before the Column of Beauty. Through the picture attached to the column moved "a mixed and confused bustle of coaches, footmen, and cornets: men with their hearts in their hands; and an indistinct cavalcade of shapeless things without heads, called smiles, sighs, vows, desires, faintings, languishments, and adorations." As they looked at the picture "a fat but sprightly young woman" hurried up and putting a bundle down began to sort through her wares in order to barter. In the bundle were "thick legs, red hair, brown skin, and small-pock marks in abundance." After the attendants agreed to accept the woman's goods in exchange for beauty, but before she sat in the ebony chair, the narrator flipped the picture over, exposing the reverse side. Consisting "of scandal, spleen, jealousy, anguish, perjury, and ruin," that side showed what the woman would receive along with beauty in the trade. "No sooner" did she see "the faces of this ugly set of monsters, than, snatching up her bundle, she ran as fast as her thick legs could carry her, tumbling, head over heels, at every heap in her way, and getting up as she best could without staying to look behind her." Horrified by what she saw on the mount, Miss Frolic begged the narrator to give up dreams of fame, awake, and "return with her to the lower but happier world."[5]

In *Vice in Its Proper Shape* (1789) a sea captain returned from the East Indies, bringing back a "curious little treatise" which described the instructive sights seen by a man and his children. While walking one day they came to a row of small sheds; on a board above the largest was written "WAL*KINBEHOL* DANDLE*ARN, which signifies, *Walk in, behold, and learn.*" A Brahmin, named Wiseman, invited them to enter the sheds, saying there were several things to be seen "which might contribute to the entertainment and instruction" of "pretty fellow travellers." In the sheds were animals into which the souls of naughty children had transmigrated. In the body of an ass, the children learned, was the soul of Jack Idle. Since early education, Locke taught, made men good or evil, useful or not, it was clear that Jack had not been "a great friend to learning." "His aversion to the useful arts of reading and writing" had been such that he had "an indifferent knowledge of the alphabet." When he died, he was "just able to scrawl his own name in characters which were scarcely legible." One morning as he dawdled on the way to school, Tom Sharper and Dick Lockwit convinced him to play hookey and go fishing. For an hour the boys enjoyed "pretty good sport." Then, Tom's line got tangled in weeds. Unable to free it himself, he persuaded Jack to disentangle it by climbing a sloping tree, a branch of which hung over the water. Unfortunately, the branch broke, and Jack tumbled into the water and drowned.[6]

In early children's books learning, and this included moral education, separated man from animal. The child who neglected his studies appeared to behave unnaturally, so much so that even Nature rose against him. In *The Friends; or, the History of Billy Freeman and Tommy Truelove* (1801), Billy Freeman was "very good natured and obliging, but at the same time so great a dunce, that at four years old he could scarce tell a letter." When Billy crossed a stile to visit Farmer Killbacon, Towzer, a dog, pulled him into the hog-trough. To end his "fright," Goody Kill-bacon gave him a custard pie. Billy had little time to enjoy it, for Farmer Killbacon's turkeys flocked together and chased him out of the yard. "At that instant" Squire Martin happened by and seeing Billy crying "asked what was the matter? Si-Si-Si-Sir, I, I wa-was going to p-p-play in the farmer's yard, and the turkies hissed me out: And that is not all, the great dog barked at me, and pulled me into the hog-trough. Pho! Pho! said the gentleman, I am sure both the dog and turkies are good natured to all boys and girls who learn their books." The squire then sat on a bench and taking Billy "between his knees" took out an alphabet book. When he discovered that Billy was unable to "tell" his letters, he preached to Billy, saying, "the dog and turkies may well bark and hiss at you; every one will laugh and make sport of you if you thus continue a dunce; for there are few who know how to be idle and innocent; by doing nothing we learn to do ill." The squire then put the alphabet book back in his pocket. Billy immediately began to cry because he wanted the book. The squire said he would give Billy many little books if he learned his letters. Later that day when Billy went home, he asked his father to teach him the alphabet. The turkeys, the dog, and the prospect of Squire Martin's books inspired Billy, and he did so well that the squire let him read all his little books. Billy's father was also impressed. "Seeing the great desires his son had to be instructed," he "bought him a very pretty poney," and Billy, now controlling an animal instead of being controlled by them, took "leave of his papa and mamma" and "galloped away hearty as a grigg, till he came to the academy, which was kept by Mr. Allworthy." [7]

Among the other animals which the Brahmin Wiseman showed the children was a magpie containing the soul of Dorothy Chatterfast, a monkey with the soul of Monsieur Fribble, a snake containing that of Abigail Eviltongue, and a pig containing that of Anthony Greedyguts. Like poor Jack, Anthony was not a friend to education. He "loved eating much better than reading; and would prefer a tart, a custard, a plum-cake, or even a slice of gingerbread, or an apple, to the prettiest, and most useful little book you could present him with." At eleven he was "such a perfect dunce" that he could scarcely

From *Vice in Its Proper Shape.*
Courtesy American Antiquarian Society.

tell his letters. The next year he ate a dozen penny custards in a single sitting and "thereby gorged his stomach, and threw himself into a mortal fever." Resembling Bunyan's Interpreter, characters like the Brahmin often appeared as guides in children's books. In some books like *Vice in its Proper Shape*, the guide was almost as exotic as Bunyan's conductor; in others an attempt was made to domesticate him. Occasionally the result was silly. In Richard Johnson's *Juvenile Rambles* (1786), Wisdom took Miss Charlotte and Master Billy on a series of instructive walks through the natural world. For a final ramble Wisdom led the children to a cemetery where he discussed the deaths of small children. Typically the stories told were cautionary. When a farmer discovered him robbing his orchard, Dicky Flight fell from a tree trying to escape and broke his leg in two places. The break was so bad that Dicky was forced to have his leg "cut off, and he died before it was well." In the ordinary turn among the tombs, almost everything was matter for a sermon; consequently Wisdom let little pass him by. "Bless us, master Billy," he said, "what beautiful flies are hovering over the graves of these departed little ones! They too have only a little time to live, and perhaps even a few hours may strip them of all their gaudy apparel, and reduce them to the last state of nature." Like the flies, Wisdom himself was soon to depart, not however to a better or far-off world, but mixing the mundane and the miraculous, he took the coach for London, telling the children, "I shall soon see you again."[8]

Although allegories blended the ordinary with the unusual, few ended with guides taking coaches for London. Most, however, reflected contemporary belief in education and taught lessons about life in this, rather than the other world. Instead of journeying to heaven and the Celestial City, Master Headstrong and Miss Patient traveled to the Land of Happiness in *The Adventures of Master Headstrong, and Miss Patient* (c. 1802). On setting out for Happiness, Headstrong met three other travelers: Patient, "an elderly staid female called Reason," and Passion, a youth "rushing on like a torrent." Reason volunteered to guide Patient and Headstrong. Patient accepted the offer; but finding the pace too slow, Headstrong ran ahead with Passion. Taking a wrong turn, they reached the Palace of False Pleasure in which "a number of both sexes assembled, dancing, singing, and drinking the most agreeable liquors." At the upper end of the main hall "sat a lady richly habited, of a most excellent shape and complexion, as far as her skin was discovered; but she wore a veil over her face, as if from modesty, and which *Passion* judged to be the thin covering of excellent beauty." Traditionally Passion was unable to discern truth, and instead of being beautiful, the lady was "a most ugly, loathsome witch."

Having forsaken Reason, Headstrong's journey consisted of a series of instructive tribulations. The Palace of False Pleasure led to the "Realms of Disappointment," where Headstrong fell into a pit. Reflection helped him out, then told him to avoid "the broad pleasant path that is straight before you and keep the rugged narrow way to the left." Following Reflection's advice, Headstrong caught Reason and Patient whose plodding pace had proved faster than that of Passion. *The Adventures* contained a wealth of allegorical characters and places: Hope and Fancy who deluded Headstrong, Experience who directed him out of a wasteland, Caution who saved him from the Cave of Infamy, and Fortitude who encouraged him to go through "the *bitter water of Repentance*" so that he reached the Temple of Virtue and was able to enter the Land of Happiness with Patient and Reason. Although Headstrong swallowed the black water of repentance, he did not die. Unlike *The Pilgrim's Progress*, which directed pilgrims away from this life, *The Adventures* showed how reasonable and moral behavior helped a person achieve earthly happiness.[9]

In drawing so heavily upon *The Pilgrim's Progress*, *The Adventures* was unusual. In *Some Thoughts*, Locke maintained that children delighted in variety and change and were practically incapable of concentrating attention on any subject for a long time. Eighteenth-century publishers studied Locke and built their books for children on his description of the child. As a result many children's books were miscellanies in which allegory was only one ingredient in a blend of fables, riddles, poems, maxims, alphabets, moral stories, jokes, and games.[10] Accordingly, only part of *The History of Master Jackey and Miss Harriot* (1787) was allegorical. When he was eight years old, Jackey was sent to the village school by his father Mr. Gracemore, a tradesman. Jackey's cousin Tommy accompanied him. At school Jackey "was so constant in his good behaviour to every body, that the whole village talked of nothing else." The Earl of Fairfame, whose estate was a half-mile outside the village and who was "remarkable for his generosity and benevolence to the poor," heard about Jackey. After Goody Creamer, who supplied him with butter, assured him that Jackey was the best boy in the village, the earl gave Jackey a new watch and invited him and Tommy to visit his estate.

On the boys' arrival Lady Fairfame showed them the garden. The instructive centerpiece of the book, the garden was allegorical. Two gates stood before it. The right-hand gate represented the road to virtue and "was planned with the utmost simplicity, or rather rudeness," as cypress hung over it, ivy wrapped around its pillars, and "time seemed to have destroyed all the smoothness and regularity of the stone." Two stone champions with raised clubs guarded the entrance while dragons and serpents "were seen in the most hideous attitudes." Behind the gate the way appeared dark, and only the inscription *"Previous to Virtue"* tempted Jackey and Tommy to enter. In contrast the architecture of the other gate, the road to vice, "was light, elegant, and inviting." Flowers hung down the pillars while "nymphs in the most alluring attitudes beckoned." Over the gate was written *"The descent is easy"* while behind it the path "seemed gay, luxuriant, and capable of affording endless pleasure." Jackey and Tommy decided to enter the garden through this gate. At first the way was pleasing, but soon the sky grew dark, the path became winding, frightful rocks hung over their heads, and eventually they lost their way amid "gloomy caverns, unexpected precipices, awful ruins, heaps of bones, and terrifying sounds."

When they were "sufficiently impressed with the horrours of what they heard and saw," Lady Fairfame addressed them, explaining, "My dears, you now see the terrible termination of the road to vice, I would have you learn from what you now see before you, that, *Vice however specious at its first appearance, terminates in endless misery.*" Then taking them by the hand, she led them through a hidden door back to the right-hand gate which they now entered. In a short time, the forboding entrance was left behind, and they discovered "beautiful cascades, beds of flowers, trees loaded with fruit, and arbours of jessamine and roses." From this little walk, Lady Fairfame said, "you may learn, that, *The road to virtue terminates in happiness.*" [11]

Vice in its Proper Shape was built around the exhibition of instructive curiosities, a device which Bunyan used in Christian's viewing the *"Rarities"* of the Lord of the Hill and the contents of Interpreter's *"Significant* Rooms." Lending itself to variety, the device provided the framework for many allegorical tales for children. It furnished, for example, the structure of *The Lilliputian Auction* in which Charly Chatter disposed of the effects of his late uncle Timothy Curious, a "celebrated Lilliputian Virtuoso," who had "not only collected what was rare and curious, but what would likewise be beneficial to Mankind." Among the items auctioned was an instructive Brazen Head, which unlike "many other Brazen Faces" never lied. When Master Careless asked it, *"What was the best Game to play at?* To the great astonishment of them all, the Head immediately opened its Mouth, and replied:

Make your Book your Diversion,
for that's the best Game;
You'll find it will bring you both
Profit and Fame." [12]

Perhaps the most popular collection of rarities in early children's fiction was *The Exhibition of Tom Thumb; being an Account of many valuable and surprising Curiosities which he has collected in the Course of his Travels* (1787). Collected "for little masters and misses," Tom said, "who are little and good like myself," the exhibition was held "in a large commodious room at *Mr. Love-good's* No. 3, in *Wiseman's* buildings, at the end of the upper end of *Education-Road.*" Among the objects exhibited were the stone with which Master Stephen Hot-spur killed his brother and a diamond found by "Messrs. *Temperance* and *Wisdom*, in one of the walks of *Paradise*, exactly upon the spot where stood the evening bower of *Adam.*" The diamond shed "an agreeable lustre, even in the darkest place" and when worn next to the heart contributed "greatly to the health of the body" and filled "the mind with a pleasing serenity." On entering Mr. Lovegood's building children were welcomed by the Advice-bird who said he hoped they were "wise enough to attend to the useful instructions which his master's curiosities are intended to suggest." If he saw that children listened and were willing to follow his suggestions, the bird displayed his beautiful feathers. For a naughty boy or girl, however, he assumed a different appearance.

To give you an opportunity of seeing this, Mr. *Love-good* generally sends into the street either for *Jack Idle, Anthony Greedyguts, Stephen Churl,* or one or other of their wicked companions; who no sooner enter the room, but the *Advice-bird,* instant divesting himself of his former beauty, begins to swell and increase his size at a surprizing rate, as if he was changed by the power of magick, until in the space of a few minutes he becomes an ugly vulture; in which frightful shape he immediately flies upon them, and pecks and scratches them until he has fairly driven them out of the door.[13]

From *The Lilliputian Auction*. Courtesy American Antiquarian Society.

THE
LILLIPUTIAN
AUCTION.

TO WHICH

All little MASTERS and MISSES

ARE INVITED BY

CHARLY CHATTER,

WALK IN

Young Gentlemen and Ladies,

A Going, a Going, a Going!

The World's an Auction, where by Young and Old,
Both Goods and Characters are bought and sold.

PHILADELPHIA:
Published by JACOB JOHNSON,
Nº 147, Market Street.—1802.

From *The Exhibition of Tom Thumb.*
Courtesy American Antiquarian Society.

Although allegorical exhibitions in early children's books were invariably didactic, they were certainly more playful than those in Bunyan. Following Locke's directions, publishers of children's books blended amusement with instruction. The mixture varied, but often amusement seemed to take precedence over instruction. The Lilliputians, Giles Jones wrote, in *The Lilliputian Masquerade* (1787), "having had a quarrel with the Tommy-thumbians their neighbours, concerning an affair of no less importance, than, Whether, when a Cat wagged her tail, it was a sign of fair or foul weather, much scratching ensued." After the two groups had "kicked and cuffed each other to some purpose," an old lady named Reason "told some of the very wisest senators of both parties, that they were all fools to quarrel about what did not any way concern them—for that the only sign of a Cat's wagging her tail, was, that she had a tail to wag." Both parties acknowledged that Reason was right and concluded a peace. To celebrate, the King of Lilliput decided to give "a grand Masquerade, to which all the principal persons were invited."

The masquerade was instructive, and Sir William Wise, "a Lilliputian of great repute," attended so that he could comment on the entertainment to his son Peter Prudence, Esq.

Because wisdom despised outward show, Sir William wore "a plain domino." His mask was full of eyes and had a padlock over the mouth, "signifying that a wise person should see every thing and say nothing." As an allegorical world paraded past, Sir William instructed his son. The first figure to appear was Squire Clumsey of Tumbledown Lane. Although he was extremely fat and suffered from the gout, the squire disguised himself as "the nimble footed Harlequin," thereby making "himself ridiculous to every one." "This is often the case with those who are self-conceited," Sir William observed; "they want to appear to be what nature never fitted them for—and by those means become contemptible." "Let no one desire to be greater than Providence has designed he shall be," Sir William continued, "for all who give ear to pride become laughing stocks to their neighbours." Following not far behind the squire were four Misses: Misconduct, Misfortune, Mischance, and Mistake. Misconduct had a scornful expression on her mask and held up her right hand to push Good Advice aside while she greeted Folly cordially with her left. "She will never reform," Sir William said, but will "run counter to reason all her life-time." Among other participants in the masquerade was a grave philosopher carrying a candle and lantern and carefully searching "for a man who KNOWS HIMSELF." In the dress of a miser, Adam Avarice reminded Sir William of the inscription on a tombstone in Lilliput. "Reader," it stated, "beware immoderate love of pelf; / Here lies the worst of thieves—who robb'd Himself." Seeing a shoemaker dressed as a blind fiddler, Sir William remarked, "Sly rogue, he plays the merriest tunes in order to make people caper and dance about, that they may wear out their shoes the sooner, and he have the more custom; tho' he pretends to be a blind Fidler, he is cunning enough to see his own advantage, and makes the people frisk about to a fine tune." [14]

Although allegorical devices were used for secular, or for moral rather than doctrinaire, ends in most early children's fiction, some writers for children continued to use them for strict evangelical purposes. Learning technique from both religious tradition and children's books, George Burder in *Early Piety; or, Memoir of Children Eminently Serious* (1806) produced a text which was evangelically serious and which also appealed to children's delight in change and variety. Master Billy and Miss Betsey Goodchild, Burder wrote, attended a "genteel boarding school," run by Miss Lovegood, "a lady of singular piety and wisdom; remarkably fitted for the education of youth." Like Squire Martin, Miss Lovegood "never failed graciously to reward" her pupils when they "did well." Unlike the squire, however, she did not encourage them to read playful alphabet books. Instead she rewarded them when they were "diligent in reading their bibles, in learning their catechism, in secret prayer, or when they could give a good account of the sermons they had heard on the Lord's Day." Proficiency in studies did not bring Master Billy a pony but a blessing. When Billy and Betsey arrived at home for the Christmas holidays, they immediately fell on their knees and "begged their parents blessing." In tears, their mother could not speak, but Mr. Goodchild, "raising them up in the most tender manner, said, 'May JESUS bless you both!' and kissing them, added, 'God be praised for his mercy, in giving me to see my dear children again!' "

Because they were good, John Benevolent, Esq., invited the children to his country house to view his "many curious things." "Nothing pleased them better than a gallery of fine pictures, each of which had a *spiritual meaning*." One picture showed a "poor man almost drowned" being pulled out of the water by a "good prince" who had thrown him a rope. The prince was Jesus while the poor man was Everyman and the rope, the children learned, showed "how we are saved by *faith*." After the picture gallery, the children visited Benevolent's museum where their guide was "a venerable dissenting minister." The first room in which they were led "contained a vast variety of serpents, snakes, adders, and such like frightful creatures; many of which though beautiful to look upon, were terrible when alive; having sharp stings, and mortal poison, under their tongues." Having learned his lessons well at school, Billy recognized the reptiles. "These destructive creatures," he said, "put me in mind of that old and subtle serpent, who first persuaded Eve to sin against God, by breaking his commands." The minister agreed and as a gloss added, "I hope you know that Christ, the friend of sinners, came, according to his promise, *to bruise the serpent's head.*" [15]

Collections of stories were common, in part because they provided a structure for the miscellany that Locke's assertion about children's delight in change seemed to mandate. Often children gathered at school, as in Sarah Fielding's *The Governess* (1749), or on special occasions, as in John Newbery's *The Twelfth-Day Gift*, and recounted their experiences, told tales, or read excerpts from other publications. Bringing the Goodchilds to a Twelfth Day assembly with other right-minded children such as Miss Mild, Master Prayful, and Master Serious, Burder used the device to provide enticing variety. Although all were evangelical, different kinds of stories were told at the assembly: allegory, moral tale, and the almost obligatory account of the joyful death of the young believer. From the point of view of the parent who wanted to educate his child for life in both this and the next world and who thought *The History of Master Jackey and Miss Harriot* a useful tale, the allegory recounted by Burder's Master Considerate was probably, at the very least, wrong-headed. A hermit, Considerate began, set out to discover if Providence really guided men's actions. On his journey, the hermit met a "beautiful youth," and together they traveled through a series of allegorical experiences that seemed to teach that Providence controlled people's lives. One evening the two stayed at the modest home of a man "content and benevolent" who entertained them graciously and discussed religion with them. The next morning, "just before they departed, the youth went to the cradle, in which was a pretty infant, (the pride and joy of its aged father,) and broke its neck." Seeing this as terrible recompense for their host's decency and generosity, the hermit fled from the youth in horror. The youth, however, would not let him escape, and turning into an angel explained his action, showing in the process that God in his great love for humanity did govern the events of daily life. "The child of our pious friend," the angel said, "had almost weaned his affections from God; but to teach him better, the Lord, to save the father has taken the child. To all but us, he seemed to go off in fits, and I was ordained to call him hence—the poor father, now humbled in tears, owns that the punishment was just." [16]

Although he did not ameliorate his evangelical message, Burder learned technique from popular children's books as, correspondingly, the first publishers of children's books drew from religious writing, adapting allegory to their ends. By the end of the eighteenth century, most allegory written for children had been thoroughly secularized, and the rest, like that of Burder, had been influenced by contemporary children's books. One allegory which was not secularized and which drew directly upon Bunyan for message and method was *The Infant's Progress, from the Valley of Destruction to Everlasting Glory* (1821) by Mary Sherwood, the best of the early nineteenth-century evangelical writers. Although not typical of the main stream of eighteenth-century children's literature, *The Infant's Progress* reflected the religiosity of the Evangelical Movement which had begun to publish numbers of children's books by the 1820s.

In the preface Sherwood encouraged children to search for her meaning almost as if they were playing a game, albeit a serious one. "Now as nuts and almonds are hidden under rough shells, and as honey is concealed in the bells and cups of flowers," she explained, "so there is a hidden meaning in every part of my allegory, which I hope you will be enabled to draw forth for your profit. In the meantime, my dear children, I pray God to seal instruction upon your hearts, and fill you with that heavenly wisdom, whose price is far above rubies." [17]

The Infant's Progress described the journey to the "gates of heaven" of three small children—Humble Mind, not quite ten, and his two little sisters, Playful and Peace. When Evangelist turned the steps of their parents toward "the shining light," these "pretty babes" had been left behind "in their father's house." With them was "as ill favoured and ill conditioned an urchin as one could see, whose name was *Inbred* or *Original Sin.*" Inbred Sin never left the children; he stayed in their house, lay in their bosoms, accompanied them on walks, and ate his meals with them. There was nothing done in the family "great or small, in which this busy one did not meddle." At Evangelist's urging, the children left home and became pilgrims. On their journey they passed through a series of instructive experiences. In *The Infant's Progress* right education did not prepare the child for this world but for the next, and Sherwood attacked what she saw as education's emphasis upon the secular. Not long into the pilgrimage, Humble Mind was led astray by Mr. Worldly-Mind who took him to his school. "These are the men," Evangelist preached, "who think themselves wiser than their Maker, and who turn aside many young persons from the right way, in order to fill them with such knowledge as only puffeth up, and tendeth to destruction. They take the sling and the stone from the hand of the youthful pilgrim, and put on him the armour of Saul; they rob him of his Bible, and fill his mouth with the words of man's wisdom." By such people more "young pilgrims" were destroyed, Evangelist concluded, "than by thousands of the open enemies of our Lord." [18]

Children's books themselves were a manifestation of belief in the formative effects of education, and Sherwood laid the critical rod on heavily in an attempt to purge educational corruption. Having escaped from Worldly-Mind, Humble Mind met Mr. Lover-of Novelty who showed him his garden, adorned with "fanciful decorations" and filled with "all kinds of vanities." Along its twisting paths wandered "teachers of superficial accomplishments." As soon as Humble Mind appeared, "certain of these teachers of vanities came and spread their toys" before him: "to wit, pencils and paints, maps and drawings, pagan poems, and fabulous histories, musical instruments of various kinds, with all the gaudy fopperies of modern learning." Unknown to Humble Mind and to the children who received fashionable, worldly educations, just behind the garden was "a howling wilderness full of wild beasts which used to come in the night and commit dreadful ravages in the place; there being no fence, or wall between the garden and the wilderness." In contrast to the seductive amusement provided in Mr. Lover-of Novelty's garden, true instruction was provided by Law, a stern taskmaster who ran a school on Interpreter's estate. When Filthy-Curiosity interested the children in "earth-nuts" and they eagerly grubbed up the ground "while *Inbred-Sin* gaily crowing and clapping his sides, maliciously splashed mud and mire" on their "white garments," Law "laid sorely on their backsides with a scourge." [19]

The Infant's Progress taught children to reject this world. To this end at Palace Beautiful, Prudence showed the children a rarity, "a magic glass" presented by Mr. Spiritual-Man. The glass was actually a magic lantern, and when a candle was inserted in it, pictures reflected on a wall before the children. Depicted was a wide plain full of large towns, "all scattered over with rubbish." Above the plain was "a glorious heaven"; beneath was "a yawning grave going down to the very pit of hell." In the middle of the plain stood "a very unsightly old man clothed in filthy garments"; at his right hand was his father Satan. Unable to stand straight, the man could only look at his feet. While the children watched, he began "to rake and scratch all the muck and rubbish together"; while doing so, he appeared "not only to become vicious, but to be filled with an indescribable fury." At this point Law appeared and beat the old man "until he was glad to leave scraping the muck and dung together, and to sit down quietly upon the heap which he had already collected."

While the old man sat on his possessions, Satan called his servants and instructed them to help his son. While Art painted him red and white, concealed his sores, and taught him to smile, Fashion clothed him with "gaudy garments," and Light-Mind's "train," her "teachers of elegant accomplishments," began to educate him. After this was done, "certain persons, wise in their own conceits, came to the old man, with many learned professors, putting certain books into his hand. He received the books, and after reading therein, he rose up inflated with vanity; and his manner was as if he were mocking at the Most High." Then leading him to the top of his rubbish heap, the old man's teachers placed a crown upon his head and bowed before him. While they were bowing, however, "one came behind and struck him; upon which he lost both his crown and his rich garments, and suddenly falling down, he rapidly tumbled from precipice to precipice, till he sunk into the pit and totally disappeared." At the end of the show, Piety asked the children what the pictures represented. Playful observed that the old man was "the emblem of what we are by nature." Prudence agreed, adding "you saw all that Art and Learning, and Fashion, and Elegant Accomplishments could do for this old man."[20]

The Infant's Progress was powerful. Instead of vacillating wildly between instruction and inappropriate amusement, it was unified, built single-mindedly after the instructive model provided by Bunyan. Instead of being a miscellany, mirroring the changing moods and tones of its contents, it was pervaded by a narrow but vital evangelical fervor. Along with being the source of the book's power and thus success, this narrowness was also the source of its limitations. While the Evangelical Movement attracted many people, and was strong by 1820, the middle classes—and these seem to have included the majority of moderately well-off evangelicals—believed that childhood education, of which learning, if not necessarily fashion and elegant accomplishments, was an important part, should prepare a child for this world and the next. Although they thought that education like life was a serious matter, they did not reject the world, and indeed, many were remarkably successful in it.[21] By the 1820s, unlike the 1780s, when a handful of firms published the great majority of children's books, most of which were thematically and structurally similar, the world of children's literature had grown remarkably diverse in tone and theme. Even as Mary Sherwood and her sister Lucy Cameron wrote tracts and books to train children in serious habits of thought, much of the allegory in print was latitudinarian.

Most eighteenth-century critics of children's literature were ill at ease with the imagination, and they attacked fairy tales for awakening the imagination without providing useful, moral lessons for the understanding. Because it drew upon religious tradition for its appeal to the imagination, allegory escaped general condemnation. Filled with the marvelous and the exotic, eastern or oriental stories resembled both allegory and fairy tales. Like fairy tales, these stories became popular. Thus the author of *Modern Arabia Displayed* (1811) explained, "The flattering reception which the 'Arabian Nights Entertainments,' has in all languages experienced, contributed, in no small degree, to induce the author to adopt the oriental mode of composition, as most pleasing to youthful taste."[22]

"Among the questions which are most interesting to the progress of morals and the cause of truth," a reviewer wrote in discussing a volume of "Arabian Tales" in the *Monthly Review* (1793), "is the utility of that species of fiction which is supported by supernatural aid; and, if it have been, or may here after be, useful, what ought to be its limits? That fables or tales of this kind seize, hurry forward, and enrapture, the undisciplined imagination of youth, there can be no doubt; and that they therefore tend to awaken curiosity, which otherwise might continue dormant, is highly probable:—but it is no less certain that they likewise have a tendency to accustom the mind rather to wonder than to inquire; and to seek a solution of difficulties in occult causes, instead of resorting to facts." Although the reviewer's attitude toward eastern tales was mixed, he stressed that they were inferior to instructive stories furnished with the domestic and the familiar. "Between the moral utility," he wrote, "of fables built on the marvellous, and of those which originate in true pictures of life and manners, there can be no comparison."[23]

This hesitation to condemn the eastern story resulted from the conventional ends for which it was used. Unlike most fairy tales, eastern stories became vehicles of instruction, relying on the familiar devices of the domestic moral tale. Thus, the eastern story blew life into Burder's venerable clergyman, turning him into a hermit. Often resembling Old Testament prophets, hermits frequently spoke in biblical rhythms. "Hearken, ye children of the dust, to the words of ZAKIN," the "Arabian Hermit" urged in *The Selector*; "despise not the instructions of the aged. The thorny paths of adversity have taught me wisdom, and the lamp that directs my feet was lighted in the dreary habitation of Poverty." In general early children's books celebrated simplicity and a modest life and criticized great ambition and luxury. In doing so, children's books often praised country living at the expense of urban living. Having retired from cities, far from luxury, hermits were well suited to become spokesmen for those important truths which people seemed prone to lose sight of amid the moral chaos of city life. Not all critics were comfortable, however, with the use of an exotic setting and exotic characters to preach conventional religion. In the *Guardian of Education* (1803), Sarah Trimmer attacked a collection of "Siamese Tales." After acknowledging that the book taught "many good moral lessons," she concluded that the collection was not "favourable to the Christian cause," criticizing the presentation of religious truth under the guise of pleasing fiction. "We cannot," she wrote, "allow that those things, which alone are worthy to be called TRUTHS, stand in need of any art or embellishment to recommend them to the attention of unsophisticated youth. They present themselves in the most inviting manner, in their own original form, *the written Word of God.*" "Surely," she concluded, "it is a great affront to the *divine Majesty* to introduce the ALMIGHTY, as an agent in a fictitious tale—a degradation of the office of the MESSIAH, to ascribe to a Genii (an imaginary being) that mediation which belongs to the SON OF GOD alone—and to make Divine Providence a poetical machine, to bring about miraculous events, which never did, nor according to the analogy of the Divine dispensations ever will happen."[24]

Few eastern tales and characters fared so badly in the *Guardian of Education.* Much as Burder worked the techniques of secular children's literature to his doctrinaire end, so writers of children's fiction adapted the characters of eastern tales to their uses. After a seafaring life, the hero of *Hamlain; or, the Hermit of the Beach* (1799) inherited a cottage and a decent annuity and retiring from society lived alone near the British seacoast becoming a repository of moral wisdom. According to Trimmer, he was "a *Christian Philosopher*" and she praised *Hamlain,* saying the hero's "*reveries*" did not resemble "those *wild vagaries* which result from the indulgence of fancy."[25]

In most eastern stories for children, the exoticism was merely gaudy, alluring dressing. Although Virtudeo could suspend animation by pressing an alabaster tablet he wore next to his heart and could convey speech and understanding to inanimate objects, the writings found among his possessions after death consisted of commonplace observations. Thus in *The Manuscripts of Virtudeo* (1801), possession of genie-like magic did not transform the hero into an inspiring sage; and when, considering education, for example, Virtudeo criticized sending girls to boarding school, he concluded mundanely that "the duties, the amusements of women, I mean of virtuous women, are all domestic." Each evening in *The Governess* (1801), Mrs. Corbett told her students instructive stories. The widow of a clergyman, she was careful to tell acceptable, moral tales. To hold the children's attention, however, she often adorned her truths in eastern dress. "Among the caliphs one more than all the rest," she began one evening, was renowned "for the goodness of his temper." To learn his people's grievances, Haroun Abraschid frequently wandered alone through his kingdom in disguise. One morning at sunrise, as he walked beside a river, he saw an old man talking earnestly to his grandson. "In wantonness," the boy had caught a "water-worm," and "having thrown it on the ground, had lifted up his foot to crush it." The old man reproved him, and as the caliph drew near, said to his grandson, "do not take away that which is not in thy power to give. He who gave life to that insect, gave it also to thee: how darest thou violate what he bestowed? Shew mercy, and thou will find mercy." [26]

Astonished at "hearing beggary and rags so eloquent," the caliph asked the old man his name and address. The old man replied that he was called Atelmoule and said he lived in a nearby cottage. An hour later officers carrying "a robe of state" appeared before the cottage and informed Atelmoule that he had been appointed vizier. The officers led Atelmoule "full of wonder and confusion" to the caliph, who said, "you are next the throne: forget not your own lesson. Shew mercy and you shall find it." "Mean time the sun was warm," and the worm "whose life the new vizier had saved, opened its shelly back, and gave birth to a fly." Enjoying "his new-born wings with rapture," he "buzzed about," then "settled on the mule that carried the vizier, and stung him." The mule "pranced," and unaccustomed to riding, Atelmoule fell to the ground where he was "killed by a stroke of the creature's heel." When an account of Atelmoule's death was brought to the palace, "even those who had murmured at the sudden exaltation of the man" pitied "that death he owed to his virtue." Some even criticized providence, "so daring and so ignorant is man." Superior to the rest in virtue, however, the caliph raised his hands to heaven and blessed the name of the prophet, crying, "I decreed transitory honours to Atelmoule, but thou has snatched him to those that never fade—to Paradise." The ending did not satisfy Miss Wentworth, and she said that "it was a naughty fly" that stung the mule and "made him kill so good a man." Although "The Mount of Fortune" was an allegory and the account of Atelmoule an eastern tale, the stories taught similar lessons. As the narrator had fled from the Mount of Fortune to lower, less exalted regions where he could live a simpler, less anxiety-ridden life and from which he could ultimately be elevated to heaven, so Atelmoule had been saved from unhappiness, temptation, and possible damnation. "The poor fly," Mrs. Corbett explained, was "but a weak instrument in the hands of our great Creator, perhaps to snatch the virtuous Atelmoule from impending danger; for who can answer, whether his morals would have remained untainted amidst the splendour and vice of courts; or might not envy at this unexpected preferment, have raised him enemies that would never have ceased pursuing him until covered with disgrace they had brought him to shame and death."[27]

Eastern stories also used rarities, or the paraphernalia of fairy tales, for often the only difference between the two was the instructive uses to which the rarities were put. In Edward Kendall's *The Adventures of Musul* (1808), a "wealthy grandee of Persia" gave his son three miraculous gifts: a ring which made all who saw him love him, a jewel capable of procuring anything he desired, and a cloak which could transport him wherever he wished to go. Although the gifts appeared miraculous, they were actually attributes of the young man's character. The ring was amiableness; the gem, genius; and the cloak, an active mind. During his adventures, Musul was seduced by *"false pleasure,"* and becoming a "slave to luxury" lost his good character. He then suffered terribly, catching leprosy and being pursued by a lion. His travails, however, were all for an instructive best, for as a genie later told him, his sufferings were "the means of restoring you to the treasures you had lost: the misfortunes themselves have brought back into your heart and mind the virtues which they had lost."[28]

Occasionally allegory borrowed the trappings of the eastern story. Lucy Peacock's *The Adventures of the Six Princesses of Babylon, in their Travels to the Temple of Virtue* (1785) was an eclectic blend of fairy tale, allegory, and eastern story. Defeated in battle, the king of Babylon and his queen took refuge in a lonely desert in a foreign land where the fairy Benigna visited them and informed them that "the Oracle" doomed them "to eternal exile, unless raised again to empire by the virtues of your children." After transporting the king and queen to an island, Benigna took charge of the young princesses' educations. She waved her wand and "an elegant gold chariot appeared, drawn by eight snow-white swans." After she and the princesses entered, the chariot "mounted the air, and in a short time, losing sight of the deserts of Babylon," they "arrived at a spacious grotto." There, as the years passed, she instructed "them in the most useful and entertaining parts of learning, at the same time taking care to instil into their minds the love of virtue." Eventually she informed them that each was to go on a quest for one of the "*Six Wonders*," hidden "as a trial of your constancy." The "happiness or misery" of their lives, she warned, depended upon their success. If they succeeded, "peace and prosperity" would attend them, but if they failed, they would bring down "shame and infamy."

The wonders for which the princesses searched resembled Musul's gifts or the curiosities collected by Timothy Curious. Miranda looked for the Distaff of Industry which "by applying one end of it to your right hand," Benigna said, "you are instantly put in possession of the thing you desire." Taken from "the River of Good-nature," Florissa's wonder, A Bottle of Water, was "endowed with the power of reconciling all differences." The Spear of Truth, for which Clementina searched, had the "power of overcoming all evil enchantment" while the person who was "fortunate enough to obtain" Bonnetta's Mantle of Meekness immediately became "beautiful as an angel." Orinda's Magnet of True Generosity, Benigna explained, was capable of transferring the pleasure one felt to another, and Matilda's White Wand of Enchantment had the "power of rendering the most disagreeable objects in nature agreeable." On their quests the princesses visited allegorical places such as the Floating Island of Disappointment, the Labyrinth of Error, and the Castle of Avarice, meeting instructive characters like Gentle Reproof, Flattery, the Fairy Delay who was the Daughter of Idleness, the Hermit of the White Rock, and Prince Manfred Knight of the Shield of Moderation.[29]

"Education has properly become the polished handmaiden of

religion," the author of *Constance and Caroline* wrote in 1823. By the end of the eighteenth century, education was not simply a handmaiden. In children's books, it was the monarch, and although doctrinaire writers like Mary Sherwood tried to restore religion to the throne, they were not successful. According to Sarah Trimmer, *The Adventures of the Six Princesses of Babylon* was "a vehicle of good moral instruction." A better, or at least more contemporary, vehicle was rapidly becoming popular, one that would convert the matter of allegory and even the eastern tale to its own moral and instructive, if not religious, ends. This was the school story. The most interesting, because it was transitional, of the early school stories was *The Prettiest Book for Children; Being the History of the Enchanted Castle; Situated in one of the Fortunate Isles, and governed by Giant Instruction* (1770). Ostensibly written by Don Stephano Bunyano, Instruction's secretary and "a distant relation of the famous John Bunyan," *The Prettiest Book* adapted the paraphernalia of the eastern tale and that of Bunyan's Interpreter and his House to suit the educational climate of the time. Wearing a flowered gown and hairy cap, waving a white wand, and having a long blue beard, Don Stephano resembled an Arab sorcerer, not a Christian. In habits, though, he was conventional and despite his dress behaved like a good little boy. As soon as he got up in the morning, he said his prayers, washed his face and hands, and combed his beard. Like his secretary, Instruction was exotic in appearance. He was ten feet tall and had a gold beard and gold hair which hung over his shoulders "in flowing ringlets." On his head sat a green turban decorated with gold and diamonds while about his waist he wore a purple vest embroidered with pearls. He was so handsome, Don Stephano declared, that "if some of your English ladies were to see him, they would either wish that he was reduced to the common size, or that they themselves were born *giantesses*." Despite his seductive Turkish or Arabian appearance, however, Instruction was a Christian, who believed the Bible was the best book in the world and who said his prayers every morning and evening. His wife was Lady Good-Example, and his daughters were Piety, Patience, Charity, Sobriety, and Prudence.[30]

The Enchanted Castle was built on "the *Seat of Education*," the smallest of the Fortunate Isles. Despite the gaudy, magical world in which it was located, the castle itself was decorously symmetrical and seemed almost an emblem of a rational, moral education. Each of its walls being eighty feet long, it formed a perfect square. "A spacious and a very beautiful court" paved with stone was in the middle of the square while in the center of the court a fountain cast up "water as pure as crystal, to a most surprizing height." Tutors lived in the castle, and the children of both the rich and poor traveled "hither to be educated" from other islands. As sinners avoided Interpreter's House, so Instruction refused to admit children who believed that birth, not education and good behavior, determined success in life. "No man can be so great, or so rich and powerful," Instruction said, "as to have any right to excuse himself from his duty. Some little boys, indeed, because they are gentlemens sons, and are finely dressed, and eat and drink, as we say, of the best of every thing, are silly enough to think that they may do all manner of wickedness and mischief. But these are very stupid and naughty children; and if they were even to set their feet in the *Enchanted Castle,* or even to come near to the door of it, the good giant would spurn them out of his sight, or perhaps do something worse with them." [31]

In *The Prettiest Book* Bunyan's allegorical devices became vehicles for moral education. As Watchful the porter challenged pilgrims before the house built by the "Lord of the Hill," so the porter of the castle was Mr. Alphabet. He refused entrance to bad and to ignorant children, these last who because education shaped the good adult were almost certain to be bad. If a child did not know his letters, Alphabet sent "him packing like a dunce and a blockhead." Once admitted to the castle, children examined instructive curiosities, much as Christian viewed the "*Rarities*" of the Lord of the Hill, and the contents of Interpreter's "*Significant* Rooms." First children came to the picture gallery where they were met by Mr. Interpreter, who like his namesake showed them instructive pictures, including Mr. Dutiful's depiction of Absalom's death, Mr. Good's painting of the cruel steward, and Mr. Mannerly's picture of the "foaming bears" pursuing the children who mocked Elisha. After the gallery, children visited the museum where Mr. Set'em-right, the caretaker, pointed out rarities like the Moneycup, which turned all money placed in it to dust and thus taught "the real value of your money." Beyond the museum lay the library; over the door in the language of the Isles was inscribed, "THEF EAROF THELOR DIS THEBE GINING OFWIS DOM, and means in English, The Fear of the Lord is the Begining of Wisdom."[32]

At the beginning of *The Prettiest Book*, Don Stephano criticized contemporary children's books. Petty writers, he wrote, "stuffed their little books with so many out-of-the-way expressions, and so many words which are borrowed from the learned and other languages" that the insides of many books "were as fine and tawdry as the gilt paper on the coverlids." Consequently the books did not teach children "plain good sense" but "only taught them to talk *gibberish*." Like his secretary, and to some extent resembling Mary Sherwood, Instruction suspected the "gaudy garments" of fashionable education. For him a good education was practical, increasing understanding and forming character. When he met the children in the library, he showed them a parrot, who could read and talk and "was no stranger to Greek and Latin." Unfortunately, the bird only parroted knowledge and did not understand the things it memorized. "Such Parrots," Don Stephano wrote, were "to be met with in many a fine library in England." "I hope, however," he explained, "that all my little readers, when they take a book into their hands, will be resolved to understand it as they go along."[33]

In a review of *The Governess*, Sarah Trimmer criticized the story of Atelmoule, saying it was "too puzzling for children." As Don Stephano worried about the "fine and tawdry" distracting children from "plain good sense," so others like Trimmer were concerned that the *"language of figure"* was puzzling. Despite Instruction's emphasis upon the growth of understanding, the allegorical and eastern furnishings of his castle were fine and ingenious. If education determined character and success, then allegorical ingenuity like the alluring labyrinth in Lady Fairfame's garden in which Jackey and Tommy lost their way could mislead readers. As the parrot read but did not understand, so the decorative surface of allegory could so interest children that they would become fascinated with it and miss a book's lessons. Despite its use by religious writers like Sherwood, not all evangelicals were comfortable with allegory, and in the *Evangelical*

Magazine (1806), Gaius warned that it led people to "thirst after the froth of human fancy to the neglect of the sincere milk of the word." An important ingredient of early children's books, allegory was not banished from the nursery. Suspect, however, among believers—both those in "the word" and in education— allegory would lose stature in the nineteenth century.[34]

2

* * * * *

School Stories

llegory and the first school stories were closely related, using some of the same instructional devices and often teaching similar lessons. Transformation of the Enchanted Castle into an academy and Instruction into a schoolmaster would almost change *The Prettiest Book* into a school story. The children's exploration of rooms in the castle would then become an educational progress through forms and beyond various temptations. In contrast to allegory, which often appeared a world apart, the school story appeared as a recognizable, albeit diminutive, world. "A school may be styled," Elizabeth Sandham wrote in *The School-Fellows* (1818), "the world in miniature." As Christian left the City of Destruction and began a spiritual progress toward eternal life, so the schoolboy left the protecting, and confining, family to begin an educational progress through life. The boy, Ellenor Fenn wrote in *School Dialogues for Boys* (1783), emerged from under his mother's "wing into that LITTLE WORLD, a SCHOOL." Although

31

this little world seemed more familiar than that of allegory, the characters which inhabited it were generally allegorical. In Sarah Fielding's *The Governess*, the first and most influential eighteenth-century school story, among Mrs. Teachum's pupils were Dolly Friendly, Lucy Sly, Nanny Spruce, Henny Fret, and Jenny Peace. Among *The Little Female Orators* (1770) at boarding school were Dolly Goodchild, Betsy Thoughtful, Deborah Mindful, and Sally Readwell, while attending Mrs. Propriety's class in *The Village School* (1817) were Katy Saucy, Bet Dirty, Ned Rattle, Sukey Giddy, and Charles Mindbook. In *School Dialogues for Boys*, Mr. Aweful the master, Mr. Wiseman the usher, and Mr. Sage the assistant taught an allegorical cast of children including Candid, Sensible, Worthy, Spiteful, Meek, Pert, Flaunt, Frisk, Easy, Tinsel, Flippant, Subtle, Mildmay, and Chatter.[1]

To reach the Celestial City, Christian had to learn to reject the temptations of the world and to stand firm against worldly pressure. Similarly, if a schoolboy wanted to progress along his "Road" to success, he had to learn to say *no*. "The first thing necessary for a boy to learn, at going to a great school," Sensible informed Sprightly on his arrival at Mr. Aweful's school, "is to be able to say, NO, with a firm and manly assurance." Some books placed this denial in clear religious perspective. "To avoid every vice, and to *dare* to refuse, when to comply would be criminal, often requires so much resolution as to be justly compared to 'striving to enter in at a strait, or (narrow) gate,'" the author of *The Pleasures of Benevolence* (1809) wrote. "In this, as in other acts of virtue," she continued, "the first entrance to the path is the most rugged, and those who have conquered the difficulty of a *first* refusal, generally find the following ones more and more easy, till at length they have not unfrequently the satisfaction of feeling themselves more respected even by those who would have led them astray from the path of duty, than if they had weakly complied with their solicitations."[2]

Although he received heavenly aid, Bunyan's Christian could be seen as alone and ultimately responsible for his salvation. School stories put great stress upon the individual's determining his own future. To become successful, the student like Christian had to acquire not only the ability to withstand temptation or pressure but the knowledge that he had a duty to himself that outweighed secular calls. *"Reverence thyself,* was a maxim laid down by the antients, which deserves to have been written in letters of gold," a clergyman advised his daughter before she left home in Mary Pilkington's *Mentorial Tales* (1802). "Let me entreat you," he urged, "scrupulously to follow it, and you can never deviate from that which is *right."* "Young as you are," Mary Ann Kilner explained to children in *A Course of Lectures for Sunday Evenings* (1783), "you have been instructed, that there is a God who observes all your actions; you have been taught your duty to him as your Creator and Preserver: you know likewise what are your obligations to your fellow creatures; and that a regard to a right conduct, and the practice of virtue, is a duty that you owe to *yourself.—*It is a part therefore of the performance of those duties, to do all in your power to improve in knowledge; to learn every day more and more in what those obligations consist." [3]

The student who reverenced himself acted carefully and deliberately; impulsive behavior was almost certain to lead one astray. "If we accustom ourselves to act without consideration in *trifles,"* Mr. Rotchford warned Charles in *The Rotchfords* (c. 1783), "it will not be long before we shall proceed upon the same sandy foundation to commit actions of the greatest importance." Since early impressions and thus actions had lasting consequences, turning aside from a road built upon sand to that raised upon a firm educational foundation was difficult. Unlike Christian, who lived for the next world and sought only God's approval for his actions, schoolchildren were educated for this life. As a result they frequently confused popularity with success and erred through the desire to please. In *School Occurrences* (1782) Miss Greedy refused to share a cake which she received from home and instead locked it in her bureau. When Greedy left the room, Miss Pry suggested to the other students that they open the bureau and eat the cake before it spoiled. Several girls tried their keys in Greedy's bureau with no success; then Pry recalled that Miss Sprightly's key opened the bureau. At first Sprightly refused to give the girls her key, but under pressure she lost, as she said, "the right way" and gave them her key. Before the cake was divided, however, she struggled and regaining the way refused to eat any. Although schoolmates accused her of being "squeamish, and affectedly scrupulous," she responded that she "regretted nothing but that she had not had sufficient resolution to persist in her refusal of the key."[4]

More threatening to resolution than scorn was ridicule, "the most dangerous weapon," Hannah More wrote, "in the whole arsenal of impiety." Reflecting fashionable disdain for serious matters, "*persiflage*," that "cold compound of irony, irreligion, selfishness, and sneer," More explained, "has of late years made an incredible progress in blasting the opening buds of piety in young persons of fashion." "When first I came to school," Laura wrote in *Correspondence between a Mother and her Daughter at School* (1817), "I was in great danger of acquiring that silly habit of laughing at every thing, and every body, which, I believe, is almost universal among the commoner sort of school girls." "But I see now," she continued, that instead of its being "a sign of *cleverness*, it proceeds from vacancy and idleness, more than any thing else; and sometimes from envy and ill-nature." In school stories the moral, if not necessarily religious, virtues were an essential part of education, and the child who could not resist being ridiculed out of his faith was too weak to make successful educational progress. "Firmness," Richard Johnson wrote in *Moral Sketches* (1802), "represents a faint image of eternity, and is the perfection of all the virtues, since, without the assistance of the former, the latter could have no stability." "When I knelt down the first night to say my prayers," Supple, a new student at Mr. Aweful's, recounted of a former school, "they called out, '*a Methodist!*'" "What did you do?" Sprightly asked. "I never durst kneel any more, for shame," Supple replied, adding that he knew he was "doing ill, yet had not the courage to brave the jests of my naughty companions." "Be as compliant as you please in things indifferent," said Sensible who overheard the conversation and who served as Sprightly's guide; "let others choose whether you shall drive a hoop, or play at leap-frog;—but where *right* and *wrong* are concerned, be *firm*."[5]

Allegorical books like *The Adventures of Master Headstrong*, *The Infant's Progress*, and even *The Prettiest Book* taught only general educational or religious truths and appealed to both boys and girls alike. In contrast, school stories usually were written for either boys or girls but not for both. In part the differentiation mirrored contemporary education in which boys and girls above the lower classes attended separate schools. In part, however, it reflected the age's strong belief in the formative influence of childhood reading. Since the success and ways of behavior thought proper for men were not the same as those considered proper for women, children's books, and in particular school stories which focused directly upon education, often described a different educational progress for boys than for girls. The difference between books written for girls and those for boys was especially great in attitudes toward one manifestation of firmness, fighting. With the exception of books written for lower-class boys which often viewed fighting as socially disruptive and instead taught the passive virtues of humility and resignation, school stories for boys frequently included fights. By the end of the eighteenth century, with the exception of books written from an evangelical bent, most literature for children stripped Christianity of particular doctrine, leaving it a faith of general morality and good deeds. As a consequence, although fights in school stories in part reflected Christian's lonely struggle with Apollyon, they also looked forward to Kingsley's muscular Christianity in which the believer fought not simply in the Valley of Humiliation for his own soul but in the social arena as the champion of the weak and the oppressed.

The heroes of the first school stories usually fought aristocratic foes. In early fiction for children, most of which was written for and embodied the aspirations of the growing middle classes, there was little room for an aristocracy. Because its wealth and position were inherited, its very existence denied that education determined a person's moral, economic, and finally social success. In an ideal educational world, no man would inherit prestige or power but would instead be educated for it. Achieving the right education and consequently position would then depend upon work, not privilege. In school stories, hard-working, middle-class boys thrashed aristocrats, in the process either driving them out of school or converting them to belief in the importance of education. Even when they were not overtly allegorical, the names of students involved in fights in these stories usually revealed their social classes and thereby their characters. In *Tales of the Academy* (1820), the two leading pupils in Mr. Osgood's school in the village of Muchlore were Adolphus and Ernest. Although born with "most genius," Adolphus, resting on his inheritance, neglected his education, and as a result Ernest excelled him first in studies and then, because of his work, in virtue.

Although Mr. Osgood did not approve, fagging existed in his school. One Saturday after the boys received their weekly pocket money, Ernest saw one of Adolphus's fags crying and discovered that Adolphus had taken the boy's money and given it to another fag to buy apples. "I suppose you owed him the money," Ernest said. "No," the boy answered; "he told me I *must* lend it to him; and because I wouldn't lend it, he said he would take it, and pay me at the half-year's end (in the language of the academy, not at all)." Although interfering with another student's fag violated custom, Ernest had been educated to support decency, and he retrieved the boy's money from the gardener selling apples. When Adolphus appeared, Ernest told him his apples were still with the gardener, adding, "If you want them, find some more honest means to obtain them." Like Apollyon before Christian, Adolphus behaved histrionically. He turned pale; his lips quivered with rage, and he "fiercely enquired what Ernest meant by interfering between him and his fag." "To rescue the little one from your injustice and oppression," Ernest answered, "calmly, but firmly." "Secretly fearing" Ernest, as a portion of the aristocracy feared the leveling effects of education, but not knowing "how to vent his growing rage," Adolphus aimed "a blow at his little fag, who still stood trembling by." By offering both the opportunity to better their lots in life, education emblematically joined the lower, and comparatively weak, and the middle, and comparatively strong, classes. Symbolically Ernest stuck his arm out and "received the blow, casting a glance of contempt at Adolphus." Then, facing the little boy, Ernest assured him that he would protect him from oppression in the future. While Ernest was looking the other way, Adolphus hit him. Ernest, however, was not hurt, and grabbing Adolphus by his shoulders "laid him, without the effort of a blow, at his length upon the ground."

Adolphus was stunned, and although "hootings and other sounds expressive of contempt" assailed him, he refused to fight and "took to his heels, and was not seen again by his school-companions during the day." In fleeing the punishment he de-served, Adolphus refused to struggle with his weakness, and straying far from the road to virtue and success, began a sad demonic wandering. After he returned to school, he plotted against Ernest under the cover of professed friendship. Craftily, he spilled ink across Ernest's copy book, and like the snake spoiling Eden, poisoned Ernest's prize rose bush and opened a fence and let pigs into his garden. Eventually, however, his deeds were found out, and he was expelled. He then became addicted to worse vices, and after losing his inheritance gambling, be-came a highwayman. When last heard from, he was imprisoned in the hulk *Retribution*. "I had become a pest and a disgrace," he wrote, "THROUGH THOSE ROOTED HABITS OF CRAFTINESS AND DUPLICITY I ALLOWED TO BECOME MY MASTERS IN MY BOYHOOD."[6]

Characters resembling Adolphus appeared in many children's books. Representing a class and perhaps its ultimate fate, these children were so indulged that they did not study or work. As a result they could not endure hardship or meet challenges. When reprimanded or threatened by middle-class children, they almost invariably asserted the superiority of their births. In a society in which more and more people believed that the only superiority of consequence was determined by education and individual effort, the appeal to rank failed. In Mary Pilking-ton's *Biography for Boys* (1809), an aristocratic Henry Clifton threw a rock at and killed a leveret belonging to Horace Lacells, a poor orphan. Despite Henry's being in the protecting com-pany of his brother Charles, Horace challenged him. Although they outnumbered Horace, the two Cliftons fled. Charles es-caped but Horace caught Henry. "Do you suppose I fight with mere plebeians," Henry said when cornered. Horace ignored Henry's remark, and twisting a cane out of his hand, began to beat him across the shoulders. Almost immediately Henry begged for mercy and offered to pay Horace for the leveret. "Keep your money for a better purpose," Horace replied, "and remember that though a *gentleman* cannot condescend to *fight* with a *plebeian*, a *plebeian* has much gratification in *thrashing* a *gentleman*."[7]

From Mary Pilkington's *Biography for Boys*.
Courtesy American Antiquarian Society.

BIOGRAPHY

FOR

BOYS;

OR

CHARACTERISTIC HISTORIES,

CALCULATED

To impress the Youthful Mind

WITH AN ADMIRATION

OF

VIRTUOUS PRINCIPLES,

AND

A DETESTATION OF VICIOUS ONES.

BY MRS. PILKINGTON.

PHILADELPHIA:

PUBLISHED BY JOHNSON & WARNER,
No. 147, MARKET STREET.

1809.

In emphasizing the importance of education for this world, there was the danger of teaching children to overvalue worldly things and worldly behavior. If education, Hannah More wrote, was "a school to fit us for life," then, she reminded readers, life was "a school to fit us for eternity." In part aristocrats were villains in school fights because they represented the seductive and corrupting influence of luxury. At the end of the eighteenth century, social critics almost routinely blamed the aristocracy for undermining the morality of the middle classes, arguing that the upper classes set poor standards for emulation by living in a luxurious fashion. "The seeds of false-refinement," Mary Wollstonecraft wrote, "undermine the very foundation of virtue and spread corruption through the whole mass of society." "Elevation in life inspires neither sense nor discretion," A Lady warned in *New and Elegant Amusements for the Ladies of Great Britain* (1772); "pomp, grandeur, honours, fame, dignity, or splendour will not breathe the pure gale of happiness, unless reason, virtue, and prudence lend their softening aid."[8]

Not only did aristocrats suffer beatings as representatives of luxury in children's books, but many stories described the errors of parents who aped luxurious behavior and gave their children educations which schooled them for neither life nor eternity. *The History of Jacky Idle and Dicky Diligent* (1806) described the unfortunate effects of, as Jane West put it in *Letters to a Young Lady* (1806), the "rapid increase of wealth to families that have not, either by habit or education, been taught the proper use of it."[9] Jacky Idle was the son of a tradesman, who having inherited a fortune from a relative, quit the solid middle-class world in which he belonged, and moving from the city to the country adopted a style of living which he thought aristocratic. Believing that money, not education, made the man, he paid little attention to his son's studies and allowed him to be spoiled by his wife. When Jacky eventually went to school, Mrs. Idle warned the master "never to chastise him, nor even to force him to learn any thing against his inclination," observing "that a depth of education was necessary only to those who were hereafter obliged to work for their labour."

Attending school with Jacky was Dicky Diligent, who, because his parents were poor, realized the importance of education.

During the holidays, Dicky visited Jacky. Mrs. Idle "loaded her son's stomach with cakes and sweetmeats," so much so Jacky "grew dull and pale, and soon afterwards sick indeed." Instead of feeding her son the plain provender of a good education on his recovery, Mrs. Idle gave a party and inviting the "neighbouring gentry and people of fashion" exposed him to debilitating fare. During the party an old lady exclaimed, "What a pity it is that such a smart young gentleman, as is master Jacky, should spoil his fine eyes by reading, and hurt his stomach by pressing against a desk while writing. Gentlemen of fortune have no business with the sciences; they should be left to the labour of poor people." Although Dicky Diligent remained silent, his face revealed his thoughts, and Mr. Freeport, a wealthy merchant sitting nearby, asked him if he disagreed. "I do not know how to answer you, sir," Dicky replied, "for the old lady must certainly know better than I." The answer satisfied Freeport, and he offered the boy a position as clerk in his counting house. Dicky's diligence brought rewards; after some years, he became Freeport's partner and married his only daughter. In contrast Jacky, whose education had not prepared him to progress through life, did poorly. After receiving his inheritance, he "launched out on the dangerous ocean of the wide world, without any compass to steer by, without the least ballast to keep his vessel steady, and without any knowledge how to direct the helm." As a consequence, sharpers stripped him of his money and then, treating him like an uneducated animal, advised him to "return to the country, and there get your living by looking after hogs, sheep, and other cattle."[10]

Fighting in school stories for girls differed from that in books for boys. In the latter, fights frequently represented an allegorical struggle between good and evil often embodied as a struggle between classes. On the level of the individual the fight marked a stage in development in which the rightly educated boy proved himself firm enough to overcome obstacles and worthy of continuing his progress toward success. In books for girls physical struggles rarely occurred between individuals; instead fights represented the general breakdown of social order, as the domestic and "passive virtues" which women ideally embodied bound society together. Although women were not entitled to places in Parliament, they were, Jane West wrote, "*legislators* in the most important sense of the word." The home was a microcosm of the nation and was the "proper sphere" for women, Mrs. Taylor wrote. Although men had "much to do with the world without" and "*our* field of action" was circumscribed, she declared, women who discharged their duties at home "may produce effects equally beneficial and extensive."[11]

Fielding's *The Governess* began with a fight which revealed the importance placed upon education in early children's books. The governess, Mrs. Teachum, gave a basket of apples to Jenny Peace, her senior girl, to distribute among her schoolmates. One apple was bigger than the others, and although Jenny parceled the apples out as fairly as possible, all the girls coveted the large apple and began to quarrel. To quiet them, Jenny offered to divide it. When this failed to halt the bickering, Jenny threw the apple over a hedge. Even this did not restore calm, and a fray erupted as the girls fought over who should have had the right to the apple. As desire for an apple led to the expulsion of those first children Adam and Eve from Eden, so it introduced discord into the school world. In contrast to the Bible and *The Pilgrim's Progress*, however, education, not right religion, restored harmony. Although education and religion were closely linked since Mrs. Teachum was the widow of a clergyman, they were nevertheless separate, for, not God or a minister, but Mrs. Teachum instructed the children "in all proper Forms of Behaviour." No other fights occurred in *The Governess*. Having curbed the outbreak of original temper, if not sin, Mrs. Teachum directed her pupils' progresses so that they would enjoy successful lives and be "obedient to their Superiors, and gentle, kind, and affectionate to each other."[12]

In school stories for girls great stress was put upon the passive virtues, "fortitude, temperance, meekness, faith, diligence, and self-denial," as Hannah More listed them. "Nothing is more conducive to female happiness, or more certain to insure the affection of those with whom we live, than a yielding forbearing temper," M. Woodland wrote in *Bear and Forbear* (1809); "it not only produces that harmony which is so desirable in families, but teaches fortitude and patience; two qualities which cannot be too highly estimated, and which young women cannot too assiduously cultivate." Instead of fighting an individual to over-come a symbolic obstacle, girls were taught to conquer the urge to fight. "The regulation of the temper," Priscilla Wakefield wrote in *Reflections on the Present Condition of the Female Sex* (1798), "is of all qualities the most useful to conduct us steadily through vexatious circumstances." In contrast, regulation of the temper did not always overcome evil in boys' books, and good boys often fought out of a sense of virtuous indignation. In *The Disgraceful Effects of Falsehood* (1807), Henry Cathcart "was as much beloved for the sweetness of his temper, as he was ad-mired for that spirit which would not suffer the *defenceless to be oppressed.*" When he returned to school after an illness and learned that Adolphus Fitzhue had abused his brother Edward, a fag, "the fire of indignation sparkled in his eyes, and without even replying to the account which had been communicated, he immediately hastened to Fitzhue's room." Ignoring Fitzhue's claim that he was "rather too much of a *gentleman* to *fight*," Cathcart grabbed him by the collar and thrashed him "with all his strength."[15]

In *Anecdotes of a Boarding-School* (1795), a girls' story, the attitude toward fighting was very different. When Martha en-tered Mrs. Steward's school, some of her classmates, including Miss Grumpton, Miss Sneak, Miss Lapwing, and Miss Stone, ridiculed her good manners and religion. When Martha asked her mother how she should behave, Mrs. Beauchamp wrote, "Gentleness and forbearance should at all times be the char-acteristics of a young lady's conduct, even to those who offend her." Following her mother's advice, Martha tried to ignore her persecutors until one day when Miss Grumpton crept behind her and snatched a letter from Mrs. Beauchamp out of her hand. When Martha tried to retrieve the letter, the bad girls passed it about the room. Martha became frantic, and losing her temper, tore half a yard of binding from Miss Grumpton's shirt. A fight began, and soon all the girls in the room were involved. Hearing the commotion, Mrs. Steward rushed in and found Martha "en-deavouring to bite the hands of a Miss *Fangly*, a great girl, who was holding her by the arms to prevent her going to her letter, and at the same time, making the most use she could of her feet, to induce her to set her at liberty." Instead of being transformed into a righteous champion like Henry Cathcart, Martha's loss of temper turned her and her schoolmates into animals. "My dear," Mrs. Steward told her, "though offended, we are not to suffer our passions to transport us beyond all bounds, and permit ourselves to kick and bite like dogs, who have no understanding or reason to guide them." [14]

In school stories for girls, the emphasis put upon controlling the passions usually turned potential conflicts with external opponents into internal struggles. Because it encouraged rivalries that could grow heated and develop into open conflicts, competition was frequently discouraged. Mrs. W., her governess, Laura wrote in *Correspondence Between a Mother and Her Daughter at School*, "takes great pains to check in us a spirit of competition and rivalry; while she endeavors to inspire us with the genuine love of knowledge, and with a true taste for our acquirements; urging us to be more ambitious to excel *ourselves* than to excel each other." In Maria Edgeworth's story "The Bracelets" (1800), Mrs. Villars awarded a prize for "successful application" at the end of each school year. The two leading candidates were Cecila and Leonora. After her mother's death, Cecila was raised by her father. Although he attempted to fill a mother's role "in the best and kindest manner, he had insensibly infused into his daughter's mind a portion of that enterprizing, independent spirit, which he justly deemed essential to the character of her brother." As a result Cecila's virtues "were more estimable in a man, than desirable in a woman." In contrast, Leonora, who had been reared by a mother, "had a character and virtues, more peculiar to a female." Her judgment, Edgeworth wrote, "had been early cultivated, and her good sense employed in the regulation of her conduct; she had been habituated to that restraint, which, as a woman, she was to expect in life, and early accustomed to yield." Since she had been practically raised as a boy, Cecila delighted in competition and won the prize for application. Success, however, did not bring lasting satisfaction. As soon as she received the award, Cecila ran exulting down a flight of stairs and knocked over little Louisa, breaking a china doll which Louisa had just received from her mother. As the doll broke easily, so Cecila's happiness, built not upon solid feminine restraint but upon a masculine enjoyment of competition, shattered quickly. Cecila laughed when she broke the doll and was rebuked by Leonora. Cecila was unhappy from this moment until she won the inner struggle against ambition and cast a vote she thought would break a tie between Leonora and herself and give Leonora an award for "most amiable." [15]

Inner struggles "to excel" a selfish, or the clearly related ambitious, self, provided the substance of fights in school stories for girls. For the most part, the battle against, as Jane West put it, "this insatiable monster, a rage for distinction" appeared as a personal struggle against vanity and the superficial attractions of aristocratic luxury. The "phrenzy of accomplishments," Hannah More wrote, "is no longer restricted within the usual limits of rank and fortune; the middle orders have caught the contagion, and it rages with increasing violence." In early children's books, vanity and luxurious living were responsible for the deaths of many children. Curing the contagion was difficult and in books for girls depended upon an education which created immunity to luxury. In appealing to the middle classes, early children's books not only preached the danger of living luxuriously but also taught that if children from families of rank and fortune received proper educations they would reject luxury, and embracing temperance and self-denial, would become true aristocrats, in effect spiritual and moral members of the middle class. In *The Mother's Gift* (1787) Mrs. Forbes sent her niece Harriet to Mrs. Lawes's school, apologizing that the girl had "the Misfortune" of being "a person of Quality." Although Harriet had "been taught the Accomplishments that make a Figure in the World" and could sing, dance, play the harpsichord, and understand "every Form of good Breeding," she was "entirely deficient in every Part of useful Knowledge" and "ignorant of the Duties which are the Improvement of Life." After a struggle with herself, Harriet overcame vanity. Instead of remaining merely a figure, or the sum of worldly accomplishments, she grew into a substantial person. She received a proper education and so progressed that she recognized her duties and led a useful, benevolent life. "All who are acquainted with her," the author wrote, "had Reason to bless the Time when the wild Shoots of Pride and Extravagance were pruned, and the Buds of Virtue and Religion grafted on her Heart." [16]

"Felicity dwells not with princes; she is not the guest of the great ones of the earth," Elizabeth Somerville wrote in *The History of Little Charles and his Friend Frank Wilful* (1808); "she has long since fled from palaces, and retired to the scenes of simple nature, to dwell in rural quiet, and become the companion of the harmless village swain." Living amid luxury in an unnatural social system that emphasized birth rather than moral and intellectual worth, children of quality like Harriet were often seen as unfortunate. Rank and the seductive attraction of material goods prevented them from attaining that simplicity which Somerville celebrated as an ideal and which brought a pure vision and then a wholesome life. Unless circumstance swept them out of their palaces or a kindly relative undertook their educations, they wandered about unhappily, aware that something was wrong with their lives but unable to do anything. In *Evenings at Home* (1797) little Lord Linger was bored and dissatisfied. "Tired of doing nothing" and thinking that a ride would brighten his day, he ordered his horse saddled. After getting his boots on, however, he decided instead to go out in his low chair. Once again, though, he changed his mind, and when his ponies were almost harnessed, he decided to go into the cornfield and see how his pointer hunted. Unhappily this did not hold his interest long, and he spent the rest of the morning attempting to find something that amused him. After becoming bored by billiards, geography, Virgil, and even his "London made bow in its green case, and the quiver with all its appurtenances," he once again decided to go for a ride. With a servant following him, he "sauntered" for "a mile or two through the lanes, and came, just as the clock struck twelve, to a village-green, close by which a school was kept." The door of the school burst open, and out ran "a shoal of boys, who, spreading over the green, with immoderate vociferation, instantly began a variety of sports. Some fell to marbles—some to trap-ball—some to leap-frog. In short, not one of the whole crew but was eagerly employed. Every thing was noise, motion, and pleasure." Seeing Jack, one of his father's tenants, Lord Linger asked him if he liked school. When Jack replied "pretty well," Linger asked if he had much time to play. When Jack said that they could play from twelve to two and then again before supper, Linger responded that the time seemed "very little." "But," Jack answered in justification, "*we play heartily when we do play, and work when we work.*" Jack then ran off to play trap ball, and Lord Linger said to himself, "I wish I was a schoolboy." [17]

Right education would have made Lord Linger happy and would have turned him, as it did Harriet, into a useful and successful person. At Mr. Allworthy's academy in *The Friends*, Master Ashton complained that Master Wills had taken his place in the classroom, saying that "superiority of birth and fortune" entitled him to first place. In response Wills pleaded superior learning. To settle the dispute, Tommy Truelove told a story which illustrated the comparative values of learning, and of birth and fortune. A great man in one of the "Islands of Solomon" in the South Seas, Tommy began, owned a house near the ocean where he spent much time hunting and fishing. Overgrown with reeds, a long slip of land lay between the sea and the rich man's property. The land was owned by a poor but honest basket maker whose livelihood depended upon the reeds. Having failed to buy out the basket maker, the rich man resolved "that it became not a man of his quality to submit to restraints, in his pleasures, for the ease and convenience of an obstinate mechanic" and he ordered his servant to burn the reeds down. When the basket maker complained, the rich man had him beaten, whereupon the basket maker took his grievance to the king. In passing it should be noted that although early children's books generally had democratic or leveling tendencies, few references were made to the monarchy. For the most part children were simply told to honor the king, much as they were told to say their prayers. Although Tommy Truelove's story taught the superiority of learning to birth, the king existed beyond the conflict as an almost infallible judge. When the rich man justified his behavior arguing that the poor man displayed "unmindfulness of the submission due from the vulgar to gentlemen of rank and distinction," the king reminded him that the rich man's great-grandfather had been "a cleaver of wood." In response the rich man raised the specter of revolution, muttering that "this way of thinking" would give dangerous thoughts "to the commonality." The king then ordered Yanhumo, his Captain of Gallies, to strip both men and leave them naked on a remote island. Here the rich man was educated and outgrew the misfortune of being a person of quality. When natives discovered the two men on their island, they threatened to kill them. The rich man could do nothing, but obtaining some reeds, the basket maker wove a coronet for the natives' leader. The basket maker's skill so impressed the natives that they spared the men. The basket maker then set about teaching the natives to weave and was treated as a great man while the man of "quality" gathered boughs for him and became his servant. After three months in this menial position, the rich man reflected and said if they were rescued he would share his possessions with the basket maker. Eventually they were rescued, and the rich man stuck to his word, dividing his property so that the two extremes of society, the rich and the poor, met in what in effect was a harmonious and ideal middle. After hearing the story, Ashton wept and asked Wills's pardon, and one can assume became a better person and a spiritual member of the middle class.[18]

"The sphere of feminine action," Priscilla Wakefield wrote, "is contracted by numberless difficulties, that are no impediments to masculine exertions." Much as fights in school stories for girls were confined to an internal rather than external sphere, so Harriet would use her knowledge and exercise her duties more in the domestic than in the public world. Although men were given "a firmer texture of mind" than women and would ultimately be exposed to "that consummate knowledge of the world to which a delicate woman," Hannah More wrote, had "no fair avenues," the progress of all children in school stories was confined to a comparatively limited landscape.[19] As Christian had to hold fast to religion and remain on "the Road" to reach the Celestial City, so children's books discouraged students from prematurely wandering into the wide world where they could be distracted from proper education. Making educational progress was difficult, and students who ran away from school usually were either bad or weak. *The Adventures of Timothy Thoughtless* (1813) described the sufferings of a small boy who fled boarding school. Timothy was the son of a confectioner who "by his own industry and attention to business" became wealthy. Although Mr. Thoughtless did not ape the aristocracy, his son was spoiled literally and metaphorically by indulging in the insubstantial sweets made possible by wealth. After Timothy became sickly, Mr. Thoughtless sent him to Greengrove House, a boarding school. Instead of dining on luxurious "sweet articles," students ate hearty meals, and Timothy soon grew both healthy and "forward in his learning."

Timothy spent two happy years at the school; then, inevitably, Will Grumble, who had been expelled from other schools, appeared in the green grove. Like the serpent in Eden or the apple in Mrs. Teachum's school, Grumble brought discord. "His joy was to tell one boy that Master Such-a-one had said different falsities of him, and then he would go to the other with similar lies, till he had produced a quarrel or a boxing match." When the rest of the boys were at play, he crept into the schoolroom and blotted copy books. Like Adolphus in *Tales of the Academy*, he destroyed gardens, pulling up flowers and breaking fences. Because of his "crimes," innocent boys were flogged. He criticized the school and the master Mr. Stubbs so cleverly that students "began to think themselves very badly used, and became discontented, careless, and refractory." As a consequence, Stubbs became more severe, and unhappiness spread. One day Grumble stole a book from Master White's play-box. When asked about it, he, like every other boy in school, denied knowledge of the theft. A week later, "as Timothy was watching a large snail crawling up the wall of the barn, which was old and full of chinks," he discovered the book hidden between two bricks. Stubbs, who was on his way to the stables, saw Timothy take the book from the wall and concluded he had stolen it from Master White. So great was his anger "at finding a thief in one of his scholars, as he supposed," Stubbs did not listen to Timothy's explanation and instead beat him with his riding whip and declared he would flog him the next morning before the entire school.

Timothy decided to write his father, but Grumble, who had witnessed the beating, convinced him to run away from school with him. The next morning Timothy fled with Grumble, but like Headstrong in the company of Passion, soon found the way difficult and became lost. In leaving school and thereby the education which determined both moral and economic success, Timothy practically condemned himself, like those who took the wrong gate in Lady Fairfame's garden, to "*endless misery.*" At times the landscape through which he and Grumble wandered resembled Hell. Exhausted, the two boys eventually fell asleep, only to be awakened by a storm. "The lightning flashed as if all the heavens were on fire, and the thunder shook the ground where they stood with its dreadful explosions; the wind bent the branches of the trees in the hedges, mingling its loud howlings with the thunder; and the rain, rushed down upon them in torrents." To escape the rain, Grumble took shelter under a beech. Just as he reached the tree, however, "a prodigious limb, torn off by a sudden gust of wind, fell upon him with a frightful crash, dashing out his brains upon the spot." In undermining his and other boys' educations, Grumble had earlier destroyed all possibilities for positive development and his early death like that of Jacky Idle was fortunate and inevitable. "Thus ended," Walker wrote, "the life of that wicked boy, who, had Providence suffered him to live, would in all probability have grown up in wickedness, till some of his actions would have brought him to the gallows."

Since early experiences had lasting consequences, finding one's way back to school or to the right educational road was not easy. Education taught control and discipline, and as uneducated Grumble had, in a sense, been at the mercy of his evil impulses, so Timothy who had rashly rejected education was now at the mercy of unrestrained elements within society. After being chased and bitten by dogs, he eventually fell asleep again, this time to be "suddenly awakened by someone pinching his cheek." Timothy was horrified to find "a beggar woman stooping above him. Her face was haggard, and withered, and frightfully marked with small-pox." She wore rags and on her back was a filthy child. Beside her stood a boy, Teddy, Timothy's own age, without hat, shoes, or stockings. "Pray, don't kill me!" Timothy cried in terror. "What money have you got, you little thief," the woman answered and ordered Teddy to search him. Timothy's money did not satisfy Teddy, and after taking his hat, handkerchief, and knife, he said, "I think, mother, I should like his shoes." " 'Oh, what shall I do? what shall I do?' cried Tim, in a grievous tone of voice; 'Oh, that I had never left Mr. Stubbs.' "

"Give over your piping and snivelling," the woman cried, adding "or I'll be after stripping your carcase, and murdering you.—Come, pull off this green jacket and trowsers, and change cloaths with the lad." In running away from school, Timothy had unconsciously turned away from education, which was responsible for the differences between men. Without an education, Timothy was doomed to be a Teddy, and after the beggar woman left, he wandered aimlessly. Instead of making an educational progress during which he gradually disciplined himself and thus asserted control over circumstances, he became the pawn of circumstances and the emblem of the uneducated man. He joined a group of potters headed for a fair. When they deserted him, a vagrant fiddler and ballad singer made him beg. Only luck saved him from being murdered or becoming a thief. For a while, he lived in a poorhouse; then he was apprenticed to Sam Sturdy, a master chimney sweep. Eventually he obtained a piece of paper, and because he remembered his letters wrote his parents, who rescued him and sent him, repentant, back to Greengrove House.[20]

Many versions of Timothy's story appeared in children's fiction. Because education shaped the adult and as in the case of Billy Freeman raised the child above the animal and an animal like existence, the stories emphasized loss. Outside school, children were stripped, first of their clothes and then often of their lives. Because the heroine of *Sophy; or, the Punishment of Idleness and Disobedience* (1819) did not want to learn her book, she ran away from home. Becoming lost, she was given shelter by a farmer's wife. Unfortunately Sophy had so drifted from proper instruction and lost her way that she did not want to work and she left the farm. A beggar woman then found her, and after robbing her forced her to "become the companion of beggars" and to "lead a vagrant wandering life." Deprived of the sustaining direction which a nourishing education would have provided, Sophy eventually starved to death.[21]

Unlike controlled educational experiences, undisciplined wandering usually did not lead to growth. Sophy died, and Timothy only learned that he wanted to return to school. As Christian had to remain on the road to reach the Celestial City, so children had to remain in school not only to succeed in life but to remain alive. Outside school life was anarchic and instead of controlling circumstances by resisting temptation, the child was controlled by circumstances and instead of growing by denying experience was ruined by experiencing. Much, however, as the middle classes in the eighteenth century generally held that a religiosity like that of Bunyan inhibited a child's educational progress and thus his future, so a growing number of writers criticized educational practice, and children's literature, arguing that they, too, were narrow and limiting.

Experience in its multiplicity, they claimed, taught better than schoolmasters, and tales like the school story which confined children to a world within walls undermined development. Experiences like those endured by Timothy Thoughtless should not have incapacitated a child but should have made him more capable. In book five of *The Prelude* (1805) Wordsworth celebrated what he called "a race of real children" and criticized educators who confined children like "engines" to a rigorous educational road. Instead, he believed, children should roam freely across "the open ground of Fancy." As their worlds expanded, so would their capacities, and unlike engines that would be knocked off the road by unusual events, real children would be able to cope with the unexpected. An education which only taught girls "all proper Forms of Behaviour" and which emphasized discipline, preaching control of the passions, was partly responsible, Mary Wollstonecraft argued, for making women inferior to men. "The regulation of the passions," she wrote, "is not, always, wisdom. On the contrary, it would seem that one reason why men have superior judgment, and more fortitude than women, is undoubtedly this, that they give a freer scope to the grand passions, and by more frequently going astray enlarge their minds." [22]

In this attitude were the seeds of different, more complex heroes, characters in whom both virtue and vice appeared and who because of their rounded natures did not lend themselves to allegory. In early children's books, however, the rounded character or individual, interesting in and for himself, did not appear. Although not all were allegorical, characters were flat instructional devices. Somewhat paradoxically, however, Locke's stress upon the formative effect of education may have undermined both allegory and the allegorical character. Wordsworth overstated his case in arguing that educators had reached a kind of instructive consensus which enabled them to mass-produce engines rather than human beings. In truth, Locke's ideas raised possibilities of endless individuality. No longer restricted to an estate or trade by birth, children, in the world of theory and of hope at least, could become and do almost anything, provided they received suitable educations. Instead of a type, the child could become an individual upon whose own initiative depended much of his future. Mirroring this state of educational belief and coinciding with the great spread of education in the nineteenth century, unique individuals began to appear in children's literature. Be this as it may, however, "new" characters were not necessarily more complex than their allegorical counterparts. Often writers simply reversed the formula which celebrated the disciplined child and made a hero, for example, out of the boy who violated convention and appeared bad but who was actually good, or the vagabond who was a dismal failure in school and who seemed to be drifting aimlessly but who was actually developing an enormous capacity to cope with and succeed in life. Although such characters superficially appeared more realistic than the heroes and villains of allegory, they lent themselves almost as easily to moral or social commentary. For those who believed that society and its institutions were corrupt and that conventional education perpetrated social evil, the character became the voice of truth or of nature. Thus uneducated children like Dickens's Sissy Jupe were transformed into child philosophers while the Teddys of the road became teachers and social scientists. Because such a character's growth usually depended upon challenging experiences or a series of challenges to society, he was often the hero of a picaresque story. At its best this attitude produced Kim and Huckleberry Finn.

Despite the occasional appearance of a character like Aladdin who because he was uneducated was able to discover the magic in a worthless lamp and transform life, few early children's books depicted the vagabond or wanderer favorably. In early children's books, the gypsy was not a romantic character traveling through worlds and time but a predator lurking just beyond the border of home or school, waiting to prey upon the disobedient child. In *Juvenile Anecdotes* (1809), Laura left her parents' protected garden and wandered into a lane where a gypsy saw her and started to rob her. "Children should not wander beyond the bounds allowed them, especially if their clothes are rich and valuable," Priscilla Wakefield wrote, "as they are liable to meet wretches, like this gipsey, who for the sake of a little money, would strip and abuse them, or perhaps carry them about as their own children, where their parent could never find them." Unlike *Kim*, which celebrated alluring mystery and the multiplicity of life, early children's books cautioned children against the unknown. "Never follow a stranger in the streets, who promises to give you cakes, fruit, or tarts to show you any fine sight," the *Boy with a Bundle and the Ragged Old Woman* (1813) warned; "never venture into narrow lanes, dark alleys, or lonesome places, with a stranger who offers to show you the way." Unlike Kim, heroes of early children's books were rarely friends of all the world. Instead of accepting life's variety and treating existence as a game, the Kim of early children's books, the hero of Mary Sherwood's *Little Henry and his Bearer* (1819), learned to say *no* and to keep to the "narrow gate."[23]

Like Kim, Henry was orphaned in India, his mother having died a year after his birth and his father having been killed in battle. Although a benevolent woman took him in, she paid little attention to him, and until age five he was effectively raised by Bossy, his bearer. Unable to speak English, he spent his time on "the *verandah*, between his *bearer's* knees," chewing "*paun*" and eating sweetmeats. He did not wear shoes or stockings but was "dressed in *panjammahs*, and had silver *bangles* on his ancles." "No one could have told by his behaviour or manner of speaking that he was not of Indian origin"; only his light hair, blue eyes, and "delicate complexion" gave him away. Exposed to servants, Henry learned many things "a little boy should not know." Even worse, his knowledge of true religion was rudimentary, and he believed that "Mussulmauns were as good as Christians." Knowing that the woman who took him in, his "mamma," sometimes went to church and accustomed to seeing natives "performing *poojah*, and carrying about their wooden and clay gods," he concluded that there were many gods and that the god to which his mamma prayed "was no better than the gods of wood, and stone, and clay, which his *bearer* worshipped. He also believed that the river *Ganges* was a goddess, and called Gunga; and that the water of the river could take away sins."[24]

This kind of broad knowledge that contributed to Kim's becoming an effective and tolerant guide for a holy man threatened to damn Henry. When he was five, however, the daughter of a clergyman arrived from England, bringing Bibles and children's books. Knowing it was "a dreadful thing for little children to be left among people who know not God," she labored to educate and to save Henry. Instructing him in English and religion, she "strove to teach him" that "there was only one true God." Henry resisted the constriction of his world, and at first he left her company and sat between his bearer's knees. That night the lady prayed for Henry, and the next day "she made him kneel down, and pray to God to give him sense to understand the truth." To convince him that there was only one true god, "she had also provided herself with one of the Hindoo gods, made of baked earth." After asking him to examine it carefully, she threw it down on the floor where it broke "into an hundred pieces." Then she said, "Henry, what can this god do for you? it cannot help itself. Call to it, and ask it to get up. You see it cannot move."

The demonstration convinced Henry, and he fast became an ideal student, albeit initially he had difficulty with the concept of sin. He did not, for example, consider lying to be sinful, "nor feel ashamed of stealing, unless it was found out. He thought, also, that if any body hurt him, it was right to hurt them in return." The lady, however, overcame Henry's difficulties, and "in a short time," his whole behavior changed. "He never said a bad word," Sherwood wrote, "and was vexed when he heard any other person do it. He spoke mildly and civilly to every body. He would return the *salam* of the poorest *coolie* in the *bazar*. If any body had given him a *rupee*, he would not spend it in sweetmeats or playthings; but he would change it into *pice*, and give it to the *fakeers*, who were blind or lame, or such as seemed to be in real distress." In just a year and a half Henry had progressed "from the grossest state of heathen darkness and ignorance to a competent knowledge of those doctrines of the Christian Religion which are chiefly necessary to salvation." At this time, the lady left to be "married to a very pious young man." Before departing, however, she urged Henry to convert Bossy so that he, too, could "be counted among the sons of God."[25]

Henry took her instructions to heart and set about saving Bossy. Much as the lady had trouble with Henry, however, he had difficulty with Bossy. When he informed Bossy that there was a country in which there were no castes and all men were "dear brothers," adding that he was going there soon, Bossy asked if he were going to Europe. Almost as if good health signified an undue concern with earthly things and sickness indicated spirituality, Henry fell ill. As his body grew weaker, both his soul and powers of conversion grew stronger. He worked hard for Bossy's salvation, and on his deathbed, his labor was rewarded. Dying, he praised God, saying, "He washed me from my sins in his own blood; he gave me a new heart; he has clothed me with the garments of salvation, and hath put on me the robe of righteousness." Turning to Bossy, he then cried, "O my poor *bearer*! what will become of you *if you neglect so great salvation?*" "O Lord Jesus Christ," he prayed in Hindu, "turn the heart of my poor *bearer!*" "Scarcely knowing what he was doing," Bossy repeated the prayer, the first prayer he ever said. Later he was baptized and renamed *John*. As the open road was no place for Timothy Thoughtless, so, despite guiding his unholy man to the river of salvation, India was no place for a proper education, and like Timothy who returned to his schoolmaster, so Henry returned to his heavenly master.[26]

In *The Way to be Happy* (1819), an old woman interrupted a group of boys playing. Some of the boys were so frightened that they ran away while others ridiculed her and called her a witch. Henry, the oldest boy, however, recognized her as the fairy Instruction. When little George, the youngest boy, did not run and simply put his hand into Henry's for protection, Instruction invited the boys to visit her castle "where she promised to make them as happy as the day was long." The path to the castle was "very much beset with briars"; eventually, though, the boys arrived, and Instruction opened the door admitting them to a large hall where they "sat down to a pretty collation of plumb-cakes, biscuits, and sweetmeats, which were brought in by four beautiful damsels, called Innocence, Health, Mirth, and Good Humour." The hall itself was supported by five pillars in the niches of which stood statues of Truth, Modesty, Natural Affection, Good-Temper, and Diligence. Instruction touched the statues with her wand and they stepped down from their pedestals and gave George presents. Diligence, for example, attached wings to George's shoulders, remarking they "will be of great service to you by and by; but they will droop whenever the old witch Laziness comes near." To protect him against Laziness, who would turn him into a dormouse, she also gave George a golden spur, telling him that if he stuck it into his side when Laziness approached his wings would "immediately resume their vigour." In early children's books Instruction possessed miraculous transforming powers. The journey to her castle was difficult, and many children fled from or ridiculed her. If a child, however, accompanied Instruction and made use of the gifts offered in her castle, he would not simply learn the way to be happy but would be happy and successful. Contrary to Burges's contention, "modern education" did not banish religion from the nursery. Instead, early children's books expanded the allegorical progress to include this life as well as the next, frequently converting "the wilderness of this world" into "that LITTLE WORLD, a SCHOOL."[27]

3

* * * * *

Robinson Crusoe

hen Hannah's parents died, she went to live with her aunt and uncle. For three years, "A Lady" wrote in *The Little Scholar's Mirror* (1812), Hannah had no playmates. Then her cousin Robert arrived from the West Indies "for the purpose of receiving a liberal education." Life in the Indies spoiled Robert, and he was lazy. Often he stayed in bed until lunch, and only rarely did he wash his face or put on clean clothes. Because Robert "knew that he should possess a large fortune, which in his opinion, rendered it wholly unnecessary to acquire knowledge," "every attempt to instruct him" was futile. One afternoon when Hannah, Robert, and their aunt and uncle were walking to a neighbor's house, they were caught in a shower. All except Robert dashed for shelter and did not get very wet; too lazy to exert himself, Robert continued his "slow pace," was soaked, and as a result became ill. Because he was so enervated, Robert declined rapidly. In hopes that stories would interest him and he would bestir himself, Hannah began reading to him. One day Hannah found *Robinson Crusoe* in her uncle's library and asked Robert if he would like to hear it. "Well," he said, "I know nothing about this Crusoe, but I will listen." The book had a miraculous influence. The tale intrigued Robert, and "the efforts made by the hero, during his abode in the solitary island, his industry and perseverance, produced a salutary effect on his mind. In a serious conversation with his uncle, he expressed his resolution of attending to his studies, and ardently wished to walk once more in the open air." Putting his wishes to effect, Robert began to exercise and soon grew healthy. Although it took more time for him to overcome his "habit of idleness" and to become a diligent student, *Robinson Crusoe* showed the way and "in a few years he became a virtuous and intelligent man."[1]

Not all readers, however, found *Robinson Crusoe* so therapeutic. What broke Robert's lethargy and stirred him to sense and health could have unfortunate side effects leading others to nonsense and illness. Calling it "one of the most interesting and entertaining books that was ever written" and noting that it had been well "employed in the education of boys, for the purpose of shewing what ingenuity and industry can effect, under the divine blessing," Sarah Trimmer still warned parents against it. "Children of very lively imaginations," she wrote, "accustomed to indulge their fancy without control in their infantine amusements, may undoubtedly, be led by it, into an early taste for a rambling life, and a desire for adventures."

Maria Edgeworth agreed. "The taste for adventure," she wrote in *Practical Education* (1815), "is absolutely incompatible with the sober perseverance necessary to success" in "liberal professions." Adventure was particularly dangerous to boys, she thought, who "from the habits of their education, are prone to admire, and to imitate, every thing like enterprise and heroism." "When a young man deliberates upon what course of life he shall follow," she wrote, "the patient drudgery of a trade, the laborious mental exertions requisite to prepare him for a profession, must appear to him in a formidable light, compared with the alluring prospects presented by an adventuring imagination." "A boy," she continued, "who at seven years old, longs to be Robinson Crusoe, or Sinbad the sailor, may at seventeen, retain the same taste for adventure and enterprise."

Robinson Crusoe was one of the most popular books in the eighteenth century. Like those of Edgeworth and A Lady, however, attitudes toward it varied. In the world of early children's literature it was an educational tract for the times, and behind both the book's popularity and differences over its potential effects lay worries about education and the influence of childhood reading.[2]

Crusoe was a secularized, middle-class version of Bunyan's Christian. Once marooned on the island, he behaved like the members of the Bettering Society, keeping a diary in which he charted moral growth and the progress he made in coping with the world. Indeed, after the shipwreck he resembled Locke's infant with a mind like a blank tablet or empty cabinet. Those ideas which he learned in England were of little use to him in this second beginning; slowly, though, as his senses sharpened, he stocked his cabinet with mental tools which enabled him to function in this world and which prepared him for the next. As members of the Bettering Society learned economics in order to become successful tradesmen, so like a merchant Robinson Crusoe learned practical skills: farming, manufacturing, and managing. The inhabitant of a pure Lockean place in which success depended on the individual, not inherited social privilege, Crusoe educated himself and fashioned his own success. For twenty-eight years he lived on the island, after which he resembled the young person who, having passed through childhood, adolescent education, and initial years of work at a trade, left home and entered society as a capable, self-sufficient adult.

Early children's books made much out of self-reliance. When Kitty Kindness gave Peter Pippin a penny, he behaved like a Lockean ideal. Adding the penny to five others which his father had saved for him, he took the money to Farmer Giles and asked him to buy a sixpenny edition of *Robinson Crusoe* for him the next time he went to town. "Now a great many silly boys," the book stated, "would have spent that penny in apples, gingerbread, or some such trash, and when they had eaten it, what better would they have been of it? Why, nothing at all. But Peter did not lay out his money in such an idle manner; whenever he got a penny, he bought food for his mind instead of his belly, and you will find he afterwards reaped the benefit of it." In warning parents against *Robinson Crusoe*, Edgeworth argued as a good Lockean that "the first impressions which are made upon the imagination . . . are seldom entirely effaced from the mind." In Peter's case, these first impressions had a happy educational effect, contributing to his self-reliance and thus preserving his life. Years later he was shipwrecked while on a voyage to the West Indies. Because he remembered his *Robinson Crusoe*, he survived, and after being rescued, he eventually, and fittingly, became governor of an island in the Indies.[3]

In *Reflections on the Present Condition of the Female Sex*, Priscilla Wakefield divided the female population of Britain into four classes and suggested courses of study appropriate to each. Wakefield devoted most attention to her third group, the lower middle class, the segment of society from which Robinson Crusoe himself came, "those, whose honest and useful industry raises them above want, without procuring for them the means of splendid or luxurious gratification." "Plain instruction in a plain garb" best suited these girls who, she thought, would become wives of tradesmen. As useful for a tradesman's wife as for a member of the Bettering Society were "a thorough acquaintance with figures" and "a methodical system of book-keeping." In contrast, dancing, music, embroidery, and a "smattering" of French were to be avoided. Worse still were plays and novels. "Nothing," Wakefield wrote, could "be more distant from the plain, sober, useful qualities of a housewife, than the excellencies of the heroine of a novel." So that they would not be led astray by indiscriminate reading, Wakefield suggested thirteen titles. Instead of preserving physical life, as *Robinson Crusoe* did for Peter Pippin, the books emphasized the practical and the moral, teaching girls to behave correctly and to be hardworking and satisfied with a life of useful industry. Among the books were Sarah Trimmer's *Family Magazine*, Jonas Hanway's *Virtue in Humble Life*, Robert Dodsley's *The Economy of Human Life*, and Christoph Sturm's *Reflections on the Works of God, and of His Providence, Throughout all Nature, for Every Day in the Year*. The only novel on the list was *Robinson Crusoe*. On his island

From *The Wonderful Life . . . Robinson Crusoe*.
Courtesy American Antiquarian Society.

THE
WONDERFUL LIFE, AND
Surprifing adventures of that
Renowned Hero,

Robinfon Crufoe,

WHO LIVED
TWENTY-EIGHT YEARS
ON AN

Uninhabited ifland,

✕✕✱✕✕✕✕✕✕✕✕✕✕✕✕✕✕✕✱✕

Written by Himfelf.

✱✱✱✱✱✱✱✱✱✱✱✱✱✱✱✱✱✱✱✱✱✱

BOSTON

Printed and fold by N. COVERLY

⁎⁎ PRICE THREE PENCE.

Crusoe resembled a tradesman, keeping accounts and methodically spending his days working. Perhaps more important than the example of sober practicality illustrated by Crusoe's experience on the island was the warning Crusoe's life provided against the dangers of "rambling," both mentally and physically. Crusoe's troubles began with his education. "Not bred to any Trade," he had not, in Wakefield's words, benefited from plain instruction suitable to his station in life. Instead of the tools of a practical education, Crusoe's head "began to be fill'd very early with rambling Thoughts," the kind, Wakefield believed, produced by novels and plays. Crusoe's childhood ramblings determined the drift of his later actions; eventually he obeyed, he recounted, "blindly the Dictates of my Fancy rather than my Reason" and his "Head began to be full of Projects and Undertakings beyond my Reach." As a result he grew dissatisfied with, as his father labeled it, "the middle Station of Life," that segment of society which provided the readership for children's books and to whose aspirations and fears such books generally appealed.[4]

In the eighteenth century many abridged editions of *Robinson Crusoe* were available for children. Most were very different from the book read today. A good number included selections from either or both of the sequels: *The Farther Adventures* (1719) and *Serious Reflections during the Life and Surprising Adventures of Robinson Crusoe* (1720). Several of the editions published before 1800 were chapbooks or small two- or three-penny versions.[5] To offset the attraction of Crusoe's adventures, these editions emphasized the cautionary aspect of *Robinson Crusoe*. Typically an edition of 1794 concluded with Crusoe's returning home after fifteen years on the island and finding his parents dead. Although they were old, Crusoe blamed himself, not age, for their deaths, and while reflecting about the property he inherited, he lamented, "I cannot have peace to enjoy it, and at this moment I really believe myself the most miserable object living, and heartily I repent giving way to the restless disposition which made me leave my parents, as from that hour I date all the subsequent misfortunes of my life." At the end of an edition of 1786, Crusoe addressed children who bought books from the publisher Isaiah Thomas, warning, "Now as many of my readers, from a wild inclination of their own, or from the advice of bad children, may wish to ramble from one country to another, they may rest assured by me, that it will only bring them into distress, for every word of my father's advice, when he called me into his chamber, I fatally found strictly to be true." Having in effect cautioned young readers against dreams of adventure, Thomas, then, in what underscores the age's ambivalence toward *Robinson Crusoe*, advertised a fuller, more exciting edition, writing, "Note.—*If you learn this Book well, and are good, you can buy a larger and more complete History of Mr.* CRUSOE, *at your friend the Bookseller's in* WORCESTER, *near the* COURT-HOUSE." In the short version much stress was put upon the advice of Crusoe's father. "What can possess thee, my child," the father said in Thomas's edition, "for wishing to leave thy native Kingdom, depend on it, travel where you will, by land or by water, never will you put foot into any country where the blessings of life are more generously disposed among all ranks of people." When Crusoe showed little inclination to follow advice, his father told him that traveling "*will bring on you many an aching heart.*" [6]

Since early impressions had lasting consequences, the appeal to duty became an important device by which parents could control children. In part Crusoe's aching heart resulted from ignoring his father's advice. In *School Occurrences*, Miss Worthy recognized her duty to obey and resisted the temptation to ramble. Mrs. Worthy sent her daughter a book in which she marked passages she thought appropriate for reading. Worthy followed her mother's instructions and when reading aloud skipped unmarked passages. Looking over Worthy's shoulder and noticing that she was not reading the entire text, Miss Pry asked why. After Worthy's explanation, Pry said, "I wonder that you do not have strings attached to your eye-lids, and that the ends are kept in your Mamma's hands." When Pry added scornfully that she was "so over-good," Worthy answered, "We cannot be too strict in our adherence to the injunctions of our parents." "You have no curiosity," retorted Pry. "Oh! yes, I have as much as you; but I do not indulge it at the expence of my *duty*," said Worthy, adding, "you recollect that disobedience was the first sin; and curiosity perhaps the inducement." [7]

Robinson Crusoe could be seen as celebrating, even rewarding

From Dorothy Kilner's *The Holiday Present.*
Courtesy American Antiquarian Society.

disobedience. Not only did the disobedience of his father lead to an exciting life, but it brought material rewards. In some respects the island became Crusoe's estate, and with winter and summer homes, he could be thought a type of country gentleman, if not a member of the landed gentry. Usually, however, disobedience in early children's books rarely led to industry and discipline, much less success. Instead of fitting a child for life, disobedience handicapped him. In *The Holiday Present* (1787), for example, Polly Ingrate's mother told her to stay away from a pond in the garden. Polly did not listen, and one day when she was playing catch, she fell into the pond. On this occasion, she was fortunate and was rescued. Her mother also warned her to avoid "a little dirty yard" where pigs were kept. Polly paid no attention, and one day when she tried to pet a baby pig, a sow bit her fingers "so bad, that one of them was obliged very soon to be taken off." Polly's obstinacy brought only painful distress. Despite being forbidden to approach an open window, Polly leaned out of a window in her mother's bedroom, and falling to the ground below, broke her back. By not heeding advice, Polly condemned herself to unhappiness, or in Wakefield's educational terms, so misspent her childhood that she could not assume the "duties" of her station. Not surprisingly, the fall crippled her, and the author wrote, "She is now a woman, and you cannot think how sadly she looks. She is never well: Her back sticks out worse than any thing you can imagine, and her shoulders are as high as her ears; and all this was the consequence of not minding what had been said to her."[8]

Polly's appearance was an outward, visible sign of her inward, moral deformity. Much like Adam and Eve, children who disobeyed a parent's instructions were frequently condemned to suffering and death. The story of "Tom Noddy and his Sister Sue" appeared in several early children's books. Tom and Sue were attractive children; unfortunately they were not obedient. One day their mother saw them teasing cows and told them to stop before they were injured. Just as she called to them, a hawk flew overhead, and a hen warned her chicks. Unlike the children who did not listen to their mother, the chicks "ran immediately under her Wings for Shelter." A gentleman who happened to be walking nearby saw and heard everything. He stopped and urged the children to obey their mother, saying, "These Chickens, though they are so little, have more Sense than you; for they know that their Mother is older and wiser than them, and therefore they always do as she bids them."

Ah! I don't care, what do you think I mind you, says Tom; I don't care what, do you think I mind you, says Sue; and away they both scampered after the Cattle. The Gentleman, who heard the Bull grumble and saw him curl up his ugly Face, called to them again, and ran to bring them back; but before he could get near them the Bull with his Horns had tossed them both into the Air, and the Cows when they fell trampled them in the Dirt, and what became of them afterwards I don't know; but this I know, that all Boys and Girls, who are not dutiful and obedient to their Parents, never come to any Good, but are, as they ought to be, always neglected and despised.[9]

Spoiled children constituted the largest group of disobedient children in early children's books. As Crusoe was the youngest of three sons and spoiled to the extent that he did not learn a trade, so the parents of such children so neglected education that their children were not suited for any station in life. Unlike Crusoe, these children rarely were reborn on deserted islands. In *The Adventures of a Silver Penny* (c. 1786), Master Billy Headstrong was "permitted to hecter and domineer of the servants, and even to call them names." Instead of correcting him, Billy's parents laughted at "his spirit and liveliness." One morning while sitting in bed, Billy began "grinding a large quantity of gunpowder in a coffee-mill." When the footman warned him, Billy told him to "go about his business for a fool. The footman did so, and in a few minutes the mill took fire, bursted, killed him, and set fire to the curtains." Such, Richard Johnson wrote, was "the consequence of Mr. and Mrs. Headstrong's giving their son so much liberty." Almost always a sign of a child's being spoiled, not parents' lack of caring, liberty was associated with idleness and led to a child's going astray and, if not being burned alive, to those flames that burned through eternity. In *The New Robinson Crusoe* (1790) Joachim Campe emphasized that Crusoe's troubles originated in his being allowed too much liberty and too little attention being paid to his education. His parents, Campe wrote, "suffered their *dear child* to do whatever he pleased; and as this *dear child* liked better to play than to work or to learn any thing, they let him play almost the whole day long, by which means he learned little or nothing." [10]

Birth amid poverty did not condemn one to unhappiness in early fiction for children. More often than not, it was seen as advantageous, for in this literature idleness and its attendant, luxury, killed more children than poverty. In contrast to the child born to wealthy parents who was often tempted by and who had time to indulge in the corrupting vanities, the poor child was forced to work. Not only did poverty protect him from luxury, but it taught industry and the value of education. "Happy," Mary Wollstonecraft wrote, "is it when people have the cares of life to struggle with; for these struggles prevent their becoming a prey to enervating vices, merely from idleness." "Few things," *A Birth Day Present* (1803) said, "are denied to resolute industry and perseverance." "*Idleness,*" the author of *The Book of Games* (1811) emphasized, "*is the bane of virtue, and the destroyer of happiness.*" "Of all the qualifications belonging to human nature," *The Child's Friend* (c. 1790) explained, "industry may be rank'd among the first." It enlivened the mind and contributed to health, the book continued, while idleness was "the cause of debility and disease." Since early impressions were crucially important, the diseases were often moral, and children's books preached avoiding idleness and using time lest in the process of wasting it the future was lost.

"Learning is like climbing up a steep ascent," Kitty's brother told her in *The Brother's Gift* (1786); "if you are not moving upwards, you will be in danger of sliding down to the bottom." For religious writers the fall was more serious than a tumble down a hill. From Hell there was no way back, and in *An Essay on Christian Education* (1812), Sarah Trimmer urged parents not to neglect early religious education. "*Satan,*" she wrote, "will assuredly be busy sowing *bad seed,* and though children in their early years are not capable of *actual sin,* the *old Adam,* the corrupt nature will spring up in them; and bad habits, very difficult to eradicate, will take root, unless *the things belonging to the* SPIRIT be cherished." In contrast to, in Campe's words, his "sauntering about and playing in the streets of Exeter," Crusoe was rarely idle on the island. His life there stood as a model of practical industry at a time when many critics thought prosperity was corrupting the middle classes and turning them into sauntering idlers who aped the aristocracy. The "rapid increase of wealth," Jane West wrote in *Letters to a Young Lady* (1806), "has principally affected the intermediate orders," families "that have not, either by habit or education, been taught the proper use of it. The first blessing which fortune seems to offer to an ill-regulated or ill-informed mind is self-enjoyment, the second distinction; hence arise luxurious modes of living, and absurd exhibitions of grandeur." [11]

Not attracted so much by luxury as by vanity and idleness, Campe's Crusoe seemed doomed to be a moral and economic failure. Only his "death" and rebirth on a desolate island, where there were no luxuries and in which he did not have time to indulge his luxurious imagination, prevented it. According to Campe life on the island saved Crusoe. Crusoe "was now become so accustomed to work," Campe explained, "that he could not live without employing his time in some useful occupation. In the latter part of his life, he would often say, that his reformation was principally owing to this single circumstance; that when he was constrained, when in solitude, and deprived of all assistance, to provide for his wants himself by persevering labour; and he would add, 'Constant employment is the mother of a crowd of virtues, as habitual idleness is the source of all vice.'" Sometimes children's books neglected the young Crusoe and focused on the island experience, seeing Crusoe as an admirable representation of the industrious man. During an especially cold winter in *The Little Islanders* (1809), Sir Robert Bonitas allowed tenants to strip trees off an island for firewood. Having read Defoe, Bonitas's children asked if they could then make the island *"Robinson Crusoe's Island."* Stipulating that they could use only "those hours which were allotted for play," their father agreed. The children's project was an instructive success, and they learned "a love of industry."[12]

Crusoe's loss ultimately led to gain, a pattern often repeated in early children's books. In *The Blossoms of Morality* (1795), Bella was an "indolent beauty." Because her father was wealthy and she was beautiful, Bella saw no reason why she should study, telling her mother, "What need have I of learning, when my parents are so rich, and you yourself acknowledge I am so pretty." When Honestus, "a young gentleman of fortune and character," met her, he considered "paying his addresses to her." Once he discovered that she was "little more than an *ignorant beauty*," however, he changed his mind. Fortuitously for her, if not for her family, Bella was "instructed by misfortune." Her father died after going bankrupt, and forced to live modestly, Bella and her mother moved into a small cottage in the country. As consolation for the loss of wealth and position, Bella reminded herself that she was beautiful. Fortunately, as things turned out, this consolation proved fleeting as she caught smallpox and lost her looks. In a passage recalling *Robinson Crusoe*, Richard Johnson addressed "youthful readers." "Be careful," he warned, "how you place too great a confidence in the possession of wealth and beauty, since they are as fleeting as the wind, and as unsteady as the vessel on the troubled billows of the ocean. Fortify your minds with religion and virtue, and a proper knowledge of the useful sciences; the storms and hurricanes of Fortune may then attack you, but you will always safely withstand their rage, and deride their fury." "Before she was a beauty without sense," Johnson wrote; "now she had lost the charms of her face, but had found those of the mind, which are infinitely the most to be valued." Two years passed, and then Honestus, who happened to be nearby on business, stopped to pay his respects to Bella's mother. At first Honestus did not recognize Bella, and after he did, began to talk to her only "out of politeness." Conversation quickly showed Honestus that the changes in Bella were more than external; he fell in love, and shortly afterward proposed and was accepted.[13]

In early children's books shipwrecks appeared almost as frequently as exhibitions of rarities. Like Johnson, writers used the wreck emblematically, warning young readers that only right education could save them from the storms of life. "You are just setting out on a voyage, which must terminate either in satisfaction and hope, or in misery and despair," Jane West wrote in *Letters Addressed to a Young Man* (1801); "A thousand dangers beset you, and not only from those tempests of adversity which no human prudence can avoid; there are many destructive whirlpools which may speedily engulph you, and many rocks and quicksands, so completely covered from your observation by a.smooth placid sea, that you can only escape them by diligently attending to the cautions which preceding adventurers suggest, and to the directions prescribed for your course." In *The Shipwreck; or, Misfortune the Inspirer of Virtuous Sentiments* (1819), Alfred Mornington at first appeared "not only *indolent* but *versatile;* continually desirous of some new acquirement, but, before he obtained any proficiency, fatigued and exhausted by application." Like Bella, Alfred was taught better ways by "the chastening hand of misfortune" and was shipwrecked in the Indian Ocean. In *Evenings at Home* Philander, who had "a considerable place about the court," lived beyond his means and was forced to retire with his family to a remote farm. There he began life anew; soon he realized that he had lost nothing of consequence while he had gained his soul. "In improved health, the charms of a beautiful country, a decent supply of all real wants, and the love and kind offices of each other," he said to his family, "do not we still possess enough for worldly happiness." "Look forward, then, cheerily," he urged, "the storm is past. We have been shipwrecked, but we have only exchanged a cumbrous vessel for a light pinnace, and we are again on our course. Much of our cargo has been thrown overboard, but no one loses what he does not miss." [14]

As useful industry distinguished Crusoe on the island from the boy in Exeter, so in early children's books it often separated the substantial middle classes from the aristocracy. In *The History of Mr. Rightway and his Pupils* (1816), Mr. Rightway became tutor to his nephew Fred, the orphaned son of Major Rightway who had fallen "victim to the ruthless and indiscriminating scythe of war." Since he was already overseeing Fred, Mr. Rightway agreed to supervise the education of the son of Lord S. who was going abroad for two years. For the young lord, arrival at Mr. Rightway's house was comparable to being marooned. Meals, for example, were relatively simple. The boy, William Sullivan wrote, "no longer beheld the same luxury and profusion; no pines, melons, nor hot-house fruits; no jellies nor sweetmeats appeared; plain roast and boiled, with an occasional fowl and fish for variety only, filled the board." Because the boy had been "tenderly reared" and "his health was delicate," Mr. Rightway urged him to dig in the garden with Fred. Also working there was a truthful rustic. After the young lord had dug for some time, "his eyes lost their languor" and his cheeks had a color "they never before possessed." " 'I declare, I think, Master Frederic, that your great folks paint,' said the gardener, 'for they look so rosy and so fair, not the brown red that the weather gives one, but such a delicate bloom of a pink or carnation, just like the young lord there.' " After hearing the gardener, the boy blushed, then answered brusquely, "I don't paint man." "I ax your noble's pardon," the gardener said, "I now sees you dont, but don't be ashamed of your looks, for *exercise* is the most *wholesome* and natural paint, and if you were only to look in the glass, you would never desire to look pale again." Along with his color, the work improved the young lord's appetite, and afterward he enjoyed a plain meal of bread and milk. The change in physical appetite foreshadowed a change in mental appetite. When Lord S. returned after two years, he was astonished by the improvement in his son's health. "The alteration in his person," Rightway explained, "is of little moment, compared with the improvement you will discover in his intellects, and above all, in his *mind* and *morals*."[15]

Mr. Rightway's educational regimen smacked not only of *Robinson Crusoe* but also of Rousseau's *Emilius and Sophia* (1762–63), with which *Crusoe* was often linked. Not only did similarities exist between the educations of Crusoe and Emilius, but Rousseau said *Robinson Crusoe* was the first book Emilius would read, calling it "a complete treatise on natural education" and writing, "I would have him indeed personate the hero of the tale, and be entirely taken up with his castle, his goats and his plantations." In *Emilius* Rousseau advocated returning to nature for education, to a Crusoe-like island of natural experience. Beginning with Locke's belief that the child was the parent of the adult, Rousseau argued that nature was a better teacher than man. As Wordsworth did later, he implicitly attacked educators who believed that childhood should be structured in order to shape the adult. "All things," Rousseau wrote, "are as good as their Creator made them, but every thing degenerates in the hands of man. By human art is our native soil compelled to nourish exotic plants, and one tree to bear the fruits of another. Improving man makes a general confusion of elements, climates, and seasons: he mutilates his dogs, his horses, and his slaves: he defaces, he confounds every thing, as if he delighted in nothing but monsters and deformity." "All wisdom," he continued, "consists in servile prejudice; all our customs are nothing but subjection, confinement and restraint. Civilized man is born, lives, and dies in slavery: at his birth he is bound up in swaddling cloaths, and at his death nailed down in his coffin; as long as he wears the appearance of the human form, he is confined by our institutions." By implication this meant that middle-class parents who were educating children so that they would be successful in society were actually corrupting them and that disobedience to parents' and indeed to society's injunctions might ultimately do more good than harm.[16]

Since institutions were corrupt, Rousseau urged that education follow nature. Man, he wrote, was "subjected by two kinds of dependence; the first on circumstances and things, which is that of nature; and the second on men, which is the effect of society. The former being merely physical, is no degree destructive of liberty, nor productive of guilt: the latter, being unnatural and disorderly, is productive of all manner of vice." "Subject your child, therefore," he concluded, "only to a dependence on circumstances; you will then follow the order of nature in the progress of his education." Few educators accepted this idea. "Let me also recommend one other rule with respect to education," Jane West wrote to her son, "that children should be early habituated to ideas of dependence and subjection: not on necessity, as Rousseau enjoins." Although the translator demurred in the preface, noting that Rousseau "allows Nature too much," Campe seized upon the educational importance of necessity in *The New Robinson Crusoe*. After abandoning Crusoe on the island without a tool, he explained,

> Necessity is the mother of invention. She teaches us many things which we should not know but for her. It is to this intent that our Creator hath formed us, and this earth that we inhabit, in such a manner, that we have different wants, which we cannot satisfy unless by the manifold efforts of invention. If ever we are masters of good sense and an active understanding, it is to these wants that we are indebted to for them: For if larks fell down out of the air into our mouths ready roasted; if houses, beds, clothes, victuals, and every thing else necessary for the preservation and comfort of our lives, grew up of their own accord out of the ground or on the tops of trees, quite ready and prepared to our hand, certainly we should do nothing else but eat, drink, and sleep, and be as stupid as brutes.[17]

For Rousseau the "method of education, by which the present is sacrificed to an uncertain future" was "barbarous," and he urged parents "not to gain time, but to lose it." Instead of books, excepting *Robinson Crusoe*, Emilius would learn from nature. With only minimal supervision, he would be encouraged to discover or wander on his own through instructive experiences. Rousseau's Timothy would not be "Thoughtless" but thoughtful and as one of Wordsworth's real children, able to cope with the unusual. In Britain the most popular writer of children's books who accepted many of Rousseau's ideas was Thomas Day, whose *The History of Sandford and Merton* (1783–89) enjoyed a large circulation. Like Rousseau, Day urged returning to a natural and nurturing educational simplicity. In Day's "The History of Little Jack" (1796), the hero was abandoned on the stoop of a tumbledown cottage inhabited by a crippled soldier and his pet goat Nanny. The soldier was so poor that he could not buy food for the infant. Poverty, however, proved a blessing. Instead of being "tenderly reared" as was the son of Lord S., the child fed simply on nature itself. Since Nanny had just lost her kid, the old soldier presented little Jack to her. She adopted him, and the boy "sucked as naturally as if it had really found a mother." Free from, in Rousseau's words, that "barbarous method of edu- cation" in "which a child is laid under every kind of restraint, and is made miserable, by way of preparing him for we know not what," Jack thrived. "It was wonderful," Day wrote, "to see how this child, thus left to nature, increased in strength and vigour. Unfettered by bandages or restraints, his limbs acquired their due proportions and form; his countenance was full and florid, and gave indications of perfect health; and, at an age when other children are scarcely able to support themselves with the assistance of a nurse, this little foundling could run alone." As Jack's body was healthy, so was his mind. Despite the old sol- dier's poverty, Jack learned to read and write. "Industry," Day explained, "enables us to overcome difficulties; in the summer time, as the old man sat before his cottage, he would draw letters in the sand, and teach Jack to name them." After the deaths of Nanny and his "old daddy," Jack was on his own. His upbring- ing made him industrious, however, and so prepared him that he was able to meet life's unexpected challenges, one of which was being marooned. Jack enlisted as a soldier for India, and when his boat stopped to take on water, he went ashore on the Cormo Islands to fetch game shot by officers. In searching for game, Jack became lost, and by the time he reoriented himself, his ship had sailed. That night Jack found "a dry cavern in a rock." After a meal of shellfish, Jack laid boughs on the floor of the cavern to make it comfortable. Then as resourceful as Crusoe, he bar- ricaded himself in by weaving branches into "a kind of wicker work." The next morning, he "arose, a little melancholy indeed, but with a resolution to struggle manfully with the difficulties of his situation." Until his rescue several months later, Jack coped well, living a "tolerably contented life," and enjoying "perfect health."[18]

In advocating what he saw as simple, natural education, Rousseau attacked luxury and wealth. In a historical twist, however, critics at the end of the eighteenth century often associated Rousseau's educational ideas with fashion and indulgent wealth. For them his call for parents to lose time evoked aristocratic decadence. "Suppose for one instant," began Prudentia Homespun, the solid, British narrator of Jane West's *The Advantages of Education* (1803), "that the rage for idleness (I beg pardon, I mean refinement; I always mistake those words) should spread." In a world in which rigorous education enabled people to make their way, the only people who did not need to progress financially were the wealthy. Since an education was not necessary to their children's attaining means, such people could indulge their children in idleness or toy with fashionable educational refinements like Rousseau's ideas. Unfortunately, critics believed, structured education did more than determine financial success; it shaped morality and formed the discipline necessary to maintaining inherited position. As West wrote in *Letters to a Young Lady* that the expansion of wealth had primarily affected families that had not been educated to know "the proper use of it," so in *The Infidel Father* (1802) she examined the uses made of new affluence. The father of Kitty Muggleton was "an honest industrious farmer, whose frugal habits" enabled him to save fifty pounds a year. Convinced that childhood learning was important, he determined to give Kitty "a good *edication*." Unfortunately farmer Muggleton did not seek plain instruction for Kitty. Instead he sent her to boarding school for seven years. "In an evil hour," West wrote, "Kitty Muggleton was removed from her father's rustic dwelling, and exchanged her homespun dust-gown for a hanging-sleeve coat, and laced peak, her domestic employments for learning bad French, executing miserable drawings, and squalling out of all time and tune."[19]

After returning home from school, Kitty married Peter Jones, a wealthy ironmonger. Having rejected the solid virtues of the middle class for unsubstantial refinement, Kitty nagged her husband until he changed his last name to Fitz-John. Later after Peter became mayor and then Sir Peter, she decided to give her children, Melisandriania and Artremidorus, a fashionable education and hired Mr. Babble to tutor them. Rousseau in fictional dress, Babble had several revealing quarrels with Eleanor, an old servant of Sir Peter's. "My system of governing," Babble lectured her, "consists in not governing at all. You are only to teach by action, example, inference, and circumstance. Suppose you wished to prevent them from cutting themselves, how would you proceed?" When Eleanor said she would tell the children not to touch a knife, Babble answered, "Then you would impede their natural liberty, and weaken the power of experience." To teach Melisandriania to swim, Babble urged throwing her into and making her stay in a cistern until she was forced to swim in order not to drown. "Nature, all-wise instructress!" Babble said, "will soon direct her infant limbs to those movements that will enable her to float upon the water, and thus before she is susceptible of fear she will instinctively acquire an art that may preserve her life." "In the pearl fishery and on the coast of Terra del Fuego," he continued, "women make the most expert divers. In the South Sea islands they glide from rock to rock like sea-nymphs, and sport amidst tornados and hurricanes. In Greenland they accompany their husbands in their boats, soothing their labours with their soft society, and partaking both of their labours and their triumphs. Whether their bodies glisten with train oil, or whether meandering lines of tattoo diversify their tender limbs, whether perforated noses admit the pointed fish-bone, or their ears are lengthened by wooden wedges, these happy females, unrestrained by our voluptuous ideas of decorum, practice this graceful agile art, which I hope soon to see the favorite accomplishment of the British fair." Because of her opposition to Babble's educational ideas, Eleanor was dismissed. Babble, himself, however, soon followed her. To teach the children self-sufficiency, he adapted an episode from *Emilius* in which the boy was allowed to wander the streets. Although Emilius was closely watched, he believed that he was rambling on his own. In allowing Artremidorus and Melisandriania to roam "through the streets of W——," Babble planned a drama of " 'hair-breadth 'scapes' to teach his pupils, what an ordinary instructor would have thought it sufficient to have forwarned them of, namely, that the undertaking was full of danger." Unfortunately Babble's plans did not produce the intended results. A dray ran over Artremidorus, crippling him for life while "one of those miscreants who, in many populous towns make a trade of stealing and plundering unprotected children" stole Melisandriania and returned her only after receiving a large reward.[20]

Unlike Rousseau's theories, which critics often condemned as crippling, related ideas in Robinson Crusoe were rarely criticized severely. Although writers like Maria Edgeworth pointed out dangers, the book escaped broad censure, partly because editions like those of Isaiah Thomas warned children against rambling and partly because the book lent itself to a Lockean educational reading. Moreover, Defoe was English, and unlike those of Rousseau, his writings were not associated with the French Revolution. Robinson Crusoe did not, of course, escape criticism in early children's books. Although such criticism was more often than not implicit and general, some was explicit and particular. Usually, though, this criticism was good-natured as educators showed that the book's ostensible practicality was actually impractical, if not silly. In Tales of the Academy (1820), Paul attended Mr. Osgood's school in the village of Muchlore. Paul was "a youth of a singular and somewhat romantic turn of mind" and "of all the remarkable characters of whom he had ever read, whether kings, conquerors, heroes, statesmen, philosophers, poets, or sages, he neither envied the success, the splendor, the glory, nor the wisdom: his sage, his philosopher, his hero, his king was—Robinson Crusoe." During playtime, Paul wandered the woods which surrounded Muchlore. "The common forms of society," the narrator explained, "its habits, ceremonies, and established usages, appeared to him but so many bars to the felicity which, he was persuaded the recluse must enjoy without hindrance or molestation."

In the school yard, Paul built a hut, and after furnishing it with a rickety table, he entertained classmates, serving them an unpalatable homemade wine, brewed from "unripe currants, gooseberries, sloes when in season, preserved with due proportions of waters, and sugar, and a small quantity of spirit, in bottles, buried, for the space of a few months, under ground."

While copying Crusoe, Paul echoed Rousseau, lamenting "that such institutions as academies should ever have been allowed to exist." "*School* fetters," he said, "appeared to him of all the shackles to which human beings were subjected by the harsh customs of society, the heaviest and most intolerable." During winter vacation when only he and Osric, a student from the West Indies, remained at school, Paul decided to build a hut outside the school yard. Ideally, Paul told Osric, he would like to build the hut on an island. Having lived on a real, not a fictional, island, Osric asked Paul practical questions. Where, he wondered, would Paul obtain the tools with which to build the hut. When Paul answered that he would get them from a shipwreck, Osric asked if he could swim. The difference between fictional and practical living was not only great but irritating, and Paul replied, "No, I protest, I never thought of that. But you interrupt one so." Always practical, Osric continued questioning Paul. When Paul responded to a query about food and said he would sow corn and plant potatoes, Osric observed that corn and potatoes might not be native to the island and wondered where Paul would get seeds and cuttings. Paul then said if he could not find corn or potatoes he would eat local plants. How, Osric inquired, would he know which ones were safe.

Despite Osric's reservations Paul built a hut, albeit not on a faraway island but in a nearby haulm field. With a crude chimney and a simple opening for a window, the hut was constructed with bushes and branches. Inside, Paul parched peas and roasted potatoes which he obtained from school. Like little Jack, he was tolerably comfortable, at least until the evening his schoolmates returned from vacation. Mr. Osgood met them in a coach, and as they approached the village, one noticed "the uncommonly vivid effect of the setting sun upon the western sky." "Vivid indeed!" Mr. Osgood exclaimed, "the splendour appears more than natural!" Unfortunately Paul had set fire to his hut while roasting potatoes, and as the coach came around a curve in the road its occupants saw that "the school-house, the village spire, and the lofty poplars, all stood in seeming darkness, as contrasted with the strong red light of the sky behind them." Because there had been a long drought, the hut, the stubble in the fields, and the hedge trees "burnt with a fury inconceivable." Only a shift in the direction of the wind and the road which formed an avenue between the fields and the school saved the academy. Along with the hut, Paul's romantic turn of mind disappeared. Never again was he "troubled with longings for a desert island, or a lonely hermitage; nor ever again thought of assuming the habits and characters of Robinson Crusoe."[21]

4

✳ ✳ ✳ ✳ ✳

The Foundling

rosperity, says the Arabian proverb," Hannah More wrote, "fills the heart till it makes it hard; and the most dangerous pits and snares for human virtues are those, which are so covered over with the flowers of prosperous fortune, that it requires a cautious foot, and a vigilant eye to escape them." Having lost position, and really identity, Crusoe worked and in the process saved his soul. "*Humility,*" Sarah Trimmer wrote, was "the ground-work of Christianity." In early children's books it was more difficult for a child of wealthy parents to achieve humility than it was for a poor child to become wealthy. Humility and the low soil from which it seemed to spring naturally formed the basis not simply of Christianity but of temporal success. "Caroline Montgomery," a tale began, "was unfortunately born in that situation of life where wealth and indulgence alike contributed to the gratification of all her wishes." Typically *The Juvenile Story-Teller* told the instructive histories of Tom Racket and Jemmy Meekly. Racket's father

81

was a wealthy merchant who amassed goods worth one hundred thousand pounds; in contrast Meekly's father was "a poor humble tradesman," barely able to afford the cost of his son's schooling. "Always the first in school, and the last to depart from it," Meekly "was surpassed by none in diligence and progress. Except upon learning he knew he had nothing else to depend, that his future advancement or miscarriage in life, depended wholly upon the most trifling or bad use of the time within his power." Unlike Meekly, Racket did not think learning necessary to his success, and he idled away hours, refusing to "mope in school." Since education not only enabled people to achieve means but also to maintain what wealth they possessed, Racket was bound to fail. When his father lost his fortune, Racket became a poor ostler. In contrast, Meekly married his master's daughter and achieved "comfort, decency, and respectability."[1]

Only children were particularly susceptible to ruinous indulgence. Fanny Daudle, *The Juvenile Biographer* (1787) stated, "was an only Child, and therefore, as is too often the Case, was a ruined one; that is, was suffered to do just what she liked, without any one being permitted to contradict her." Fed the "richest Things," Fanny was "not put upon her Legs until she was eighteen Months old." She was so pampered that at six she was "crooked both in her Legs and Shape." The physical crookedness reflected mental waywardness. Not only was she a "constant Plague" to servants, but she "could hardly tell a great A from a House"; and whenever she was asked "to take a Needle in her Hand," she was overcome with "Vapours." Without an education, Fanny was doomed, and one day she scorned advice, walked in the rain, and caught a cold. Not having a cousin to cure her with *Robinson Crusoe* as Hannah did Robert, Fanny declined rapidly and died at age twelve.

In contrast to the only child, children from large families worked. In the process, they saved body and soul. In *The Nabob* (1807), Mary and Catharine Wilson were daughters of a farmer. Getting up at five in the morning, they milked the cows, then worked in the family garden. Later they attended the village school, where they learned to read, spell, write a "fair hand," and do arithmetic. "Accustomed to bodily exertions from their childhood, and inured by necessity to frequent exposure to the sudden changes of the weather," Mrs. Rice wrote, "they grew up hardy, healthy, and well formed. The rose bloomed on their cheeks, and the tranquillity of their countenances indicated the purity of their hearts."[2]

If more siblings meant less for each child, and thus constituted a blessing, then the child who had nothing at birth could be seen as particularly fortunate. Washed ashore into a desolate world without family and with only the possessions he scraped together from wrecks about him, the foundling was a significant character in children's books. Since education determined a person's lot in life, stories about foundlings often illustrated both the advantages of education and the dangers of being born into wealth. By not belonging to a family, a class, or indeed society itself, the foundling was the quintessential mobile person, the outsider who because he did not belong was free to determine his future. In *The Foundling; or, The History of Lucius Stanhope* (1798), Richard Johnson adapted *Tom Jones* to the educational mood of the late eighteenth century. Lucius's "parents deserted him in his infancy, and left him in a basket, suspended to the knocker of the door of the good Sir John Honeycomb." At the time Sir John and Lady Honeycomb had a son two months old. Much as Allworthy did with Tom and Blifil, they raised the boys together and treated them as brothers. At five, however, the boys were informed of the differences in their births. The boys continued to study under the same masters, and no distinction was made between them except "Lucius was not permitted to accompany them in their visits. This mark of superiority was a flattering object to their son, which filled his youthful mind with ideas of the greatness of his birth, and by degrees made him very indifferent about his studies." In contrast "Lucius wisely perceived, that the only chance he had of getting into the world, and supporting himself with any degree of credit, was to attend to his studies with indefatigable industry. Thus, while the parade of birth and riches interrupted young Sir John in the progress of his learning, the want of them laid the foundation of the future greatness of the prudent Lucius."[3]

Young Sir John made no educational progress. Because he had money, he became part of a fast crowd at Oxford. Receiving only a modest allowance, Lucius "met with no importunities

From Richard Johnson's *The Foundling.*
Courtesy American Antiquarian Society.

from the rich and idle to draw him aside from his business";
and as he had disciplined himself, so he established a reputation in law. Sir John grew jealous, and much as Blifil did with
Allworthy, so slandered Lucius that the Honeycombs disowned
him. Like Tom, Lucius was forced out into the world, but unlike Tom, education had shaped him and he did not wander
aimlessly, a prey to sensual desire. He traveled to London and
articled himself to an attorney. In contrast young Sir John wasted
his money in riot, then became a gambler in order to recoup his
losses. After her husband's death, Lady Honeycomb tried to reform him, but eventually "gave herself up to despair, and died in
a consumption" after which Sir John diced away the remainder
of his estates. Without wealth or family, Sir John was now in the
position of Lucius at the beginning of the book. As he himself
had come from nowhere and had been found, so Lucius discov-

ered Sir John in an obscure public house. Clothed only in rags, Sir John resembled a poor foundling. Lucius became Sir John's benefactor and provided him with an education that taught both moral and economic law. Learning to scorn "the parade of birth and riches," Sir John became middle-class, so much so that he was truly deserving, and when an uncle died in the West Indies and left him a fortune, he remained contemptuous of former companions and "happy in having Mr. Stanhope for his bosom friend and companion."[4]

Although more melodramatic than Johnson's book, Mary Pilkington's *Henry; or, the Foundling* (1801) made the same points. Having been given an infant at his master's door, Old Richard, a servant, brought the child to Mr. Coverley. "Alarmed at the bare idea of being called upon to fullfil duties that must be attended with a drawback to his *own enjoyments,*" Coverley told Richard to take the child to the parish workhouse. When Richard found a note saying that the person who protected the child would "be amply rewarded," Coverley became avaricious and relented. Also living at Coverley's home, The Grove, were a niece and two nephews. At his death their father left money to take care of them. Unfortunately, Coverley taught "arrogance and pride" to the boys. Some four years after he appeared at The Grove, Henry received a sixpence for reading well. When Coverley walked into the nursery, Henry proudly showed it to him whereupon Coverley "demanded who had been fool enough to waste such a sum of money? and for what reason it had been given to the little brat?" Addressing his older nephew Ned, Coverley said, "I hope you will always know the distinction there ought to be between a *beggar* and a *gentleman;* and remember I took the boy in to keep him from *starving,* not to put him upon a level with your *brother* and *yourself.*" When little Emily asked why Henry could not be taught to read, Coverley answered that "he must get his bread by *labour,* not by *learning.*" After this he "snatched the book" which Henry "still held, out of his hand, threw it into the fire, and walked immediately out of the room."[5]

After this incident Henry's position in the household worsened. He was banished from the table and treated as a servant. "This unexpected degradation," though, "had a striking effect upon the little foundling." Instead of becoming soft and vain like Coverley's nephews, he grew tough and independent and "for the first time in his life gave symptoms of that loftiness of spirit, which at future periods he had reason to display." Although he was treated with haughtiness by Mr. Bradshaw the tutor, Henry knew education was important and struggled to learn, receiving help from Old Richard and Emily. Impressed by Henry's pluck, Captain Manly, a relative of Coverley, adopted Henry and paid Coverley a hundred pounds a year to care for the boy. Before returning to sea, Manly also arranged for Henry to study with Mr. Parkinson, a minister who lived nearby. Two other boys studied with Parkinson. One, fourteen-year-old Percival Pembroke, was the son of "a baronet of immense fortune, who having totally ruined his boy's disposition by never suffering him to be contradicted, placed him under Mr. Parkinson's protection, under the hope of his being able to conquer those vices, which an excess of indulgence had been the means of producing." Since early experience shaped the adult, there was little that could be done for Percival, short of marooning him on a desolate island. At Mr. Parkinson's home, Percival was the typical aristocrat, weak and arrogant. In the past Henry had played trap ball with Percival as Ned Coverley's dependent and as a result had never played "with spirit." Now made independent by Manly's kindness and by his own exertions, Henry was a different person. In a game of trap ball, he and Charles Coverley beat Percival and William Parkinson "hollow." Percival was enraged. Not only did he treat Henry with "insolence and scorn," but he accused him of cheating, "making use of the most scurrilous language." For a time Henry "received this insolence with the contempt it justly deserved." Finally, however, he was provoked "beyond the power of patience," and he hit Percival, then "placed himself in a posture of defence." Like Adolphus in *Tales of the Academy* Percival proved a coward, and refusing to fight, walked away muttering "he would not *disgrace* himself by *fighting* with a *paltroon*." [6]

Resembling the heroes of school stories, Henry fought for goodness as well as against oppression. When Old Richard broke his leg, Henry nursed him back to health, in the process becoming sick himself. He befriended Peggy Cobham, who became deranged after a bull killed William, her sweetheart. Henry gave her money and listened patiently to "her *unconnected* tales of William." Henry persisted in this kindness although it was misunderstood. Bradshaw spread the rumor that Peggy was his mother, saying it was "not likely a boy of twelve years old would spend all his pocket-money in the support of an idiot, unless he was convinced that she had a *natural claim to it.*" When Coverley lost his money and that of his niece and nephews, Henry wrote Manly and told him to take care of the three children, saying that he was used to hardship and could get a job. As a foundling, Henry had been forced to make his way. In doing so, he became truly noble, and eventually he turned out to be the lost son of the Earl of Penton, his virtues having earned him a family and honors.[7]

Several variations on the foundling appeared in early children's books. Among the most common was the story of the child from the West Indies. Sent from a luxurious life in the colonies to Britain to be educated, the child became a temporary orphan. No longer pampered, the child first suffered, then studied and became a good, decent person. Typical was *Matilda, or the Barbadoes Girl* (1817). Sent to England to live with the Harewoods, she had been spoiled in Barbados. "Carried about" by servants, she rarely walked and as a result stooped. Tyrannical "over all whom she deemed her inferiors," she called the faithful maid who accompanied her from Barbados a "black beetle." Marooned in a serious middle-class world, far from the indulgences of the colonies, and with a Friday whom the Harewoods freed from tyranny, Matilda reformed. In Mary Pilkington's *Tales of the Hermitage* (1800), Mrs. Cleveland became the guardian of her nieces, Emma and Eliza, aged fifteen and sixteen. After the death of his wife, the girls' father gambled away a fortune. Before doing so, however, he accustomed his daughters to luxurious living. In the hands of a French governess, the girls' education had so concentrated upon the ornamental and superficial that when they arrived at Cleveland Vale, they found plain living and plain virtue unappealing. When Mrs. Cleveland asked them to accompany her to local Sunday school, they refused. "I cannot suppose," Emma said, "we shall derive much entertainment from hearing a parcel of dirty children read and say their catechism." Later after listening to Emma read Italian,

Mrs. Cleveland volunteered to correct her pronunciation. "But as I really have no passion for knowledge," Emma responded, "and happen to possess so large a fortune as to render it unnecessary for me to take the trouble of attending those accomplishments which girls in less elevated stations are *taught* to *consider necessary*, I must beg leave to decline your *offered instruction*."[8]

Because they had received poor educations, Emma and her sister were not simply ignorant but also incapable of managing anything, including wealth. Shortly after Emma refused Mrs. Cleveland's offer, she and Eliza learned that their father had lost their fortunes at the gaming table. In hopes that the loss would so shock the girls that she would be able to change their characters, Mrs. Cleveland lied and told them that she also had lost her means. Knowing the girls would not change if they remained at Cleveland Vale, Mrs. Cleveland said her loss made it necessary for them to move, and for a year she and her nieces lived in a cottage in a remote part of Wales. Comparative poverty and the Crusoe-like isolation proved blessings. The girls assisted their aunt in small charities and learned to read and draw. "The Park and Kensington gardens were both forgotten," and they began to appreciate the natural, both within themselves and in the unspoiled country surrounding their cottage. By the end of a year the girls had changed so much that Mrs. Cleveland exposed her ruse and told them that she had made them her heirs. The girls' fortunes were now the substantial intangibles of character, and fittingly they attained economic as well as moral success. "Your sentiments and ideas," Mrs. Cleveland said, "have happily now taken a different turn; you have felt *adversity*, and know how to pity it; you have acquired a habit of amusing yourselves without the *aid of variety*, or the *arts of dissipation*; and you will return to the world in a temper of mind calculated to *enjoy* its *pleasures* with *moderation*."[9]

Education and industry formed character and were responsible for success. Along with inherited wealth or position, even the gifts of fortune, those of heredity itself were suspect. Exceptional talents could undermine industry, and by making achievement too easy could produce an idler and ultimately a wastrel. "The man of a middling genius," Richard Johnson wrote, "who is frequently forced to walk in the humbler paths of life, and to

whom fortune has given a liberal and prudential turn of thinking, frequently steers his course through life with more ease,
reputation, and comfort, than he to whom fortune has been so
liberal in those gifts." In Barbara Hofland's *The Son of a Genius*
(1814), Mrs. Lewis was upset when she heard her son called a
genius. Everyone she knew to whom the word had been applied,
she said, had been injured by it. "Young people whose more
moderate talents, or less vivid imagination, have preserved their
minds from being inflated by this silly method of extolling that
which implies no merit, since it exacts no exertion, will learn,"
she declared, "that much may be gained by industry, even where
nature has not been liberal, and that the attainments for which
men in all situations, and all ages, were most esteemed, were
the result of patient investigation, unwearied diligence, and in-
cessant labour." [10]

Beauty was thought especially dangerous and if not a curse,
at least a snare to virtue. Along with the temptations to which
privileged birth made her susceptible, Matilda in *The Barbadoes
Girl* had the misfortune to be beautiful. "Such are the temptations handsome people are troubled with," Mrs. Harewood
explained, "that they are much more frequently to be pitied for
the acquisition than envied for it." In *Anecdotes of the Clairville
Family* (1802), Mr. Clairville commended his three children to
the care of his sister at his death. Having been raised by "a selfish, proud, unfeeling governess," the children had received poor
educations. Catharine, age eleven, "had been taught to consider
every one as her inferior, whose fortune was not equal to her
own" while Elizabeth, who was nine years old and was beautiful, "despised every one that was ordinary, and feared and hated
every one that was handsome." One day their aunt took the
Clairvilles to visit the Beverleys, the widow and children of a tal-
low chandler. Dorothea Beverley was deformed and in walking
with the Clairvilles offered Elizabeth her arm " 'or rather shoulder I should say,' said Dorothea, 'for though I am much older
than you, you are considerably taller than I am; the misfortune I
met with in my infancy, mamma says, has stopped my growth.' "
"Misfortune indeed," responded Elizabeth, "I would not for the
universe have that nasty ugly hump on my shoulder." "Since it
is there," Dorothea answered, "I must endeavour to be content;

and though my body is deformed, be particularly careful that my mind is graceful." Arrogant in the possession of looks, Elizabeth did not listen to Dorothea's good advice. Fortunately, however, smallpox robbed her "of some share of her beauty." Not surprisingly the loss of the inessential led to substantial gain. "When grown to a woman, she frequently said, heaven justly chastised for the value she set on her personal beauty, nor once regretted the want of that which when possessed of, made her vain and envious." [11]

In Elizabeth Somerville's *Charlotte, or the Pleasing Companion* (1803), Sophia Bartlet initially appeared blessed by birth. The only daughter of a rich merchant, she was beautiful, strong, and high-spirited. Worried about the temptations into which Sophia's good health and fortune might lead her, her mother encouraged a friendship with Phoebe, a poor cottager. One day on a walk with her mother and Phoebe, Sophia ran about "in her usual rude manner." Although warned against it by her mother, she climbed a high bank from which she fell and dislocated her knee. The fall was fortunate. The accompanying injury and the fever stripped Sophia of beauty and strength. "Sophia," Somerville wrote, "recovered slowly, but the fever had made such ravages in her before handsome countenance, that she had no longer any reason to be vain from the weak cause of personal beauty: she had also a very great lameness in one of her knees, which would, in future, prevent her leaping over ditches, climbing, and seeking amusements fit only for boys. She now took the greatest pleasure in the society of her mamma and Phoebe, whom Mrs. Bartlet brought up as a companion for her daughter." In time Sophia "ceased to regret" the change in her person and "at length became one of the most accomplished and amiable young women of the age, beloved for the benevolence of her heart, while in the height of her beauty she was neglected and despised." [12]

Much as the shipwreck separated Robinson Crusoe from the world and its temptations and thus contributed to his moral growth, so a handicap isolated a child and could be seen as contributing to healthy development. Margaret Hurry's *The Faithful Contrast; or, Virtue and Vice Accurately delineated* (1804) told the story of the two Perry brothers. The younger, Alfred, "was a boy of a brilliant, rather than a solid understanding; and possessed that lively disposition, which, in childhood, is too often mistaken for sense. Nature had endowed him with every advantage of face and person." In contrast Alfred's older brother Henry was deformed. From a fall in infancy, "he had contracted a deformity, which had not only injured his shape, but his health: and his face, which was much marked with the small pox, had no feature which was not ugly." Alfred's talents and beauty made him his parents' favorite, and they indulged him "with almost idolizing fondness." While Alfred was always in the parlor being caressed and praised, Henry was neglected and "seldom suffered to leave the nursery." The Perrys' fondness for Alfred set an example for the servants, who indulged Alfred and treated Henry with "cold indifference." Even worse Henry suffered from severe pain. The catalog of seeming misfortunes which plagued Henry, however, actually separated him from temptation and contributed to his subsequent happiness. "One indulgence he was allowed, and one only," Hurry wrote; "as he was incapable of much exertion or exercise, he early discovered a taste for reading, and the master of a school, very near the hall, was suffered to attend him." At four Alfred was on the way to a bestial existence; he "scarcely knew his letters" and ridiculed his master, calling him a "stupid drone." [13]

When Alfred was eight and Henry nine, the boys were sent away to school. At first Alfred's appearance "gained him many admirers," and students compared his person with "the deformity and sickly appearance of his brother." As education brought success, though, so Henry's "amiable disposition, and the powers and charms of his mind" eventually secured "him many friends" among the "judicious and worthy." Unlike Henry, Alfred did not study. Falling in with a mischievous group of boys, he indulged in the school story's equivalent of gambling: robbing orchards. One day when he overheard Alfred plotting to rob the flower garden of Mr. Saunders the master, Henry urged his brother to reform. Unhappily, "his kind intentions were treated with ridicule, his expostulations with contempt, and he was bid,—to remember that it was not every one who could sit hours pouring over a book, till they were stupified: for although such amusements were very well for a broken back and lame leg, they would not do for boys of any spirit." The spirit in Alfred was demonic. What he needed was to be shipwrecked and stripped of his hereditary gifts so that he could be educated.

Sadly, the wreck did not occur, and one morning some time later Alfred asked Henry to retrieve his hat from the master's garden. When Henry reminded Alfred that students were not allowed to go into the garden, Alfred said the favor would save him from a flogging, then promised that if Henry granted his request he would be "in future guided wholly by your advice." Much as Will Grumble in *The Adventures of Timothy Thoughtless*, and Adam and Eve in Eden, Alfred and his companions had spoiled the garden. Amid "a confused heap of ruins"—broken pots, a battered hedge, and ruined flowers—Henry found Alfred's hat.[14]

When Mr. Saunders discovered the destruction, he called the school together. All the boys denied that they had gone into the garden except Henry who would not "utter a wilful falsity." When the gardener reported seeing Henry in the garden and Mr. Saunders asked him why he had gone there, Henry refused to explain. Blamed for the destruction, he "received a correction so severe, that he was unable, for some minutes, to return to his room." Later when an usher who believed Henry innocent urged him to reveal what happened, Henry said only that "he was not the offender." As a result of his handicaps, Henry had developed strength of character, and even when "the many little privileges which, to Henry's infirmities and Henry's pursuits, were invaluable" were taken away, "he scorned to complain" and endured injustice until truth came out. Some days later amid the ruins of the flowers, the gardener found a knife marked with the letters A. P. When the master asked Henry if he had used the knife to destroy the plants, Henry said he had not. Angry at Henry for telling what he thought was a lie, Saunders then addressed Alfred, saying, I "command you to tell me when, and for what purpose, you lent this knife to your brother." When confronted with the knife, Alfred broke down and confessed that he and four others had ruined the garden. Although Henry pleaded for Alfred and his companions and they received "a remission of punishment," "the obloquy of their conduct" remained with them. Unable to outgrow the weaknesses brought on by "every advantage of face and person," Alfred associated "only with the idle and profligate" and at age thirty was killed in a duel, "the consequence of a quarrel at one of the taverns he frequented." In contrast Henry lived a rich life; "his enlarged and cultivated mind, the kindness and generosity of his disposition, and the excellence of his heart, made him respected and beloved by all who knew him." [15]

Stories which turned loss into gain did more than caution readers. They offered reassurance and hope to children who came from poor backgrounds or who believed themselves weak or untalented. If he were willing to work and study, even the most disadvantaged child could achieve success and happiness. *The History of Tommy Titmouse* (1798), the title page stated, was the biography of "A LITTLE BOY, who became a Great Man, by minding his Learning, doing as he was bid, and being good-natured and obliging to every Body." Because he was "so very little," indeed almost handicapped, Tommy's schoolmates "often used to joke him." This "never fretted him," however, and "he generally answered, 'As little as I am, I need not care; a little boy may make a great man at last.'" On one occasion Tommy's fellow students tied him on the back of a butcher's dog. Frightened, the dog ran away and "carried him quite out of town, when it was after school-hours in the evening." Although Tommy was lost, he never strayed from the path to greatness. At the edge of a forest, he met "the Old Man of the Woods," almost an allegorical representation of Wisdom, who, after entertaining him and providing him with directions so he could find his way home, urged him "to mind your learning." Even when he went to the fair with Nurse Trueby, Tommy was not distracted from his goal and "was particularly delighted with the show of Whittington and his Cat. 'For if so poor a boy as he came to be Lord Mayor, and ride in the gilt coach, by his industry (says he) who knows what good luck Tommy Titmouse may have?'" Tommy's studies and work brought rewards; and after moving to London and becoming "a fine man" worth "an immense deal of money," Tom visited his childhood friends. "When he came in his own coach into the town where he had formerly lived," the neighbors cried, " 'Is it possible!—Can this fine gentleman be the same person, that, when a boy, we used to call Little Tommy Titmouse?' And the old folks shewed him to their children, crying, 'Look there! and see how learning and good behaviour can make a little boy a great man.' " [16]

By the late eighteenth century, Tom Thumb had become a reassuring example of the good effects of education. Although the marvelous had not vanished completely from his life—at his birth a solar eclipse occurred and "tis supposed, stinted his growth, and made him almost invisible"—he achieved his uniqueness as much through study as size. In *Tom Thumb's Folio* (c. 1780) his father was "greatly disconcerted at having such a tiney toy of a child" until "a very learned gentleman looked at him thro' a great pair of spectacles" and said he "would be a very little man and a very great man." Is it a great head, a strong arm, a big body, or a large leg that constitutes a great man, the gentleman asked. "No," he said, answering himself, "it is wisdom and virtue, and that only which can make us great and happy. A great brute, or a great bear, or a great blockhead, may be made by other means; but a great man cannot be formed without wisdom and virtue." Although Tom appeared at the Round Table in *The Lilliputian History* (c. 1795), he was no longer the figure of fun and bawdry he had been in chapbooks, being swallowed by the Red Cow and titilating the ladies of King Arthur's court by running at their bosoms with a bulrush. Now he was king of the Lilliputians, a character who surprised everyone by having "so much Sense in so Small a Body." Tom ruled Lilliputia with wisdom, and when Gog and Magog heard about "The Advancement of Learning," they led an army of giants against the kingdom. With their troops organized under the command of "Gothic Heroes" like Ignorance and Superstition, Conceit and False Glory, and Revenge and Cruelty, the giants stood little chance against Tom's learned forces: the Alphabetical Infantry, the Royal Regiment of the Primer, the Orthographical Grenadiers, the Intrepid Sons of Syntax, and the Mathematical Heroes.[17]

Besides offering reassurance and teaching the necessity of education, stories which turned loss into gain can be seen as secularized versions of those evangelical or godly books which celebrated the pious deaths of righteous children. In such books, losing the world led to gaining heaven. In separating the child from temptation, a handicap provided the opportunity for religious studies and soul-saving piety, not an education which brought temporal rewards. "When she was six years old," the author of *Memoir of Jane Evans* (1825) wrote, "Jane met with what was then probably considered an unlucky accident, but which she was afterwards led to regard as a gracious dispensation." In a fall Jane bruised her hand so badly "that she could never again use it freely" and so injured her back "that she became quite deformed, attended with extreme delicacy of constitution and great bodily suffering." Separated from other children by her injuries, Jane "passed the early part of her life in habits of retirement and strict morality." As the Perrys indulged and corrupted Alfred, so other children, indeed all members of the family of man, constituted a danger to Jane. "Had she enjoyed more constitutional health and vigour," she might not have devoted her time "to prayer, meditation and study of the Scriptures" but might have associated "with companions whose conversation and employments" would perhaps have tended to "corrupt and vitiate her mind." As the heroes of early children's literature struggled against misfortune to achieve success, so Jane won her way to heaven. After Mr. Saunders discovered Henry had not destroyed the garden, he addressed the boy, saying, "Come to my heart, and let me tell you all the admiration and love I feel for you." After Jane's suffering, she was called to the heart, not of an earthly master, but the heavenly one. Like Henry, she became better because she was forced to struggle, and as she died, she addressed onlookers, crying, "Shout! shout! why dont you all shout? let me hear you shout aloud, Victory! Victory!" [18]

In godly books a righteous death was the ultimate blessing, and the disease or handicap that made a child aware of Mary Sherwood's Inbred Sin was not a misfortune. In such books love of life was usually seen as love of the world and worldly things. As Sophia Bartlet's high spirits led to disobedience and unnatural boyish behavior, so good health was often a sign of inward corruption while sickness was a sign, if not of virtue, at least of the rejection of this world. In the *History of Henry Fairchild and Charles Truman* (1819), Henry heard Charles singing "Jerusalem, thou blest abode." Charles used to "be a rosy-cheeked little fellow," and when Henry saw him, he immediately noticed the difference in the boy's appearance. When asked what had brought about the change, Charles said he had not been "right well since about the time when poor miss Augusta Noble was buried." After the funeral Charles, in the company of his father and Samuel Hill the parish clerk, had looked at the coffins in the Noble family vault, then, along with John Barnes the bricklayer, had helped seal the vault. In the tomb there had been much religious conversation, and, Charles recounted, "I felt my heart within me all burning with love for the dear Saviour." "At the same time," he said, "that I became so full of these thoughts I became sick, and have been wasting ever since, and yet no one knows what is the matter with me; but I know that it is the will of God that I should depart hence and be no more seen." In wasting Charles was gaining, and his sickness, like that of Sophia, led to a new and better life.[19]

As Tommy Titmouse wanted to be a great man and knew that learning would make him one, so children in godly books wanted to go to heaven and knew how to get there. Even the fair with its temptations and kinship to Bunyan's worldly Vanity Fair did not divert Tommy Titmouse's attention from his goal. Similarly nothing this world had to offer could turn the heroes and heroines of godly books away from heaven. The more they lost, the closer they knew they were to success. In *Memoirs of the Lives of Hannah Hill, George Chalkley, and Catharine Burling* (1815), Hannah "entirely made death her choice, and would often say that she had rather die and go to God, than continue in this world of trouble." In George Hendley's *A Memorial for Children* (1806), nine-year-old William Quayle "never expressed the least desire for life" in his last sickness. Instead he "wished to be removed to his heavenly Father's house," saying "I would rather die than live." When he became seriously ill, Robert Hill exclaimed, "Oh, I am happy all over! I know I shall die." When offered medicine, he pleaded, "Dont give it to me, for it will do me no good, for I shall die. Do let me die; for if I live, perhaps I shall sin against God." The day before Lucy Cole died, she asked for a looking glass. "It being brought," Rebekah Pinkham wrote in *A Narrative of the Life of Miss Lucy Cole* (1830), "she took it pleasantly, gazed upon her deathly countenance, and observed:

'Ah! lovely appearance of death.'" At the end of *A Memorial*, Hendley addressed his young readers, saying, "If you become like these dear children of whom you have been reading, then your friends and your parents will love you, and God will love you; and when you die you will go to heaven, and have a crown upon your head, and a golden harp in your hand, and sing the praises of Jesus for ever."[20] Outside of evangelical writing, few early children's books saw heaven so clearly. Loss led to gain, but instead of reflecting the lovely appearance of death, early children's books pictured the successful Lucius and the benevolent Sophia. For such characters heaven was a goal, but it was not immediate. This life came first.

5

❋　❋　❋　❋　❋

Pamela

ho could have dreamt," Aaron Hill wrote after reading *Pamela*, that "he should find, under the modest disguise of a *novel*, all the *soul* of religion, good-breeding, discretion, good-nature, wit, fancy, fine thought, and morality?" *Pamela*, he predicted, "will live on thro' posterity, with much unbounded extent of good consequences, that twenty ages to come may be the better and wiser, for its influence." By the end of the eighteenth century, Hill's enthusiasm notwithstanding, there was disagreement about *Pamela*'s influence. In his *Essay on Novels* (1793), Alexander Thomson praised "moral RICHARDSON's enchanting page," declaring that "in point of originality, and power of wielding the passions at his pleasure" Richardson was "inferior only to the immortal SHAKE-SPEARE." According to the *Eclectic Review* (1805), however, Richardson's most finished characters were "amiable moralists," not well-instructed Christians. Religious writers were uncomfortable with the novel as a genre, warning readers, much as crit-

ics of fairy tales warned parents, that it could excite the imagination and undermine morality. The "direct tendency" of novels, the *Christian Observer* (1805) argued typically, was "to hurt the heart and mislead the imagination." Critics were particularly worried about the influence of novels upon the lower and the lower middle classes. The "sentimentality of their Abigails, the heroic gallantry of their Footmen, and the rhetorical gallantry of their Shoemakers," Thomas Munro wrote in 1787, "are more particularly the characters which do a material injury to that part of the nation, who, when they have shut up shop, wet their thumbs and spell through a novel." "Nothing," Priscilla Wakefield stated in *Reflections on the Present Conditions of the Female Sex*, "can be more distant from the plain, sober, useful qualities of a housewife, than the excellencies of the heroine of a novel."[1]

Jonas Hanway agreed and began his *Virtue in Humble Life* (1774) by explaining that he addressed his "labours to the *simple* rather than the *refined* in taste," adding that he esteemed "piety and simplicity, as qualities with which the lowest in condition are *rich*, and *without* them the highest *poor*." *Virtue in Humble Life* contained instructive dialogues between Thomas Trueman, a farmer, and Mary, his daughter. Mary, Hanway emphasized, was "not introduced under the ambiguous circumstances of a *Pamela*." She was "not elevated," Hanway wrote, "with hopes of riding in her coach, not taught to inveigle a young master, but reminded of the advantage of being *honest* and *pious*, agreeable to her mistress, and perchance of being one day married to a laborious *honest man*."[2]

In 1769 Newbery and Carnan published an abridged edition of *Pamela* for children. The book was a success and remained in print for the rest of the century, appearing in at least thirteen editions in the United States and being listed in 1800 in Elizabeth Newbery's *Catalogue of Instructive and Amusing Publications for Young Minds*. Much, however, as attitudes toward the novel were mixed, so despite the book's popularity, attitudes toward *Pamela* and more importantly the Pamela figure in early children's books were, to use Hanway's word, "ambiguous." In part *Pamela*'s popularity stemmed from its being like *Robinson Crusoe* an educational fable for the times. In children's books, as I pointed out earlier, there was little room for a hereditary aristocracy. Not educated for or to maintain its position, the aristocracy was usually seen as corrupt and so morally weak that it appeared doomed. Only when an aristocrat rejected the importance of birth and accepted the notion that education shaped the adult, thus effectively becoming middle class, was he able to develop into a moral and capable adult. As an aristocrat Mr. B. had been indulged and had not received a proper education. Only when he took Pamela, the middle-class girl, as his teacher and her letters as his book did his real education begin. In marrying Pamela, he embraced middle-class attitudes and showed that he deserved his position and could manage himself, becoming Trueman's honest man. Revealing the extent to which his views on education had changed, Mr. B. gave "Mr. *Locke*'s Treatise on Education" to Pamela after the birth of their son Billy. Not only did Pamela follow Locke's suggestions in raising Billy, but she wrote Mr. B. a series of letters in which she discussed Locke's ideas, thereby continuing Mr. B.'s education and ensuring that he understood the importance of education.[3]

As prosperity spread in the eighteenth century, making society more mobile and seemingly more Lockean, many critics thought that wealth was corrupting the middle classes. Instead of providing children with an education which schooled them for life and eternity, parents, critics believed, were misled by the promises inherent in Locke's educational views. Dazzled by the possibilities for advancement in society and then by the "ornamental" surface of aristocratic life, they forgot the criticism of the aristocracy implied in Locke's educational ideas, and copying "their betters," provided children with educations which taught the "showy" rather than the useful. "Tradesmen and mechanics," Priscilla Wakefield wrote, "are fond of bringing up their daughters in what they term a genteel manner; that is, sending them, at a very inconvenient expence, perhaps as half-boarders, to an elegant boarding-school, where they presently imbibe a desire of emulating their superiors in dress, shewy qualifications and fashionable folly." "The injudicious practice" of bringing up girls above reasonable expectations, Wakefield continued, "originates in a common opinion, that a good education is more valuable than a dowry; the sentiment is a just one, the error consists in a misapprehension of what constitutes a good education: No system of instruction can be properly denominated good, which is not appropriate to those who receive it." According to the *Annual Register* (1759), "the improper education given to a great number of the daughters of low tradesmen and mechanics" undermined virtue. Every village near London, the *Register* declared, had "one or two little boarding schools, with an inscription over the door, *Young ladies boarded and educated*. The expense is small," the article continued, "and hither the blacksmith, the ale-house-keeper, the shoe-maker, etc. sends his daughter, who, from the moment she enters these walls, becomes a young lady." Although the "parent's intention" was "an honest one," the result was disastrous. "How disappointed will be the honest shopkeeper," the *Register* stated, "if, at an age when he thinks proper to take his daughter from school, he should expect any assistance from her!" "Though ignorant of every thing else, she will be so perfect in the lessons of pride and vanity," the article continued, "that she will despise him and his nasty shop, and quit both, to go off with the first man who promises her a silk gown, and a blonde cap. In short, the plan of these schools appears to me much better calculated to qualify the scholars to become, in a few years, proper inhabitants of the Magdalen house, than to make of them industrious frugal wives to honest tradesmen, or faithful servants." In lamenting the spread of the "contagion" of luxurious behavior to the "middle orders" where she said it raged "with increasing violence, from the elegantly dressed but slenderly portioned curate's daughter, to the equally fashionable daughter of the little tradesman, and of the more opulent, but not more judicious farmer," Hannah More urged upper-class women to live less luxuriously and set better examples for society. "The prevailing manners of an age," she wrote, "depend more than we are aware, or are willing to allow, on the conduct of the women; this is one of the principal hinges on which the great machine of human society turns."[4]

Although Pamela was not born to the class addressed by More, her conduct set an example for young readers and showed that right female behavior could precipitate a reformation of manners. Instead of sinning, Pamela resisted the contagion of luxury. When threatened by Mr. B. armed with showy finery, she longed for plain clothes, her "grey russet." To some extent Pamela's successful resistance to temptation could be seen as the result of education. Not able to send Pamela to a boarding school to learn fashionable folly, the Andrewses limited their daughter's education to plain instruction, reading and writing. Although Mr. B.'s mother taught her ornamental accomplishments, such as music and dancing, she also continued Pamela's practical education by teaching her to keep accounts, a skill which she used later, much as a tradesman's wife, in looking over Mr. B.'s accounts. In the use which she made of her education, Pamela implicitly corrected More's view that the reformation of society "must begin with the GREAT." In children's books, reformation began with the middle classes and spread to the great. "From the economy she proposes to observe in her elevation," a children's version of *Pamela* (1794) declared "let even ladies of condition learn, that there are family employments, in which they may and ought to make themselves useful, and give good examples to their inferiors, as well as equals: And that their duty to God, charity to the poor and sick, and the different branches of household management, ought to take up the most considerable portions of their time."[5]

Pamela said that "the good lessons, and religious education" which she received from her father enabled her to resist Mr. B. The heroines of early children's books were often tested, although usually not by Mr. B.'s but by female acquaintances. Those girls who had received moral educations passed the tests. In *The Mother's Gift* (1787), Miss Johnson became an orphan at eight. Her aunt was "a great enemy to trouble" and sent her to boarding school. Almost immediately her schoolmates pressured her to accommodate herself to their ways. Although Miss Johnson was not imprisoned like Pamela, she was alone. At home she was accustomed to praying both morning and evening, and one evening while Miss Clark her bedfellow was playing in another room, Miss Johnson "retired to her chamber, shut the door, and locked it." While she was praying, Miss Clark returned and finding the door locked, knocked loudly. "What do you lock yourself up for," she cried when Miss Johnson opened the door; "you have no business to turn us out of this room; it is as much mine as yours." When Miss Johnson explained that she was praying,

From *The Mother's Gift.* Courtesy American Antiquarian Society.

Clark retorted, "Well, and does not my governess read prayers to us? Is not that enough?" Johnson then explained that she did not think it enough, adding that although her family said prayers together, her parents also taught her to pray alone. "Well! that is quite needless," Clark answered, "and you give up play to sit here alone, stupifying!—It is too much for me." "Do not we owe every blessing we enjoy to God," Johnson replied, "and should we not be glad to pay all the return we were able in thanks? I do not say a long prayer, but an earnest one. This I learned from my good mother." Clark had no answer, and shutting "the door very hard" returned to play.[6]

After telling them not to eat the strawberries which grew there, Mrs. Hammond, the governess, allowed the schoolgirls to walk in her private garden. With its forbidden fruit, this garden, like so many in early children's books, resembled Eden while Mrs. Hammond resembled God and the girls Eve. As soon as Mrs. Hammond left them, Miss Nixon and Miss Clark decided to eat strawberries. Miss Johnson controlled her appetite, and because she recognized her duty, the garden remained unspoiled. "I shall be very sorry," she said to the girls, "if you determine to be so naughty; but you may depend upon it, if you touch any, I shall certainly acquaint my governess." When the girls said she would be a "telltale," Miss Johnson answered that her actions were correct. "I should rejoice to prevent your fault, and be very sorry to give a bad account of you," she said; "she who deserves to be called a telltale, is one who is pleased to speak ill of others; but call me what you like, I shall do what I think right." After other similar trials, Miss Johnson's virtues won her friends and a true inheritance, the love of her aunt, who took her out of school and treated her like a daughter. The aunt was wealthy and lived in luxury. In her aunt's fashionable home religion and early education protected Miss Johnson's virtue. "When attended by servants, surrounded with flatterers, sparkling in dress, and invited to partake of every pleasure, 'still meek and lowly in heart,' she preserved her humility. Amidst the scenes of extravagance and dissipation, she practiced the charity of a Christian." As Mr. B. eventually loved Pamela's spirituality more than her physical beauty, so Miss Johnson captivated "a lover, who was less charmed with her person, than enslaved by her mind." [7]

Miss Johnson's experiences were typical, and in early children's books, girls' boarding schools frequently undermined morality. In *Anecdotes of a Boarding School*, Martha Beauchamp's parents sent her to school because they were forced to travel on business. Martha spent an unhappy first day at school; only when evening prayers came did she feel comfortable. "With her heart overflowing with the tenderest of feelings," she knelt and awaited the prayers. Unhappily Madame Brilieu read prayers in French, a language Martha did not understand. After returning to her room to sleep, Martha "slipped out of bed, and falling on her knees, began to say her prayers, whispering in a low voice, and not wishing to draw the attention of any of her school-fellows." Miss Grumpton, her bedmate, saw her kneel and asked what she was doing. When Martha explained that she was praying, Miss Grumpton exclaimed, "What are you going to say your prayers for now? Did you not pray enough below stairs?" Martha then said that she did not understand French, adding that at home she prayed every morning and evening. "*O, lauk*! I should never think of that for my part, returned Miss *Grumpton*; prayers are prayers *are not* they? whether they are *French* or *Dutch*; so pray come into bed again, or, I assure you, my governess will be *vastly* angry with you." After saying that she did not think the governess would be angry at her for praying, Martha climbed back into bed and then "burst into a flood of tears." "*Lah*, now!" said Miss Grumpton, becoming exasperated; "if you will pray, *pray away, pray away*, with all my heart; you may pray for yourself and me too, if you please, for I hate the employment, I assure you; but for *goodness sake*, Miss, do not lay and cry so; if you do, I declare I will tell my governess: *I* protest it is impossible to get a wink of sleep for you lay blowing your nose so, it is quite *nasty* to hear you."[8]

One evening sometime later, Martha asked Miss Starch, one of the teachers, for permission to pray in English before getting into bed. "Why I have never heard of such a thing in my life," exclaimed Miss Starch; "I wonder you were not ashamed to think of asking it! Say your prayers indeed in your *nightshift*! A pretty affair indeed! A fine cold you would get!" When Martha assured her that she would put on her bed gown and not catch cold, Miss Starch pointed out that prayers were said in school every evening. To Martha's objection that she did not understand them, Starch replied, "Then it is time you should *learn*." "What are you come to school for but to learn French," she asked, adding "nothing will improve you quicker than saying *French* prayers; so I beg I may not have another syllable upon the subject." Instead of improving students and thereby society, boarding school cultivated appearances, and as French prayers neglected the spirit of Christianity, so such schools undermined virtue. Like Miss Johnson, Martha's classmates ridiculed her, calling her "a *vast watery head*" always "sniveling and *piping your eye* about something or other." Receiving good advice in letters from her mother, much as Mr. B. did from Pamela's letters, Martha held fast to her faith and was able to endure the persecution of fellow students until she returned to her family.[9]

Because Miss Johnson's parents had given her a good education at home, teaching her the values of honesty and prayer, and because Martha's mother wrote her long, instructive letters, neither girl was harmed by boarding school. In contrast, boarding school ruined the daughters of Farmer Bragwell in Hannah More's *The Two Wealthy Farmers* (1795), a tract written for the lower classes. The two girls returned from school, much as the *Annual Register* predicted, "with a large portion of vanity grafted on their native ignorance" and just enough knowledge "to laugh at their fond parents' rustic manners and vulgar language, and just enough taste to despise and ridicule every girl who was not as vainly dressed as themselves." Refusing to work, they "spent the morning in bed, the noon in dressing, the evening at the Spinnet, and night in reading Novels." After starting to read one, Farmer Bragwell recounted, "I could neither make head nor tail of it. It was neither fish, flesh, nor good red-herring. It was all about my Lord, and Sir Harry, and the Captain." "I was fairly taken in at first," he said,

> "and began to think I had got hold of a *godly* book, for there was a great deal about 'hope and despair, and heaven, and Angels, and torments, and everlasting happiness.' But when I got a little on, I found there was no meaning in all these words, or if any, 'twas a bad meaning. 'Misery' perhaps only meant a disappointment about a bit of a letter: and 'everlasting happiness' meant two people talking nonsense together for five minutes. In short, I never met with such a pack of lies. The people talk gibberish as no folks in their sober senses ever talked; and the things that happen to them are not like the things that ever happen to any of my acquaintance. They are at home one minute, and beyond the sea the next."

Ruined by school, Bragwell's daughters married poorly, one eloping with a strolling player and the other marrying Mr. Dashall Squeeze, a corrupt contractor and gambler. Unlike Pamela, who learned fashionable arts from Lady B., but who was able to place them in proper perspective because of her religious upbringing, Bragwell's daughters knew little about religion. "None was taught" at boarding school, More wrote, "for at that place it was considered as a part of education which belonged only to Charity Schools." [10]

Few early children's books romanticized childhood. Children learned to be good. Only rarely were they depicted as teachers and infant philosophers in touch with moral truth beyond adults. In *A Pretty New-Year's Gift* (1786), however, Solomon Sobersides told a story in which a child educated and saved his father. After a "worthy old gentleman" gave his wealth to his son, the son treated him "with the most mortifying neglect." For four years the old man's only source of happiness was his young grandson, Tommy. One day when the son was entertaining fashionable friends, the grandfather came into the room looking for Tommy. The son disliked being interrupted and turned rudely on his father, asking how "he dared to break in upon him without leave." The old man left and went upstairs and cried. Little Tommy then came into the room and said, "Papa has made poor grandpapa break his heart; he will cry his eyes out above stairs." The father was embarrassed and tried to brazen out the incident. "Turning round therefore to the child, he desired him to carry a blanket to grandpapa, and bid him go and beg: Ay, but I will not give him all the blanket, returned the child: Why so, my dear? says the father: Because answered he, I shall want half for you, when I grow up to be a man, and turn you out of doors." The rebuke so stung the father that he reformed and a happy reconciliation occurred.[11]

As Romanticism became pervasive in the nineteenth century, children would often become voices of honest feeling, revealing truths that touched the heart but which frequently lay beyond clear articulation. In Charles and Mary Lamb's *Mrs. Leicester's School* (1811), Elizabeth Villiers was the daughter of a village curate. Elizabeth was born in the parsonage, adjoining the churchyard. Her first memory was that of her father teaching her the alphabet from the letters on her mother's tombstone. "I used to tap at my father's study door," she recounted; "I think I now hear him say, 'Who is there?—What do you want little girl? Go and see mamma. Go and learn pretty letters.' Many times in the day would my father lay aside his books and his papers to lead me to this spot, and make me point to the letters, and then set me to spell syllables and words." "In this manner," Elizabeth said, "the epitaph on my mother's tomb being my primer and my spelling book, I learned to read."

One day when Elizabeth was sitting on the stile leading into the churchyard, her Uncle James appeared. A lieutenant in the navy, James left Britain shortly after his sister's marriage and had not learned about her death. Hearing Elizabeth spell her name, James looked at Elizabeth and seeing the resemblance to his sister concluded Elizabeth was his sister's child. "Who

W. Hopwood del.   W. R. Jones ſc

*In this manner, the epitaph on my mother's
tomb being my primer and my spelling-book,
I learned to read.* Page 9.

From Charles and Mary Lamb's *Mrs. Leicester's School.*
Courtesy American Antiquarian Society.

has taught you to spell so prettily, my little maid?" he asked. "Mamma," Elizabeth replied, explaining to the reader, "I had an idea that the words on the tombstone were somehow a part of mamma, and that she had taught me." On hearing her answer, James asked Elizabeth to take him to her mother. When she led him through the church grounds into the graveyard, he thought she was "wayward"; soon, though, he learned better. The story was Wordsworthian. The spirit of Elizabeth's mother "lived" amid the green grasses, flowers, and trees of the graveyard. There impulses brought knowledge and taught Elizabeth not simply her letters but truths about life and death that lay too deep for tears. There the child taught the adult that goodness died only to be born again, in a child or a memory.[12]

Early children's books contained few characters like Elizabeth. The truth of feeling was thought too wayward to be useful. Like the imagination, feelings were suspect guides. On the sea of life only "the steady anchor of fixed principles" prevented one from being driven "with every wind," never knowing "the comfort of secure repose." With just a few exceptions, children educated adults only in religious books, many of which were built around the deaths of pious young Christians. In such books instead of being sinful creatures stained by innate depravity and standing in need of salvation, children were often emblems of the divine child. When she was six years old, Henrietta Smith in *The Infant Preacher* (1818) was present at a baptism. Henrietta had never seen a baptism before and afterward rushed home and asked her mother why she was not baptized. Henrietta's question was "so artless and unexpected, and at the same time so earnest" that her mother was struck "dumb." When Henrietta's father appeared, he tried to change the subject and asked her to go with him and pick apples. Henrietta refused, saying she could not do so on the Sabbath and urged her family to pray. She even read the Bible to her parents. Eventually Mrs. Smith became a Christian and "found the pardon and peace of the Gospel, at the feet of Jesus Christ." Like her daughter, she had a good influence upon those around her; a neighbor who dropped in for a visit "went away with an arrow of the Almighty in her heart." At the end of the book, the author inquired, "Dear children, who read this story of little Henrietta, has God given you

Christian parents?" "Have you, my dear children, ever asked your pa and ma to get you baptized? Have you ever asked them to pray with you? I think they will not be angry if you go to them with tears in your eyes, and plead with them, as Henrietta did with her parents." "Tell them," the author concluded, "that you wish to be baptized and be good children, so that you may go, when you die, and live with Christ in heaven." [13]

The heroine of Legh Richmond's *The Young Cottager* (1815) resembled the divine child, shining before adults and pointing the way to salvation. The daughter of poor villagers, Jane began attending Richmond's Saturday school when she was twelve years old. At school, the children read and studied the Bible, repeated the catechism and psalms, and sang hymns. Richmond's class met in a garden next to the graveyard, and much as Elizabeth learned the alphabet from her mother's tombstone, so Richmond turned the churchyard into a "book of instruction." "Every gravestone" became a "leaf of edification" as he found "subjects of warning and exhortation" suitable for his "little flock of lambs." Within a short time, Richmond testified, Jane "became my teacher," saying that in her "I *first* saw what true religion could accomplish." The Lord, Richmond said, had called Jane "as a child, to show by a similitude, what conversion means" and "to be a vessel of mercy, and a living witness of that almighty power of love by which her own heart was turned to God." Jane, in gaining heaven, lost this world. Not long after her conversion, Jane became ill, and on visiting her, Richmond saw that she "had acquired the consumptive hue, both white and red," and was "ripening fast for a better world." "Pray God," he said to Jane, "that this your present sickness may be an instrument of blessing in his hands to prove, humble, and sanctify you." The prayers were answered, and "as the outward man decayed, she was strengthened with might by God's Spirit in the inner man." Detailing the conversations he held with Jane, Richmond addressed the reader, saying he hoped the account would be "a menu of grace and blessing to thy soul." "And may not hope indulge the prospect," he wrote, "that this simple memorial of her history shall be as an arrow drawn from the quiver of the Almighty to reach the heart of the young and the thoughtless?" [14]

Pamela and the main characters of godly books had much in common. At fifteen and then sixteen, Pamela was a child in comparison to Mr. B. Not corrupted by a worldly upbringing, she educated and "saved" an adult. If Pamela is seen as a type of the divine child, although a partially secularized version, then Mr. B. could be seen as not simply the rogue but the nonbeliever. Instead of, in Richmond's words, however, regaining "the Paradise, which was lost through Adam" by accepting Christ, Mr. B. gained both earthly and heavenly paradise by marrying Pamela. In some religious books at the end of the eighteenth century, earthly Pamelas appeared, and like Richardson's heroine lived through puberty to make this life better while teaching loved ones how to attain the other life. The best of these accounts was *The History of Hester Wilmot* (1803), a tract written by Hannah More for girls from the lower classes.[15]

Like Pamela's parents, Hester's parents were rural working-class people; unlike Pamela's mother and father, the latter of whom had once run a school, they were neither educated nor religious. Although Hester's mother Rebecca was "clean, notable, and industrious," she had a violent temper and was as vain in her way as a frivolous, "shewy" lady. Instead of dress, Rebecca took pride in the appearance of her home. "It was no fault in Rebecca," More wrote, "but a merit, that her oak table was so bright you could almost see to put your cap on in it; but it was no merit, but a fault, that when John, her husband, laid down his cup of beer upon it so as to leave a mark, she would fly out into so terrible a passion, that all the children were forced to run to corners: now poor John, having no corner to run to, ran to the ale-house, till that which was at first a refuge, too soon became a pleasure." Besides driving her husband to drink, Rebecca prevented her children from learning to read, saying that reading would only make them lazy and that she had "done very well without it." She even kept Hester from church "to stone the space under the chairs in fine patterns and whim-whams." This decoration, More wrote, was "a trap for praise," and Rebecca "was sulky and disappointed, if any ladies happened to call in, and did not seem delighted with the flowers which she used to draw with a burnt stick on the white-wash of the chimney corners." Mistakenly, More explained, "all this finery was often done on a Sunday, and there is a great deal of harm in doing right things at a wrong time, or in wasting much time on things which are of no real use, or in doing any thing at all out of vanity." Rebecca was not concerned with substantial plain garb but only the ornamental. As a result her family was almost ruined. John spent more time at The Bell, and at fourteen Hester "could not tell a letter, nor had she ever been taught to bow her knee to him who made her." Happily for the family, however, at this time Mrs. Jones established a Sunday school, and despite Rebecca's rude behavior was so persistent that Hester was allowed to attend. Hester soon became such a good student that Mrs. Crew, the schoolmistress, lent her books. Since her mother "hated the sight of a book," Hester read after work at night or in the morning before her family woke.[16]

One Sunday night Hester's father said "he thought she had now been in school long enough for him to have a little good of her learning" and he asked her to read to him. Hester immediately "fetched her Testament." When he saw the book, John laughed and called her a fool, saying "it would be time enough to read the Testament to him when he was going to die, but at present he must have something merry." John then gave her a songbook he had found at The Bell. After looking at it, Hester refused to read, explaining that "she did not dare offend God by reading what would hurt her own soul." John became angry and calling her "a canting hypocrite," threatened to throw her Testament into the fire. "Not because she thought her daughter in the right" but because she was glad of a pretext to scold her husband, Rebecca took Hester's part. After cursing both women, John left the house "in a violent passion." Hester's troubles did not end after her father left, however, for Rebecca now grew angry at Hester, saying she "only made religion a pretence for being undutiful to her parents." Like Pamela, Hester "bore all" and "committed her cause to Him 'who judgeth righteously.'" This dispute occurred the Sunday before Mrs. Jones's yearly feast. On May Day, her Sunday scholars attended church, "each in a stuff gown of their own earning, and a cap and white apron of her giving." After church, Mrs. Jones examined the students and presented a Bible or "some other good book" to those who knew the scriptures best and those who brought the best character for industry, humility, and sobriety."[17]

During the year Hester earned at least two shillings a week. Except for twopence which she applied toward the material for her May Day gown, she gave the earnings to her mother. The day after the disagreement at home, John found himself short of gambling money and asked Hester if she could lend him a half crown. John did not know how much Hester had saved, and when she produced a box with the money she had set aside for the gown, he took it all, saying he would repay it the next morning. Unfortunately, he lost it playing all fours. The next day when Hester asked for the money, he confessed the loss. On discovering that she intended to buy the material for the May Day gown with the money, he was overcome by guilt and said he was sorry that Hester could not attend the celebration. "Yes, but I can," Hester answered, "for God looks not at the gown, but at the heart, and I'm sure he sees mine full of gratitude at hearing you talk so kindly; and if I thought my dear father would change his present evil courses, I should be the happiest girl at the feast to-morrow." As Pamela's letters and speeches softened Mr. B., so Hester's words affected her father. Walking "mournfully" away from his daughter, John thought "surely there must be something in religion, since it can thus change the heart." Where Hester was once pert, he thought, she was now "mild as a lamb"; once indolent, she was now "up with the lark." Once a vain girl who would "do anything for a new ribbon," she was content "to go in rags to a feast at which every one else will have a new gown."[18]

Like Pamela in her gray russet, Hester was adorned in virtue and received the prize Bible. She received an even better prize as she walked to church and "saw, among a number of working men, her own father going into church! As she past by him, she cast on him a look of so much joy and affection, that it brought tears into his eyes." As Mr. B. had to grow beyond his fears of fashionable society's view of his marriage, so John had to endure Rebecca's attacks. Angry at Hester for wearing an old gown to church, Rebecca beat her daughter. On discovering why Hester wore the gown, she attacked John when he came home. While her parents fought, Hester fled to her "little room" and prayed. After Rebecca rushed angrily out of the house, John heard Hester praying. Her prayers tempered his feelings, and he "fell down on his knees, embraced his child, and begged her to teach him how to pray." Slowly, John learned to pray and then to read, and as right education shaped him, he became a better man, so much so that Rebecca began to pray and becoming a Christian mastered vanity and her temper. As Pamela's virtue was rewarded, so was Hester's; instead, however, of marriage and riches, she became an underteacher in Mrs. Jones's Sunday school.[19]

Although Pamela concentrated her instruction upon Mr. B. and his immediate family and did not become a schoolteacher like Hester, she was an instructor in early children's books. Many middle-class heroines followed her footsteps from poverty to affluence. Like Pamela, the girls often experienced trials which tested their characters. Indeed sometimes a character remarkably like Pamela appeared, although under a different name. The history of Florella, John Newbery explained in *The Lilliputian Magazine* (1752), had been "sent by an UNKNOWN HAND, and may, for ought we know, have been published before." After he lost his fortune, Florella's father, "an eminent citizen who had lived in good fashion and credit," sent his oldest daughter to the home of an honest farmer "who had married a servant of the family." In following "his country sports," the lord of the manor often visited the farmer's house. Finding Florella there "in the bloom of her youth and beauty," he fell "passionately in love with her." Although a man "of great generosity," he had received "a loose education and had contracted a hearty aversion to marriage." Consequently he "entertained a design upon *Florella*'s virtue." "The innocent creature, who never suspected his intentions, was pleased with his person; and having observed his growing passion for her, hoped by so advantageous a match she might quickly be in a capacity of supporting her impoverish'd relations." One day finding Florella weeping over a letter which described her father's plight, the lord "took this occasion to make her a proposal. It is impossible to express *Florella*'s confusion when she found his pretensions were not honourable. She was divested of all her hopes, and had no power to speak; but rushing from him in the utmost disobedience, lock'd herself up in her chamber."

Not daunted by Florella's Pamela-like behavior, the young lord wrote her father saying that if he convinced Florella to become his mistress, he would settle four hundred pounds a year upon her and "lay down the sum for which you are distressed." The servant who delivered the letter gave it to Florella's mother instead of her father. On reading it the mother reacted like Pamela's virtuous parents. She immediately wrote Florella saying the lord's proposal "would throw us to a lower degree of misery, than any thing that is come upon us." "How could the barbarous man think," she exclaimed, "that the tenderest of parents would be tempted to supply their want, by giving up the best of children to infamy and ruin." "We will not eat the bread of shame," she concluded, "and therefore we charge thee not to think of us, but to avoid the snare that is laid for thy virtue." The messenger, like Mr. B.'s servants, was not to be trusted, and despite his promise to take the letter to Florella, took it to his master. The lord read it, and "moved at so true a picture of distress" carried it to Florella. She refused to see him until he said he brought a letter from her mother. Once admitted into her presence, he would not give her the letter until she agreed to read it before him. "While she was perusing it," *The Lilliputian Magazine* recounted, "he fixed his eyes on her face with the deepest attention. Her concern gave a new softness to her beauty, and when she burst into tears, he could no longer refrain from bearing a part in her sorrow, and telling her too that he had read the letter, and was resolved to make reparation for having been the occasion of it." Immediately he wrote an apology to Florella's mother. He then paid her father's debts, after which he married Florella, "making himself happy by an alliance" to the "virtues" of the "worthy family."[20]

In children's books, the very name *Pamela* was associated with virtue and hard work. In *The Adventures of a Silver Penny* (c. 1790), Pamela was the ten-year-old daughter of a farmer. Having lost her mother, Pamela took care of the farmhouse "with all the solidity of a little woman." She got up every morning at sunrise and swept and cleaned the house, after which she fed the chickens. When the farmer came back to the house for breakfast, then dinner, food was ready for him. What free time she had she spent educating herself reading "pretty books of amusement and instruction." Education was very important to characters who bettered themselves. Such characters were able to endure and overcome hardship because they believed in and worked hard to obtain educations. Frequently the girls became teachers before they made successful marriages.[21]

The most famous of Pamela's followers was Goody Two-Shoes (1765). Goody's life was instructive, and the title of her biography not only stressed education but underlined similarities between her progress and that of Pamela. *The History of Little Goody Two-Shoes*, it read, *Otherwise called, Mrs. Margery Two-Shoes. With the Means by which she acquired her Learning and Wisdom, and in consequence thereof her Estate; set forth at large for the Benefit of those,*

> *Who from a State of Rags and Care,*
> *And having Shoes for half a Pair;*
> *Their Fortune and their Fame would fix,*
> *And gallop in a Coach and Six.*

Margery's father Farmer Meanwell lived in Mouldwell Parish, which consisted of twelve farms, the leases of which were held by the lord of the manor. When Sir Timothy Gripe became lord, he conspired with Farmer Graspall to combine the farms. Eventually Graspall held all the farms except that occupied by Meanwell. When Meanwell refused to surrender his lease, Sir Timothy ordered that a brick kiln and dog kennel be built in Meanwell's orchard. This was against the law, and Meanwell took Sir Timothy to court and won. Notwithstanding the defeat, Sir Timothy went ahead with his plans. After three court cases and three victories, Meanwell was bankrupt and Graspall obtained the farm. Shortly thereafter Meanwell fell sick and died. His wife could not bear his loss, and she died from a broken heart, leaving Margery and her brother Tommy penniless orphans. Mr. Smith the parish clergyman took them in. Since Margery had only one shoe, Mrs. Smith ordered her a new pair. When the cobbler brought the shoes, Margery "ran out to Mrs. Smith as soon as they were put on, and stroking down her ragged apron thus cried out, *Two Shoes, mame, see two Shoes.*"

Margery had a new name but she did not have a new home for long. When he learned that the Smiths were caring for the orphans, Sir Timothy threatened to reduce his tithes, and the Smiths were forced to send the children away. Mr. Smith arranged for Tommy to go to sea but was able to do little for Margery. Adversity, however, proved a blessing. Seeing "how good and wise" Mr. Smith was, she concluded "that this was owing to his great Learning, therefore she wanted of all Things to learn to read." To this end she borrowed books from children and learned to read so well that she became "*a trotting Tutoress*," bartering lessons for food and shelter. The education Margery supplied was moral as well as practical. Along with spelling and reading, she taught prayers and rules for right conduct. When Polly Sullen declared she would not pray for her enemies, Margery exclaimed, "Not pray for your Enemies . . . yes, you must, you are no Christian, if you don't forgive your Enemies, and do Good for Evil." One day while in a barn during a storm, Margery heard thieves planning to rob Sir William Dove. She warned Sir William, and he was so grateful that he appointed her to succeed the local schoolmistress, who had become old. Margery was such a fine teacher, not only instructing her pupils but settling disputes between adults, that Sir Charles Jones, a wealthy squire, married her. As Margery's education strengthened her virtue and provided her with valuable skills, so it was fitting that Tommy appeared at the church just before the marriage. Having made a fortune in the Indies, he presented her with a substantial dowry. After the wedding Lady Jones devoted herself to good works: teaching poor children to read, lecturing on religion and morality, encouraging marriage by giving young couples money to purchase household items, and having acres of potatoes planted so that poor people could always find food.[22]

Also resembling Pamela was the heroine of *The Renowned History of Primrose Prettyface, who by her Sweetness of Temper, & Love of Learning, was raised from being the Daughter of a poor Cottager, to great Riches, and the Dignity of Lady of the Manor* (c. 1780). Primrose's father Gaffer Thompson was "an humble honest man, who kept a cow, a pig, and a few fowls, which, with the money he got by working in the fields, enabled him to live tolerably comfortably." One day when she was going to the well for water, Primrose met Lady Worthy, who asked if she could read. Primrose's manners charmed Lady Worthy, and after going to the Thompsons' home and discovering that Primrose never missed church on Sunday, said her prayers morning and evening, and was "dutiful and obliging to her parents," Lady Worthy asked Primrose to read. After listening, Lady Worthy "took her up in her arms, and kissed her a hundred times, and moreover, gave her half a crown to buy some books with; adding at the same time, She would look over her books at home, and pick out some to send her the next day by the footman."

Lady Worthy was true to her word and sent Primrose a parcel of instructive books. Like Hester, Primrose worked hard, not simply to educate herself but for her family. As soon as Lady Worthy's servant left, Primrose "set about cleaning her milkpails, swept out the room, did the task her mother had set her at spinning, and fetched up the cow as fast as she could, that she might get time to read some of the books." Like Goody Two-Shoes and Pamela, Primrose educated those about her. The next day she showed the books to children in the village. On seeing the books, the children "were all ready to run wild." Hearing them clamoring for books, Goody Thompson ran out of the house "with a Heigh derry down! heigh derry down! what is here to be done?" Knowing her daughter was a natural teacher, Goody Thompson told the children that if they would promise to be good, and "learn what *Primrose* will teach you," they could each have a book. The children obeyed, and while Primrose did her spinning, they took turns reading. Primrose did more than listen, however; she taught moral truths. Some years later, Lady Worthy took Primrose into service. When Lady Worthy's son William returned from Oxford, he fell in love with Primrose and much to his mother's pleasure married her.[23]

Much as Farmer Trueman criticized *Pamela*, first saying the heroine's circumstances were ambiguous and then discouraging his daughter Mary from coveting a husband and life above her station, so Primrose's marriage was attacked. In the *Guardian of Education*, Sarah Trimmer warned, "It certainly is very wrong to teach girls of the lower order to aspire to marriages with persons in stations so far superior to their own, or to put into the heads of young gentlemen, at an early age, an idea, that when they grow up they may, without impropriety, marry servant-maids." Behind Trimmer's criticism was the fear that children's books could corrupt children as easily as luxury. A sign of both vanity and an undisciplined imagination, romantic aspirations, she believed, undermined virtue and duty. Such books, she thought, were particularly dangerous to children from the lower classes. Of course, from Farmer Trueman's perspective *Pamela* itself was just as dangerous to young adults. Indeed, the edition published by Newbery and Carnan in 1769 cost a shilling and may have appealed as much to adults, particularly those in the lower middle class, as it did to children. According to the bookseller James Lackington, "the poorer sort of farmers, and even the poor country people in general" had become great readers by the end of the century. "On entering their houses," Lackington wrote, "you may see Tom Jones, Roderick Random, and other entertaining books stuck over their bacon racks." "If *John* goes to town with a load of hay," he continued, "he is charged to be sure not to forget to bring home 'Peregrine Pickles adventures;' and when *Dolly* is sent to market to sell her eggs, she is commissioned to purchase 'The history of Pamela Andrews.' " [24]

For readers like Dolly, Mary Sherwood wrote *The History of Susan Gray* (1815). "Designed for the Benefit of Young Women when Going to Service," *Susan Gray* was relentlessly instructive and would have received Farmer Trueman's approval. In rewarding virtue so splendidly and in charting the heroine's progress through an ordeal from poverty to wealth and marriage, *Pamela* smacked of the romantic world of fairy tale. In contrast, Sherwood lodged *Susan Gray* firmly in lower middle-class life. Much like *Robinson Crusoe*, the book was filled with concrete detail and the conversational equivalent of such detail, an oftentimes colloquial and richly particular speech which, if it were not socially accurate, was believable. As a result, despite melodramatic scenes and characters *Susan Gray* appeared appealingly realistic and provided an effective cautionary balance to the fairy tale aspects of *Pamela*. Sarah Trimmer praised *Susan Gray* enthusiastically, "earnestly" recommending that the book "be given to every girl on her going into service, in order to guard her, if possible, from the allurements and temptations to which she will unavoidably be exposed." "With a little accommodation to circumstances," she wrote, "it might be applied with great propriety to the higher classes." [25]

For these classes, books already existed. The best was Jane West's *The Advantages of Education; or, the History of Maria Williams* (1793), written like *Susan Gray* for adolescent girls. For West the success of characters like Pamela and Goody Two-Shoes raised romantic expectations and corrupted readers. "By delineating human life in false colours," she wrote, such books formed expectations "which can never be realized; the consequence of which is, that life is begun in error, and ended in disappointment." In her introduction, West, writing as Prudentia Homespun, warned readers not to expect "extravagance of character, or variety of incident." "Writing professedly for the inexperienced part of her own sex," she thought "it more advisable to describe life as they are likely to find it, than to adorn it with those gaudy and romantic colours in which it is commonly depicted. She wishes to convince them, that it is but seldom that they will be called forth to perform high acts of heroic excellence, but that they will be daily required to exert those humble duties and social virtues, wherein the chief part of our merit and our happiness consists." [26]

The novel began with Maria attending boarding school. She had been there for a time and knew little about her parents. Later she discovered that her father had gambled away his money, and that he and her mother had gone to the West Indies in an attempt to mend his losses. After her husband's death, Mrs. Williams returned to England with modest means and withdrew Maria from school.

Only the "ornamental plants" of education were cultivated at boarding school, and Mrs. Williams quickly discovered that her daughter's "mind ran into disorder and irregularity." When Mrs. Williams asked Maria where she wanted to live, Maria said "the metropolis." Like Mrs. Cleveland, who took her nieces to Wales, Mrs. Williams avoided fashionable society and settled in Everdon, a rural village. There she set about providing her daughter with a proper education. Religion was the first subject Mrs. Williams taught, and she began each day with prayers, after which followed exercises in drawing and French, domestic chores, and needlework. In the afternoon Maria walked or dug in the garden; in the evening she worked about the house or read, usually instructive history. During their free time, Mrs. Williams and Maria did charity work.[27]

While out walking one afternoon, Maria met her Mr. B., a Mr. Stanley who determined to seduce her. "He conceived," West wrote, "it would be no difficult matter to persuade an inexperienced girl, tired of confinement, to quit the rigid rule prescribed by a severe mother, and fly to a protector who promised freedom and pleasure." As Mr. B., however, had not reckoned with Pamela's devotion to virtue, so Stanley misjudged Maria. Although Maria had been led astray by boarding school, her mother's lessons had begun to influence her. To further his ends with Maria, Stanley cultivated Charlotte Raby, a wealthy heiress in the neighborhood who had been Maria's classmate and who unfortunately did not have a mother to cure the effects of school. Charlotte became Stanley's go-between, and when Maria visited her, she left her alone with Stanley. Gradually Maria fell in love and appeared doomed. Right education, however, saved her; one day she found her mother weeping over a book. It was, Mrs. Williams explained, an account of Lady Jane Grey who "sacrificed her judgment and her life to oblige the parents whom she respected, and the husband whom she loved." "How strongly," Mrs. Williams said, the story warned young people "to doubt the propriety of those concessions which are extorted by the entreaties of those they love." Seeing a parallel between her situation and that of Lady Jane Grey, Maria wrote Stanley that evening, saying she could no longer see him if he insisted upon secrecy.[28]

Stanley wrote Maria to dissuade her but she had learned a lesson and was unyielding. Like Mr. B., Stanley refused to be rejected, and he called on Mrs. Williams. Probing for substance behind his aristocratic elegance, she discovered that Stanley was actually a baronet, Henry Neville. He kept his name a secret, he explained, to avoid a duel. When Neville hinted that marriage was his object, Mrs. Williams behaved differently from Pamela's father. Instead of weeping in gratitude, she stated that she objected strongly "to disproportionate marriages," adding "the esteem, confidence, and reciprocal acts of tenderness, which are the basis of connubial friendship, are in some degree incompatible with the idea of weighty obligation on one side." Mrs. Williams did not believe Maria's education prepared her to contribute to or manage aspects of an aristocratic husband's life. "Those notions of economy and retirement," she said to Maria, "which I have instilled into your mind, would be improper for Lady Neville, who must encourage trade and court popularity." [29]

When Neville insisted upon talking to Maria, Mrs. Williams allowed him to do so in the belief that her daughter would discover his true character. Unsuccessful in the attempt to persuade Maria to disobey her mother, Neville proposed a secret marriage. As Mr. B. planned but rejected such a "marriage" after being educated by Pamela, so Maria, educated by her mother, spurned the offer and informed her mother. Mrs. Williams then grilled Neville about his intentions and his livelihood. Neville said his estates were "loaded with encumbrances." Fortunately, he said, a rich uncle had made him his heir; however, he wanted his nephew to marry wealth and position and would disinherit him if he married Maria. Since the uncle was old and ill, Neville added, secrecy was likely to be but a temporary expedient. Not seduced by the promise of glittering prospects, Mrs. Williams asked Neville where his uncle lived. Neville, "who fancied that this inquiry would end in a request for a direction, and conscious that his uncle's houses stood in Utopia, replied 'that he generally spent his time in travelling, and seldom staid long in any place.'" "Indeed," Mrs. Williams said, "that restlessness of disposition is rather extraordinary, when we consider his age and infirmities." Although embarrassed, Neville answered "that such a method of life was prescribed by his physicians." "His illness," Mrs. Williams said, "then must be of a different kind to those complaints with which old people are generally troubled. Rest and peace, both of mind and body, are, you know, the cordials commonly required by age." Neville could not fabricate a deceptive answer, and escape from Mrs. Williams and truth was the cordial he now seized, explaining to Maria before he left that her mother was too suspicious. [30]

In Richardson's novel, Mr. Williams the minister tried to save Pamela from Mr. B. He failed, and Pamela married Mr. B. and lived happily, even embracing Mr. B.'s illegitimate daughter and rejoicing over the new life the girl's mother Sally Godfrey made in Jamaica. Although *The Advantages of Education* contained characters similar to Sally Godfrey and Mr. Williams, their lives were different. An old friend from Jamaica, Mrs. Herbert, visited Mrs. Williams and introduced her only son Edmund to Maria. Educated at Oxford, Edmund had just returned from making the grand tour with a nobleman. Having known Neville at university, Edmund soon discovered that Neville was hiding from a Captain Seymour. Believing that Neville intended to marry her, Seymour's sister Eliza had eloped with him, only to become his mistress and then be abandoned. After hearing this tale, Edmund warned Neville against deceiving Maria. When Neville threatened him, Edmund refused to be intimidated, saying, "I again assure you, Sir Henry, that if you have dared to form a view injurious to the honour of the young creature, whom you now address, you shall not accomplish it, if it is in my power to prevent you." In this novel education determined behavior and thereby success and failure. Although West's Mr. B. did learn from his Pamela, he learned too late as indulgence and wrong education and their progeny, sin, determined the course of his life and death. On leave from Gibraltar, Seymour arrived in Everdon, determined to revenge the honor and now the death of his sister, who died in want. Having learned about Neville's attention to Maria, Seymour visited the Williamses and exposed the baronet's treachery. While at the cottage, Mrs. Williams persuaded him against violence, urging that Neville be forced to "endure the stings of conscience." During this time, Neville, like Mr. B., fell in love with his Pamela's virtue, and when Maria refused to see him again, set out for the cottage. Unlike that of Mr. B., however, his persistence did not lead to earthly, and ultimately heavenly, salvation. On the way he met Seymour carrying Eliza's body in a coach. Instead of fighting, Seymour showed him the body, saying, "Thou shalt bear a hell in thy own bosom here, and despair shall plunge thee into endless misery hereafter." Instead of giving his Sally Godfrey five hundred pounds and educating her daughter, Neville shot himself and died in black despair. "Great God!" he said to Edmund, who was at his deathbed, " 'Whither am I going, Herbert?—I have been rash—

desperate—is there any hope—any mercy, ah!—what no mercy for me—Speak,' continued he, compulsively wringing the hand of his pitying friend; violent faintings succeeded, and he expired in inexpressible horrors." Although there was no hope for this Mr. B., here or hereafter, West's Mr. Williams fared better, and after some time Edmund received Maria as reward for his virtue.[31]

In *Virtue in Humble Life*, Farmer Trueman lectured his daughter Mary on reading. Be cautious, he warned her, "what books you look into, as you are not to burn your fingers, when you mean to warm your hands: proper books, like due nourishment, feed, support, and strengthen the mind; but in this *scribbling* age, there are thousands of volumes which serve no other end, than to corrupt the heart." At the end of the eighteenth century, critics differed over what constituted due nourishment. They agreed, however, that childhood reading played a large part in shaping the adult. "All parents," the conclusion of a child's version of *Pamela* urged, "ought to be most particularly attentive to a proper cultivation of the minds and understandings of their beloved offspring; for it is a certain fact, that the tempers and dispositions of children may be modulated either to vice or virtue, with equal care." For Jane West, one of the advantages of education was that it moderated expectations and led away from Mr. B. to virtue and Hanway's "*honest man.*" In contrast, in *Goody Two-Shoes* and *Primrose Prettyface*, education, although it did not create great expectations, nevertheless led to great rewards. For eighteenth-century educators, Pamela's circumstances were, as Farmer Trueman saw them, ambiguous.[32]

6

* * * * *

Servants and Inferiors

arly children's books were filled with servants. Although some were main characters, most were minor, merely devices for teaching proper behavior. In *Some Thoughts Concerning Education*, Locke emphasized the importance of instilling "Sentiments of Humanity" in children. One of the best ways to accomplish this, he argued, was "to accustom them to Civility in their Language and Deportment towards their Inferiours and the meaner sort of People, particularly Servants." If children from comparatively well-to-do families were "suffer'd from their Cradles to treat Men ill and rudely, because," he wrote, "they think they have a little Power over them" they "will by Degrees, nurse up their natural Pride into an habitual Contempt of those beneath them." Such contempt, he concluded, could end only "in Oppression and Cruelty."[1]

Much like the character who idled time away and refused to study, the child who treated inferiors poorly seemed destined to unhappiness, failure, and early death. More often than not such a child was spoiled, and contempt for social inferiors was a sign of ruinous indulgence. After the death of his father in *The History of Tommy Playlove and Jacky Lovebook* (1793), Lady Playlove spoiled her son. As soon as Tommy "began to prattle and run about," Lady Playlove gave "strict orders" to "his nursery maid, and all about the house not to contradict him, nor ever to deny him any thing he asked for, on pain of losing their places." Tommy did not receive "the slightest check" if "he committed any fault, such, for instance, as wilfully breaking a china cup" or "throwing the hot tea in the maid's face." If corrected, Tommy cried and "then immediately his mamma, or those about him, for fear the baby should be too much vexed, endeavoured to appease him by telling him, it was not he that did so and so; but it was the cat, or Bob, or Molly, (a poor boy and girl who were servants in the house) and that they should be beat for it; and perhaps were so to please the child."[2]

Tommy's wilfulness made him practically uneducable, and he was refused admission by Westminster. Instead he attended a school run by Mr. Syntax, "one of those pedagogues who make the improvement of their scholars the least of their care." As a result, Tommy grew worse, and with the exception of Jacky Lovebook, whose father's store Lady Playlove patronized and who visited Tommy at his father's request, Tommy's friends were bad boys. One day while Jacky was visiting, Tommy said that he would not complete any more schoolwork, declaring that if "Old Syntax" corrected him, he would "cut off the knocker of his wig, and make him eat it for breakfast." Tommy's "foolish bravado" made Jacky blush and "caused the footboy, a country lad, who was waiting in the room, to laugh." So swollen with pride that he could not bear to be laughed at, Tommy seized a china plate from the table and threw it at the boy. Hitting the boy in the face, the plate "broke into a thousand pieces" and cut him so badly that "it was a very great chance he did not lose his eye." Next Tommy grabbed a pair of tongs from the fireplace, saying he would take the footboy "by the nose" and lead him out of the house. Jacky then intervened, and "with much difficulty" pacified Tommy.[3]

Tommy seemed destined to become an ignorant, inhumane adult. He was lucky, however; his history was a blend of the ordinary and the allegorical, and Wisdom concerned himself about Tommy's future. One day on the way home from Jacky's house, Tommy met some bad boys who urged him to stay out late with them and play practical jokes. The boys persuaded Tommy to lie to his mother and tell her that he ate dinner at Jacky's house. That night as the boys went about their pranks, doing such things as "knocking loudly at people's doors (after having fastened a string to the knocker, and tied the other end at the door of the next house) and then running away," they were seen by a footman. He prepared his fellow servants, and when the boys knocked at his master's door, they were greeted with horsewhips and beaten "so severely, that they were hardly able to crawl home." Not only was this the first time in his life that he had been beaten, but Tommy was humiliated because "it was done by footmen, whom he had always held in great contempt, and over whom he had been used to tyrannize in his own house." Even worse, he stayed out so late that his mother became distraught and was "seized with fits, and carried in a very dangerous condition to her bed." Guilt-ridden Tommy cried himself to sleep. That night he dreamed he was visited by Wisdom, an old man "whose hair was white as silver, and who wore flowing from his shoulders an azure robe." Wisdom told Tommy that the only way to attain happiness was to follow "the path of virtue," urging him to "make young Lovebook your friend and constant companion." The next morning, Tommy apologized to the footboy, and learning that his mother was better, knelt before her, returned thanks for her recovery, and asked for her blessing. Next, he wrote Jacky, apologizing for his misbehavior, after which he applied himself to his studies.[4]

Education and industry brought wisdom to children, not dreams, and most spoiled children who treated servants poorly met bad ends. In Mary Sherwood's *History of the Fairchild Family* (1818), Mr. Fairchild took his three children for an instructive walk in order to teach them the dangers of quarreling. On the walk, they came upon the body of a man in a gibbet. Although the body had hung for "some years," it had "not yet fallen to pieces" and remained dressed in a blue coat, silk handkerchief, and shoes and stockings. The face, however, "was so shocking that the children could not look at it." The body,

Mr. Fairchild informed the children, was that of a man who had murdered his brother. The two brothers had been indulged. Their mother did not send them to school "lest the master should correct them." Instead they were taught at home where their teachers were forbidden to punish them. Moreover, the boys were allowed to frequent the stable and the kitchen where servants "were ordered not to deny them any thing." As a result the boys behaved like Tommy and called the servants names, swore at them, and even struck them. From quarreling with the servants, the boys went on to quarreling with each other and grew "more and more wicked, proud and stubborn, sullen and undutiful." Unfortunately, their mother "still loved them so foolishly, that she could not see their faults, and would not suffer them to be checked." Eventually one brother stabbed and killed the other.[5]

"Sentiment," Hannah More wrote, was "the virtue of *ideas*, and principle the virtue of *action*. Sentiment has its seat in the head, principle in the heart." While sentiment suggested "fine harangues and subtle distinctions," principle conceived "just notions" and performed "good actions in consequence of them." Like Robinson Crusoe, the heroines and heroes of early children's books acted and in making life better for others bettered their own lots. While "singing at her wheel," young Rose heard a moan. She investigated and found an old man lying on the ground. In traveling from New York to Hartford, he had fallen ill. He stayed in an inn, but before his strength returned, his money ran out and he was obliged to travel. Rose gave him her meal of brown bread and new milk. Because her family was poor, however, her father said she should not aid the old man. Like the good Samaritan, Rose paid little attention to worldly expediency. She helped the old man into a shed near the house, brought him extra clothes to keep warm, and until he regained his health she saved the better portion of her porridge for him. Unlike the Good Samaritan who remained anonymous and received his reward in heaven, Rose became known for good deeds and "a wealthy young farmer being charmed with her virtues offered her his heart, his hand, and his fortune." "Thus was Rose," *A Gift for Children* (1796) explained, "raised from poverty, by her virtuous and good conduct, and now lives in wealth and plenty—the joy of her husband, and the pattern of all good wives."[6]

In Mary Pilkington's *A Reward for Attentive Studies; or Moral and Entertaining Stories* (c. 1800), Louisa and Charlotte went to visit their friend Miss Benson. On the way they came upon a little black boy, clothed in rags and crying. "What a frightful creature," Charlotte exclaimed; "I declare he has hardly a rag to cover him, and I vow he absolutely makes me sick." "For shame, Charlotte," Louisa answered, "is that the way you treat a poor destitute fellow-creature?" "*Fellow-creature*," Charlotte said; "do you suppose that I can degrade myself so much as to think a Negro deserves to be called my *fellow creature*." "I cannot help what you *think*," Louisa answered, "but I *know* that a Negro is *mine:* and I am persuaded if my mamma knew how unfortunate he was, she would immediately take him under her care; therefore, instead of going to see Miss Benson, I think, my dear Charlotte, we had better return home." Already hardened into "habitual Contempt," Charlotte continued alone to Miss Benson's while Louisa helped the boy. When her mother discovered that the boy had recently arrived in England and had been abandoned when his master died, "she engaged him to wait upon Louisa and herself." As instilling of "Sentiments of Humanity" in young children saved them from becoming moral failures, so Louisa's action saved her from "madness." Some years later when Louisa was in a paddock next to her house, she heard a crowd shouting, "A mad dog! a mad dog!" Terrified by the crowd, the dog leaped over the paddock gate and ran snarling toward Louisa, who screamed for help. Hearing Louisa cry, the Negro dropped his work. "Like lightning he flew to her assistance, and just as the animal had caught hold of her gown, struck him with a rake which he had in his hand, and repeated the blows until he stretched him dead at her feet."[7]

Talk did not necessarily lead to deeds, and like costly raiment, decorating the body but not touching the spirit, smacked of luxury and aristocratic decadence. In children's books accomplishing the useful or the benevolent was very important. As the individual was able to shape himself, so ideally the state could and should form itself. Not only were people who did not work likely to be corrupt, but they were a source of corruption within society. In *Evenings at Home*, Mr. Barlow, a schoolmaster, pretended to found a colony while his students played prospective immigrants. Before allowing them to immigrate, Barlow interviewed them. Those who could make practical contributions were welcomed into the colony: the miller, carpenter, blacksmith, mason, shoemaker, doctor, and schoolteacher. The tailor was allowed in after Barlow found out that he was "not above mending and botching," stressing that it would be "sometime before we want holiday suits." When he found out that he was "a working-farmer, not a gentleman farmer," Barlow allowed the farmer in, warning him, "labourers will be scarce among us, and every man must put his own hand to the plough." On the other hand, people who belonged to trades or professions which Barlow thought inessential or which produced luxuries were not allowed to immigrate. Among these were the silversmith, barber, and lawyer. When the gentleman appeared, saying, "I only mean to amuse myself," he was abruptly turned away.[8]

Admirable characters were actively benevolent and useful. They worked for themselves and others, in the process building a better and fairer world in which people who wanted only to amuse themselves had no place. Charles Howard, the hero of Maria Edgeworth's "The Good Aunt" (1810), for example, fought to improve the lot of a Creole student at Westminster. In addition to being treated poorly because he was young and a fag, the boy was looked down upon because he was a Creole. Charles himself had been left a penniless orphan when he was small. His aunt, Frances Howard, adopted him and devoted herself "to the important duty of educating a child." Until he was thirteen, Miss Howard educated Charles at home. Then because she did not believe in slavery, she sold the estates in the West Indies which provided her income. Unfortunately the ship bringing her money back to England was lost. Forced to sell her home, she sent Charles to Westminster, and buying a small house near the school, took in boarders. At Westminster, Charles met Oliver, a "lively, intelligent open hearted, and affectionate" Creole whose "*literary* education had been strangely neglected," so much so "that his ignorance of the common rudiments of spelling, reading, grammar, and arithmetic, made him the laughing stock."

Flogged three times a week because he could not do his lessons and sinking into despair because of his schoolmates' ridicule, Oliver asked an older boy, Augustus Holloway, to help him with assignments. The son of an alderman, Augustus made Oliver his fag, and although he gave the boy some help, he treated him with contempt and undermined his confidence even further. One day Charles played ninepins with Augustus. Although Oliver was studying, Augustus made him set the ninepins up each time they were knocked over. When Charles remonstrated, pointing out that Oliver needed to study, Augustus treated the boy worse. On Charles's saying he would help Oliver with his schoolwork, Augustus reminded Charles that Oliver was his fag. "Fag or no fag," Charles said "you shall not make a slave of him." "I will, I shall, I will," Augustus cried, grabbing Oliver; "I will make a slave of him, if I chuse it—a negro slave, if I please."[9]

Oliver burst into tears, and when Charles moved to help him, Augustus, who was a year and a half older than Charles, struck him and warned, "Learn to stand your ground, and fight, before you meddle with me." In asserting Oliver's right to learn and achieve a decent place in the world, Charles championed an ideal society based upon education and merit. Toppling a system which placed birth higher than learning was difficult, but children's books implied that if the middle classes persevered change was inevitable. "Before his defiance had escaped his lips," Edgeworth wrote, Augustus "felt his blow returned, and a battle ensued." Unlike Augustus, Charles was not an "experienced pugilist." He fought "with all his *soul*," Edgeworth recounted, "but the *body* has something to do, as well as the soul, in the art of boxing, and his body was not yet a match for his adversary's." "Beg my pardon, and promise never to interfere between me and my fag any more," Augustus demanded after knocking Charles down. "Never," Charles answered; "I'll fight you again, in same cause, whenever you please; I can't have a better cause." Each day during the week, Charles fought Augustus on Oliver's behalf. For Edgeworth this was not simply a schoolboy dispute. "After five pitched battles, in which Oliver's champion received bruises of all shapes and sizes, and of every shade of black, blue, green, and yellow," she wrote, "his unconquered spirit still maintained the justice of his cause, and with as firm a voice as at first he challenged his constantly victorious antagonist to a sixth combat." Like God who labored for six days to create a new world and rested on the seventh, so Charles who fought for a better social order was victorious on the sixth day. When Oliver then volunteered to be his fag, Charles put his arms around him and said, "Be my *friend*." Under Charles's direction, Oliver regained his confidence and developing into a good student became "a new creature." As Louisa's kindness to the black boy protected her from madness, so Charles's kindness and the resulting friendship between what was in effect the educated middle class and its talented but ignorant inferiors brought golden rewards. Later in the story Oliver made a discovery that enabled Mrs. Howard to regain her wealth.[10]

In a world in which education and hard work determined success, all people were potentially noble. Today's servant or Creole could become tomorrow's master, and today's master could become tomorrow's servant. Reflecting this social mobility and in the process trying to curb pride and teach humanity, children's books warned that "outward Conditions" of both wealth and poverty were short-lived. *The History of Miss Kitty Pride* (1799) described the fall of the daugher of Mr. and Mrs. Pride of Cross-street, the "proudest people" in their part of town. Kitty's mother "would not suffer her to speak to a poor child on any account, nor even to any of the misses she went to school with, unless they were dressed well." As a result Kitty's schoolmates despised her, and she asked to stop school, a request to which her mother agreed, saying "As your papa can give you a genteel fortune, you have no occasion to learn to read or work." At home Kitty spent her time frivolously, playing with dolls and looking at trinkets; sometimes she sat for hours "at her mamma's toilet," powdering her hair and painting her face. One day as she stood at the door watching "a fine young lady that went by, a poor old man with gray hairs came up to her, with his hat in his hand, and begged her to give him some broken bread; for, dear Miss, said he, I am almost starved." Instead of compassion, Kitty felt contempt and slammed the door. "Oh! Mamma!" she cried, running into the parlor, "there is a nasty old man has been asking me for some bread; he has made me sick to look at him." "I wonder such poor wretches are suffered to go about the streets! For my part, I would not go near him to give him a bit, if he was to drop down for want of it," Kitty's mother answered, and saying such people should be in the workhouse, sent "John" to chase him away. While this occurred, "a young woman who waited on Miss Kitty, was reading her bible upstairs." Seeing "the poor man going along with tears running down his cheeks," she crept out of the house and following him "slipt six pence into his hand."[11]

Pride crippled Kitty's body as well as her spirit. "To make her genteel," Mrs. Pride "made Miss Kitty wear a steel shape"; but "instead of that not having room, she grew all awry; and when she was twelve years old, she had a great hump on her shoulder." To hide her deformity Kitty wore sacks and had her stays padded. In children's books truth eventually came out, and one day while eavesdropping on the servants, Kitty heard herself described as "a lump of misery." Mrs. Pride was furious, and she turned out all the servants, including Betty who years earlier had succored the old man and who had not been present at the discussion of Kitty's appearance. Shortly after she arrived home, Betty's uncle returned from Spain where he had become wealthy. Kind and genteel, Betty soon became his favorite, and he made it possible for her to retire from service. Later he sent her in his coach to invite Kitty Pride to his house. When the Prides realized who was calling on them, they refused to receive her. This, however, was the final incidence of pride before the fall. Shortly afterward, Mr. Pride lost his money, and he and his wife were forced into the workhouse while Kitty begged "Miss Betsey" to take her as a servant. Like Charles Howard, Miss Betsey did not "lose the Consideration of Humane Nature, in the Shufflings of outward Conditions," and she took Kitty "to live with her, not as a servant, for she was not able to do any thing in the world, but out of good nature, that she might not perish." Moreover she taught Kitty, taking great "pains to teach her to read and work."[12]

With a good education, Kitty could rise from poverty to a wealth of moral, then temporal, goods. At the same time, however, that books like *Kitty Pride* celebrated social mobility and depicted virtue and education rewarded, other books, particularly those written for the lower classes, urged children to be satisfied in the station to which they were born. In part such books arose out of a reaction against the educational expectations of the times and were often written by people who believed that education was supplanting Christianity as the religion of the country. "A rage for education is one of the marked features of the great world," Jane West declared;

> the hope of forming something superior to the present race of mortals, by merely human means, is one of the wildest theories that ever entered the brain of a visionary reformer; yet it is seriously acted upon by many indefatigable mothers, who weary the patience and injure the constitution of their children by the most unremitting attention to a multiplicity of pursuits; in the hope of being able to exhibit in their own families this mechanical compound of ethical and scientifical perfection; which is to prove, that divine wisdom is not necessary either for informing our ignorance, or restraining our propensities for evil.[13]

Although many writers tried to temper educational expectations, their criticism did not lead to much literature for children until the end of the eighteenth century. Then with the disruptive effects of the Gordon Riots and later the French Revolution and with the Sunday School Movement's making great numbers of the lower classes literate, conservative writers became concerned about what the lower classes read. If Locke were right, and few people denied it—even Jane West argued not so much for the exclusion of matter but for the inclusion of religion as the core of education—in claiming education made the adult, then childhood reading was important not only for individual morality but also for the morality and stability of the nation. To counteract what they saw as revolutionary, conservatives produced literature which urged lower-class children to accept their stations. In Sarah Trimmer's *Sunday School Dialogues* (1784), young Mary discussed poverty with her teacher. If God loved them, Mary asked, why were some "good people" poor. "Because," the teacher answered, "God knows best what is proper for every one: this I am sure of, poor people will go to Heaven when they die, if they live good lives; and they will no longer be poor and distressed, but as happy as if they had been rich." The poor, the teacher continued, could do many things the rich did not have the strength to do. Poor men could plough ground, dig gardens, and drive carts while poor women could wash and iron and clean houses. Not satisfied with her teacher's explanation, Mary asked, "But why must poor people do these things any more than the rich." "Because," the teacher explained, "God placed them in a low station, and made it their duty to do so. It is *no* such hardship to be poor *Mary*, as many people are apt to think, for good people always find friends to help them in time of need; and when they are well, working gives them health and spirits."[14]

The hero of Hannah More's poem *Patient Joe: or the Newcastle Collier* (1802), thought "whatever betided" was right. Keeping Providence "ever in sight," he was "certain that all work'd together for good." Even when his son died, Joe said he was content "for God had a right to recal what he lent." Among his companions in the mines, Joe was a laughingstock. "Idle Tim Jenkins, who drank and who gam'd, / Who mock'd at his Bible" made Joe the butt of his humor. One day when Joe put his "dinner of bacon and bread" on the ground, a dog rushed forward and stole it. "Is the loss of thy dinner too, Joe, for the best," Tim asked. "No doubt on't," Joe answered before he ran after the dog. Unable to catch the dog, Joe expected the miners to sneer at him on his return. Instead he saw "horror and fear" in their faces and learned that the pit had fallen in, crushing Tim Jenkins. Joe exclaimed,

"When my meat was just now stol'en away,
    And I had no prospect of eating to-day,
    How cou'd it appear to a short-sighted sinner,
    That my life would be sav'd by the loss of my dinner?"[15]

Books written for middle-class children often contained portions urging people to be satisfied with their lots in life, warning them against the luxuries of aristocratic living. Sometimes the portions focused on servants, probably in the realization that many of today's readers were yesterday's servants. In *The Life and Perambulation of a Mouse* (1783), a footman addressed John the coachman, saying, "I cannot help *wishing* I was a gentleman." "I don't like to hear a man say so," John replied; "it looks as if you were discontented with the state in which you are placed, and depend upon it, you are in the one that is fittest for you, or you would not have been put into it." John then told a cautionary tale which illustrated the evanescence of wealth and taught that satisfaction with one's lot led to happiness. Paradoxically the heroine who was satisfied with her station usually rose from being a servant to becoming mistress of a house or farm. Mr. Speedgo, a merchant, John related, "gathered gold as fast as his neighbours could pick up stones." Unhappily, his children were raised to be "*haughty*" and "*imperious*" and "to despise every one poorer than they were." Among Mr. Speedgo's servants was Molly Mount, who "used often to say she was perfectly contented in her station, and only wished for more money that she might have it in her power to do more good." Contentment made Molly honest, and whenever she dressed Speedgo's daughters, she urged them to behave better. The girls "were prodigiously offended" and complained "of her *insolence*" to their mother. Instead of "teaching them to behave better," Mrs. Speedgo blamed Molly for "her freedom." One day the girls overheard Molly in the kitchen talking "about the *sin* as well as the *folly* of pride." The next time she dressed them, they demanded that she repeat what she said. Accordingly Molly preached to them on pride, stressing that "superior *virtues*," not riches, made one person better than another. Interpreting Molly's talk as personal criticism, they called her a "*rude, bold, insolent woman*" and had her dismissed. Molly's "fall" was fortunate. Engaging herself as a dairymaid on a nearby farm, she behaved "so extremely well" that the farmer's eldest son married her two years later. With three thousand pounds which his father gave him, Molly's husband took a "pretty farm" in Somersetshire. In the meantime Mr. Speedgo "broke all to nothing." His son went to sea, and the girls into service. Not trained to do anything, they were forced to beg for a living. Some years later Betsey Speedgo appeared at Molly's doorstep, begging for milk. Molly recognized her, and seeing that Betsey was ill, took her in, and nursed her back to health. Molly then brought Betsey's mother and sister to Somersetshire, and fitting "up a neat little house for them" entrusted "the poultry to their care." [16]

The traditional justification for a static society—that one

should be satisfied with his lot because it was ordained by God—was usually made to footmen and Marys in children's books. Unlike Joe, the middle classes were not satisfied with whatever betided. They believed that they could work and shape the future, and whenever the traditional argument for being content with a poor lot appeared in a popular children's book, as it did in Samuel Pratt's *The Paternal Present* (1804), it seemed out of step with the age. "Old, hunch-backed, lame, cripple" and "half-starved," Nahamir, Pratt wrote, begged alms before the gates of Bagdad. Nahamir had once been handsome and had a wife and six children, but suddenly his family died and a "hideous bunch of superfluous flesh" appeared on his shoulders. Then, in an accident he lost an eye; after this misfortune, he tumbled down a stairwell and broke a leg while going to aid a small boy who was being beaten. Later he stopped to help an old man slumped over by the side of a road. When Nahamir bent down, the man drew a saber and sliced off Nahamir's right arm. Finally Nahamir's business failed, and his friends forsook him.

Understandably, Nahamir thought he was unfortunate. One day as he lamented his fortune, an angel appeared and rebuked him, telling him his torments were blessings. When Nahamir asked for an explanation, the angel observed that Nahamir survived when his family died. The deaths of Nahamir's wife and children were examples of "the benevolence of heaven." If they had lived, the angel explained, the children would have been disobedient and Nahamir's wife would have betrayed him. Moreover, the loss of good looks had preserved Nahamir's life; if he had remained handsome, the angel said, he would have been involved in "a scandalous intrigue" and on its discovery would have been impaled. Even the loss of his eye was fortunate; unknown to Nahamir, the califf wanted to make him a harem guard. "Certain ceremonies would have been necessary," but the califf rejected the idea when Nahamir lost an eye. In falling down the staircase, the angel next recounted, Nahamir had been fortunate to break only one leg. The loss of his right arm was also a blessing. At a feast some time later, the angel reminded Nahamir, he had been insulted. If he had not lost his arm, he would have drawn a saber and committed a mortal sin. Even the bankruptcy was fortunate, for Nahamir would have used wealth in a detestable manner and become "an horror to thyself, and a disgrace to human nature." "Suffer patiently," the angel told Nahamir; "after death, thou shalt commence a new career, where every happiness shall be complete and uninterrupted." The angel convinced Nahamir that he was fortunate, and satisfied with his lot in life, Nahamir returned to begging, thanking "heaven, with all his heart, that he was old, deformed, blind, and crippled, and limping, without fortune, without a wife, and without children." [17]

Nahamir's satisfaction and subsequent thoughts about eternal rather than earthly things earned him a place in heaven. In most literature for children, even in that for children from the lower classes, heaven, as Molly learned, was not the only reward for contentment in one's station. In *Sunday School Dialogues*, the teacher hinted that Mary's satisfaction would enable her to better her situation. "Good people," she said, would "always find friends to help them in time of need," and since poverty was, if not a time at least a condition of need, Mary could reasonably expect her "virtue" to receive secular rewards. Nahamir aside, the belief that the individual could determine his happiness, and class, had become such a part of the age that making the case for contentment in poverty was difficult. Even conservative writers who believed that social mobility rendered the nation unstable were obliged to hint, as the teacher did to Mary, that not only would contentment contribute to mental peace but it would also lead to a better standard of living. In *The Sunday School Catechist* (1788), Sarah Trimmer blended God's will and self-interest in urging poor children to be satisfied. She wrote:

It is part of your duty to your neighbour to order yourselves lowly and reverently to all your betters; that is to say, to behave in a respectful manner to your parents, governors, teachers, spiritual pastors and masters; all these should be considered as your *betters* or *superiors*, because GOD has placed them in a higher station of life than yourselves, and put it in their power to do you many kindnesses which will render your low condition more comfortable. All rich and great people are also to be considered as your betters on this account.[18]

Perhaps the best book written for children and young people from the lower classes was Trimmer's *The Servant's Friend* (1787), continued as *The Two Farmers*. Recounting the history of Thomas Simkins, *The Servant's Friend* taught that poor people who were content in their stations were rewarded with better lives. When Thomas was ten, his father died, and Thomas went to work for a nearby farmer while his mother took in washing and ironing. Thomas's industry impressed Squire Villars, and when a place opened in the local charity school, the squire nominated Thomas. "Thank God! Thank God!" Thomas exclaimed when he heard the news; "now I shall be able to read the Bible, and use a Prayer book at church. I will take a deal of pains, mother; and, when I have learnt well enough, will read to you every evening as you sit at work." Then "taking down the Bible from the shelf, on which it was deposited in a neat wash-leather case, he eyed it with delight, and dropped a tear of joy on the cover, which he wiped away with his hand, that it might do no injury." Unlike Westminster, where Charles Howard fought for himself and others, school taught Thomas not to fight. In defeating Augustus, Charles asserted the right of the individual to determine his place in society. In resisting the temptation to fight and mastering his passions, Thomas proved himself safe and deserving of both success and patronage.[19]

The schoolmaster, Mr. Allen, set rules which maintained order. Students could not talk without permission or bring toys to school. On entering and leaving the classroom, they were required to bow to the master. Most importantly fighting was forbidden, and in his first day, Thomas almost broke this rule in defending a weaker boy from a bully. During recess, while Thomas and Jerry Franks, the head boy, were playing marbles with little Sammy Wilkins, Ralph Jennings approached and "snatching a handful of marbles" from Sammy, said, "Are you not ashamed, you two lubbers, to play with a baby? come and have a game with me." Although he was on the point of winning and was humiliated by being called a baby, Sammy "kept his tears from falling." For his part Tommy took the marbles away from Ralph and gave them "with all that he had of his own" to Sammy. "You are a stranger to me," he then said, turning back to Ralph, "but I must needs say I think you a very rude boy; what business is it of yours who we play with? besides, how can you be so unkind to Sammy? you were once as little as he yourself, and would have thought it hard if nobody played with you." Ralph warned Thomas to hold his tongue, saying, "I will give you a knock of the head." Thomas accepted the challenge, and taking off his coat, declared, "I mind a knock of the head no more than you do." In contrast to Charles, though, who battled Augustus for six days, Thomas fought only himself. "Stop," Jerry Franks interrupted, and reminding Thomas that fighting was against school rules, warned him that if he fought he would lose Mr. Allen's good will. Fearing that Jerry might complain to Mr. Allen, Ralph turned away, but Thomas "who was of a lively disposition" was not mollified until Jerry appealed to morality and self-interest. It was wrong, Jerry stated, for "any one to put themselves in a passion," particularly "poor boys, who were placed in charity schools to learn Christian virtues." [20]

"If we live long in the world," Jerry advised Thomas, "and go out to be servants or 'prentices, we must not expect every one to bend their temper to our's; it will then be our duty to study the tempers of others; and the more patience and meekness we have, the happier we shall be; therefore, the sooner we learn to govern our passions the better." Not quite convinced, Thomas asked if he were "to suffer all kinds of abuse without resentment" and to "take knocks of the head" without defending himself. "By no means," Jerry answered but then reminded Thomas that not only had he not received a blow but he was preparing to fight in a place where he was "forbidden to fight by one whose commands ought to be obeyed." In contrast to "The Good Aunt," *The Servant's Friend* did not appeal to the middle classes, urging them to fight for a better social order. Instead it simply championed order, any violation of which smacked of Adam's first disobedience. In books written for poor children, Christ was not the crusader associated with the church militant he later became in nineteenth-century school stories. Instead, he was a pacifist, converting others by example rather than the sword. "Our Lord Jesus Christ," Jerry reminded Thomas, "met with a great deal of ill treatment, and bore it all with meekness and patience; and you know all Christians should strive to be as much like him as possible." Thomas was convinced, and when

Ralph appeared and called him a coward, Thomas controlled his temper and replied, "Call me coward or what you will, Ralph, I shall not break through the rules of the school, though, were it put to the proof, I believe I could soon shew you that I have as much courage as yourself; and you had best not attack me out of school; besides, if you call me coward, the master shall know it." Thomas's masters or betters—academic, social, and eternal— approved his resolution. Because he disciplined himself and controlled his passions, Thomas became a success, ending his days not as a servant but as the servant's friend, a prosperous farmer with a family consisting of six children and many servants.[21]

Most early children's books implied that the middle classes were responsible for national morality and the future of the nation. The greatest danger to middle-class morality, and thereby to the state, was luxury. Seduced by luxury, the middle classes would not only become corrupt, but would no longer feel responsible for others, particularly those beneath them. "It has been said," Jane West wrote, "that the depravity of the lower orders is owing to the separation in the conditions of society which refinement has introduced. Unquestionably, luxury has greatly tended to alienate the minds of inferiors from their betters, by the almost insuperable bars which it has placed between their free communication." The most influential cause of the "change of manners and sentiments among the poor," she continued, was "the increasing luxury of the middle orders, who bind the extremes of society together, and consequently whose manners are the most important to the commonwealth." In contrast to children's books, however, whose world was more egalitarian than that of general society and in whose pages virtues frequently rose from the middle classes and converted the aristocracy, many other books appealed to the aristocracy to reform society. Although these appeals usually preached what in effect was middle-class morality, they assumed that the aristocracy set the country's moral tone. Because they could afford many servants, aristocrats were seen as having great influence upon the lower classes. In her *Thoughts on the Importance of the Manners of the Great to General Society* (1788) Hannah More argued that for reformation to be effective it had to begin, not with the education of the middle classes but "with the GREAT." "*Their* example," she wrote, "is the fountain from whence the vulgar draw their habits, actions, and characters. To expect to reform the poor while the opulent are corrupt, is to throw odours into the stream while the springs are poisoned." "Even the excellent institution of Sunday schools for training religious servants," she said, "will avail but little, if, as soon as the persons there educated, come into families of the great, they behold practices dramatically opposite to the instructions they have been imbibing."[22]

"From their situations" and "from all that they see of the society of their superiours," servants, Maria Edgeworth wrote, learned to "admire that wealth and rank to which they are bound to pay homage," mistaking "the luxuries and follies of fashionable life" for happiness. In children's books for the lower classes, especially religious tracts, poor children were warned against aristocratic ways. In *The Deceitfulness of Pleasure* (1798), Catharine, the daughter of an honest farmer in Westmoreland, became Lady Blithe's waiting maid. As its name implied, Blithe Hall was a pagan palace dedicated to sensual pleasure. Before the house stretched a "beautiful garden," containing "sweet flowers and fruit," an arbor, a grotto, a canal, and a temple. Many rooms in the house were as large as Catharine's parish church. Flowered carpets covered floors, and silk curtains hung from windows. On the walls were looking glasses, Catharine said, "in which you might see yourself from head to foot." Lady Blithe herself was "very handsome, and knew," Catharine wrote, "a great many fine things, such as music and drawing." Unfortunately she cared about "nothing but pleasure, and fine cloaths, and jewels" and set "a bad example to her servants." "It would have been just the same to her," Catharine wrote, "if God's holy Prophets had never written the Bible to teach us our duty, or if there had not been a church in the parish, for all she cared about them." At Blithe Hall, Catharine's behavior changed. At home she got up before five and went to bed at nine. Now she never opened her "eyes much before ten," and "it was long after midnight" before she "thought of going to-bed." At home she read the Bible every day; at Blithe Hall she did not read the Bible or say prayers.[23]

Catharine was fast being corrupted. On his lady's birthday,

however, Sir John Blithe held a feast. That night Lady Blithe got overheated dancing, and going outside to watch fireworks caught a cold which turned into a fatal consumption. On her deathbed Lady Blithe was despondent, saying that she had so neglected her duty that "it would have been better for me if I had never been born." After her mistress's funeral, Catharine was very upset. That night she fell into a troubled sleep and dreamed that Lady Blithe visited her. Wrapped in a shroud and "all shivering with cold," Lady Blithe's corpse parted the bed curtains and "in a deep and hollow voice," said,

> "Catharine, have you forgotten me? while I yet lived on earth you were brought into my service, and I fear, that by my sad example, I taught you to neglect your duty, and to choose evil ways. I now am come to warn you, that if you follow those evil ways they will, sooner or later, lead you to a place of torment. Oh! that I, while I lived on earth, had done that which is right; that I had served my God and taught my servants to do the same, that I had shunned those pleasures which end in misery, that instead of desiring fine things, I had fed the hungry, clothed the naked, and since I was not forced to work for my own bread, I had worked for the poor; happy would it have been for me had I done those things, and been pious and humble, but now it is too late, the time of trial is past, there is no repentance in the grave, remember your unhappy lady, and never wish for riches and power, which too often tempt human beings to do ill, but do your duty in that state of life to which you are called, and God Almighty will receive you when you die, into that happy place where there is no weeping."

In death Lady Blithe did her duty by Catharine. When Catharine awoke, she declared she would never again covet "riches or finery," would strive to behave herself in her "humble state," and from henceforth would be "pious, honest, and contented."[24]

In contrast to *The Deceitfulness of Pleasure*, many books warned children against servants, not masters. For Rousseau the hierarchical structure of society ensured the ruination not only of Catharines but also of Lady Blithes. Emilius, he wrote, was educated "in the country; at a distance from the mob of servants, who, excepting their masters, are the vilest of mankind." "The preposterous distinctions of rank," Mary Wollstonecraft (1792) argued, divided "the world between voluptuous tyrants, and cunning envious dependants," and because respectability was "not attached to the discharge of the relative duties of life, but to the station," corrupted "almost equally, every class of people." While Locke urged that children be taught not to lose "the Consideration of Humane Nature, in the Shufflings of outward Conditions," he nevertheless advised parents to keep children away from servants. "We are all a sort of Camelions," he wrote, "that still take a Tincture from things near us." Not only were servants "foolish Flatterers," but they provided "ill Examples." Children, he thought, were likely to follow "ill Patterns" more readily than "good Rules." Therefore, the wise parent must "carefully preserve" a child "from the Influence of ill Precedents, especially the most dangerous of all, the Examples of the Servants; from whose Company he is to be kept." In *A New Gift for Children* (1762), Charly Avidus started life happily. He "began to learn his book" well, and his mother and father, his schoolmates, and "all that knew him" loved him. As he was growing up, however, he was allowed to play with "his pappa's foot-boy, who was very wicked, and at last taught him to be as wicked as himself." When Charly gave apples to his friends, the footboy would say, "Why should you give away what you love yourself?" "When others were in misery he taught him to laugh at the wry faces they made, often telling him that good nature was a weakness, and that he ought only to consult his own happiness; so that at last he grew selfish and his heart became hard, and incapable of pity." After learning to cheat and trick people and coming to believe that torturing an animal was more fun than "learning his lesson," Charly was ruined. Eventually he joined a gang of thieves and was hanged.[25]

For the boy in danger of being corrupted by servants, school was often administered as an antidote. Removed from the low influences of home, the child was forced to study and become self-sufficient. In *The Mother's Gift*, Mrs. Newsted became ill and was obliged to entrust her elder son "to the care of a nurse." Unhappily, the nurse indulged the boy "in every thing he desired, and by this means rendered him fretful, obstinate, and passionate." When Mrs. Newsted recovered, she tried to correct her son, but he had become "so extremely idle and inattentive, perverse, and forward" that she was forced to send him to school "to receive more severe correction."[26]

Rousseau influenced Thomas Day's *The History of Sandford and Merton*. Instead of being sent to a public school which Rousseau said taught children "depraved manners" and which Day believed buttressed a corrupt class system, Day's Tommy Merton was tutored by Mr. Barlow, a minister. As Mary Wollstonecraft argued that royalty rendered "the progress of civilization a curse" and warped "the understanding," so Tommy, like Matilda, the Barbados girl, had been raised almost as royalty, a white boy in Jamaica, a land of slaves. "Several black servants" waited upon him. If he went for a walk, two slaves accompanied him; one carried a large umbrella to shelter him from the sun while the other picked him up if he became tired. Moreover as he was indulged physically, so he was spoiled mentally. The slaves "were forbidden upon any account to contradict him," and he refused to learn to read because he said reading made his head ache. By the time Tommy came to England at age six he was almost ruined. Not only was he "proud, fretful, and impatient," but he could neither write nor use "his limbs with ease" or "bear any degree of fatigue." Worried about his son, Mr. Merton sent Tommy to Mr. Barlow's house. There he was influenced by Barlow's teaching and by Barlow's other student, Harry Sandford, a hearty, good-natured country boy. Completely unspoiled, Harry was Rousseau's benevolent natural man. As life in aristocratic society damned people, so a natural democratic life could save them. Early in the book Tommy stepped on an adder, and while the snake twisted about his leg, he was unable to act. Tommy's childhood had corrupted him, and emblematically the serpent was the old serpent of Eden, slowly devouring the sinner. Only God, or God-in-Nature, could save Tommy, and when Harry heard Tommy scream, he rushed to the rescue and stripped the snake off Tommy. Under the tutelage of Harry and Mr. Barlow, Tommy grew strong in mind and body so that by the end of the book he had "learned to consider all men as his brethren and equals; and the foolish distinctions which pride had formerly suggested were gradually obliterated from his mind."[27]

In curbing his pride and becoming egalitarian, Tommy became middle-class. He saw beyond outward conditions and rejected distinctions based solely upon birth or wealth. Despite criticizing luxury and implying that education in the country was better than one in the city, most early children's books did not romanticize "inferiours" so much as Day did. Instead they linked servants to aristocratic decadence and implied that a child was better off if his parents were not wealthy. In Arnaud Berquin's "Antony and Augustus; or a Rational Education preferable to Riches," Antony Lenox's father possessed "a considerable fortune." Lenox's neighbor, Mr. Littleton, the father of Augustus, "was not in such affluent circumstances, though he lived contentedly." Knowing his son would not have a great inheritance but would have to earn his way in life, Mr. Littleton provided Augustus with "a well-grounded education, which he thought might prove of more advantage to him than riches." By the time Augustus was nine, he "was accustomed to bodily exercise, and his mind inured to study, which at once contributed to improve his health, strength, and understanding." In contrast, Mr. Lenox pampered his son. Antony was "not suffered to lift himself a chair, whenever he had a mind to change his seat," a "servant was called for that purpose." Other people dressed and undressed him, and he was so indulged that "even the cutting of his own victuals seemed a pain to him." Not surrounded by servants, Augustus resembled a middle-class Harry Sandford. "While Augustus, in a thin linen jacket," Berquin wrote, "assisted his father to cultivate a small garden for their amusement, Antony in a rich velvet coat, was lolling in a coach, and paying morning visits with his mamma." If Antony ever got out of the carriage, a great coat was put on him and a handkerchief tied around his neck. Antony's physical coddling and the bodily weakness it caused had its counterpart in mental weakness. Because the servants "had strict orders to obey him with implicit submission, he became so whimsical and imperious, that he was hated and despised by every one in the house, excepting his parents." Used to having things done for him, Antony was a poor student despite being furnished with good tutors.[28]

Raised apart from the unnatural pampering of servants, Augustus was a fine student. He resembled, Berquin wrote, "a garden, whose airy situation admits the rays of the sun to every part of it, and in which every seed, by a proper cultivation, advances rapidly to perfection." When both boys were seventeen, their fathers sent them to the university where initially they roomed together. As Tommy Merton at six was almost too old to be changed by Harry Sandford and Mr. Barlow, so it was improbable that Augustus would influence Antony. Instead of learning from Augustus's success in the university, Antony was so humiliated that he "gave loose to his vitiated taste, and wandered from pleasure to pleasure in search of happiness." Ultimately he "fell into the grossest irregularities" and returning "home with the seeds of a mortal distemper in his bosom . . . expired in the greatest agonies." In contrast, the self-sufficiency produced by right education strengthened Augustus, and fittingly he achieved great success in the law.[29]

7

✳   ✳   ✳   ✳   ✳

Liars and Tell-Tales

n *Some Thoughts* Locke wrote that virtue was "the first and most necessary of those Endowments, that belong to a Man." Without it, he said, a person would "be happy neither in this, nor the other World." As "the Foundation" of virtue, Locke explained, "there ought very early to be imprinted" on a child's "Mind a true Notion of *God*," adding that this should be accomplished by "gentle degrees" and taking the child only "as far as his Age is capable." Locke wrote comparatively little about religion on this occasion and hurriedly moved on to lying. "The next thing to be taken Care of," he wrote, was to keep a child "exactly to speaking of *Truth*." Lying, he said, was "so ill a Quality, and the Mother of so many ill ones that spawn from it, and take shelter under it, that a Child should be brought up in the greatest abhorrence of it imaginable." Let a child know, he continued, "that Twenty Faults are sooner to be forgiven, than the *straining of Truth*, to cover any one *by an Excuse*."[1]

Early children's books emphasized truthfulness. Lying, Mrs. Newton explained in *Letters from a Mother to her Children* (1780), "is a crime of so *mean,* so *base,* and *dishonorable* a nature, that people esteem it the greatest affront that can possibly be offered them, to be called by the opprobrious name of a *liar*." Invariably the insignificant lie influenced a child's character and led to unhappiness. "From an inattention to those *trifles,* which mark the rising character," Mary Pilkington wrote in *The Disgraceful Effects of Falsehood* (1807), "*originate* those *imperfections,* which *cloud* it with disgrace." In warning children against games of chance at a country fair in *The Fairing* (1788), Giles Gingerbread described the liar's family tree, stating "the gamester, the liar, the thief, and the pickpocket, are first cousins."[2]

Before Felix left for school in *Always Happy* (1816), his father urged him to remember his mother and sisters. "I would have you bear their remembrance incessantly in your heart," he said; "the recollection of their virtues will soften and improve your character, whilst the claims they have upon you will keep you steady in the path of rectitude.—Your name is theirs; do not, therefore, forget, that by staining your character, you will also cloud theirs." Felix's father knew that a spirited boy might get into mischief, and he concluded saying, "I will forgive any thing but a *lie!*" In school stories, moral lessons were more important than academic lessons. In *The Academy; or A Picture of Youth* (1808), Squire Scourhill described his expectations for his son Joseph in a letter to Mr. Macadam, the rector of a boarding school. "Make my son Joseph a scholar," he wrote, "but above all make him an honest man. I know little about your Latin and Greek, as being things very much out of my way; but this I know, that a man, if his heart be right, can look a fellow creature in the face; but without being an honest man, why he had better not live."[3]

At the Academy honesty was one of the first lessons students learned. "One holiday" young Scourhill and his friend Tom Standfast wandered into a village not far from school. There they saw an aged woman spinning beside a cottage. Nearby her grandson studied his alphabet and rubbed a cat. This peaceful scene so impressed the boys that they were about to present fruit to the child when suddenly they noticed the woman's hen on the village green, and the old Adam rose within them. "A small stone," William Mackenzie wrote, "lay at the foot of Standfast; he took it up, and wantonly threw it at the unoffending animal." The stone killed the bird, and the boys fled back to the Academy. Seeing the incident, the woman sent her son to inform the rector. Mr. Macadam then called the school together and preached to them. Although Scourhill was the only person who knew he had thrown the stone, Standfast admitted his guilt. To atone, he bought two hens which he gave, along with a copy of *Pilgrim's Progress*, to the old woman. "I have not seen it this long time," she said in thanking him; "often have I been amused with it in my earlier years; would I had leisure just now to read it!" When he learned that the woman could not take time off from work to read, Standfast volunteered to read to her.[4]

The honest child became the successful adult. In *Martin and James; or, the Reward of Integrity* (1794), young James was the hard-working son of a poor widow. Not only was he the "best scholar of his age in the village," but he managed money well. If he were given a penny as "a reward for his civility in opening a gate, or conducting a traveller through the village, instead of spending it on cakes or fruit, as children generally do, he ran with it immediately to his mother, saying to himself, 'my mammy must card a great deal of wool before she can earn a penny to buy us a loaf.'" When James was eleven, his mother died, and because he was young, he had trouble getting jobs. Farmers hired him to drive birds from their fields, but he received so little pay that he would have starved "had it not been for the humanity of his neighbours, who could not bear to see so good a boy want." At this time the father of Martin, one of James's schoolmates, died and left him four crowns. Deciding to migrate to London, Martin encouraged James to accompany him, telling him jobs were plentiful there. Although London was two hundred miles away, James thought he could accomplish the journey with three shillings. Kindly cottagers gave him the money, and he set out with a loaf of brown bread and a piece of cheese. The journey was a secular progress during which James endured hardship, resisted temptation, and then finally attained a fitting reward.[5]

On the road James befriended an old peddler, despite Martin's discouraging him by saying the peddler would beg from them. Instead of begging, however, the peddler shared his lunch with James, after which James insisted upon carrying the old man's box. While James carried the box, Martin, who now thought the peddler might have money, tried "to insinuate himself into the esteem of the Pedlar." The man was proof against Martin's flattery, noting that the boy paid attention to a stranger while he let his companion "toil on for so many miles, without once offering to ease him of his burden." To discourage James and turn the man against him, Martin knocked James off the road into a ditch half full of mud. Like Christian in the Slough of Despond, though, James struggled out of the ditch and with the man's help continued on. Later at an inn the peddler died from a stomach ailment. While the old man declined, James wept, but the peddler consoled him, saying, "Do not grieve, my child, if you continue to be honest and good, God will raise you up a friend when I am no more." Then he asked James a favor. Ten years earlier, the peddler recounted, the mayor of S., in whose service the peddler had spent his youth, lent him forty crowns to furnish his box. From his profits, the peddler said, he had saved forty crowns, and giving James "a leathren purse," he asked him to deliver it to the mayor.[6]

The peddler also bequeathed James the contents of his box. When opened, however, it was "filled only with a heap of stones." Having left the inn earlier, Martin was suspected of having stolen the goods. James now faced a sixty-mile journey with only twelvepence. Since he had so little money, he ate blackberries and sloes from hedges for lunch and bought a half-penny roll and skim milk for dinner. Overtaken by a storm on the second day, he paid a farmer threepence to allow him to stay in his barn. A one-armed sailor also asked permission to remain in the barn, but because he only had fourpence to last for a fifty-mile trip, he could not pay the farmer threepence. Rather than see the sailor turned out into the storm, James paid threepence for the man. The next day James was exhausted and almost succumbed to temptation. Looking at the money, he thought of the worldly goods it could purchase: the cottage in which he and his mother lived and an adjoining piece of land owned by Farmer Gosling.

Once owner of house and land, he thought, "I could then get honest Ralph of the mill to assist me in cultivating it, and the produce would perhaps make me one of the richest cottagers of our village." Since the peddler was dead, no one would know about the money, he reasoned. Like Christian on the road to the Celestial City, the honest child triumphed over temptation. "No," James concluded, "though I could hide my crime from all the world, I could not from God; it would be known to him." Not even great want, James decided, could excuse taking the property of someone else; and putting the coins back into the purse, he said, "I am sure money must be very dangerous to put such wicked thoughts into ones head—I will trust in God, and endeavour to pursue my way to the Mayor." The journey did not become easier, and James considered taking enough money to make his trip less difficult. Then he would tell the mayor the peddler entrusted him with less than forty crowns. But again he stood fast and resolved to die rather than be guilty of falsehood and a breach of faith.[7]

Just as James reached this conclusion, a carriage approached. Unconsciously, he opened a gate for it, and he was given six-pence, "like manna sent from heaven," James said. The money was, of course, a kind of manna. Although honest children often suffered in early children's books, they always received rewards. The next day when James began to fail again, becoming "ex-tremely faint and weary," a cart drew near. Sitting in it was the sailor who, after recognizing James, immediately gave his place to him. When the driver of the cart learned about James's kind-ness to the sailor, he insisted that both ride with him, and he drove James to within a mile of S. On arriving at the mayor's house, James delivered the money. While he was there, Martin was brought in on suspicion of robbery. James begged the mayor to pardon Martin, and because James had behaved honestly, the mayor granted his request and Martin disappeared, "over-whelmed with shame and disgrace." In contrast, James's integ-rity so impressed the mayor that he helped the boy obtain a good education after which James became the mayor's secre-tary. On his death, the mayor left James "a considerable legacy," and James bought "a little estate, about a mile from his native village, upon which he lived happily to the end of his days."[8]

In school stories there was no greater fault than dishonesty. In stories for boys, heroes often misbehaved, and indeed mischievousness, if it were not calculated, was sometimes seen positively, as an indication of natural spontaneity. In contrast, devotion to studies occasionally appeared as a sign of the sort of self-concern that led to duplicity and dishonesty. In *The Two Boys* (1810), George and Henry Manship attended a school run by their father, a clergyman. The characters of the boys were different. "Glowing, passionate and fiery," George was "quick and enterprising, with a great deal of volatility, and great generosity of disposition." As a playmate, he "was courted," but "among the steadier boys, he was rarely seen." Although he had less shining abilities than George, Henry made more scholastic progress. Patiently he watched "the slow unfoldings of science, and his perseverance in conquering the difficulties of it, promised him a rich reward." Unfortunately Henry's devotion to scientific study made him calculating. In his actions, "a certain subtilty and closeness" was apparent, and he lacked George's "generosity of spirit." While Henry passed his free time in "sober walks, with boys like himself," George flew "over the play ground, at cricket or ball, or some athletic game."[9]

Mr. Manship forbade archery at school. George and his close friend Frederick Fitz-Adam, however, paid little attention to school rules, and one day when they were in a group of boys shooting arrows, Will Morris lost an eye. The accident so terrified most of the boys that they disclaimed responsibility. In contrast, George and Frederick did the right thing and assumed responsibility. "Mr. Manship," Fitz-Adam said, "may punish us for disobedience to his orders, but shall not condemn us for want of humanity or falsehood: let us bind our handkerchiefs round Will Morris's eye, and you and I George lead him in." Although Manship punished the boys, their honesty impressed him.

Some months later, "several boys united in pilfering, not only from the gardens and orchards of some neighbouring farmers, but also from hen roosts and pigeon houses." "The prey, when obtained," they took to the house of Betty Simpson, "an old woman who not only for a trifling emolument undertook to make it ready for these young epicures, but also furnished them with drink." Deviation from honesty led to drink, and the boys were

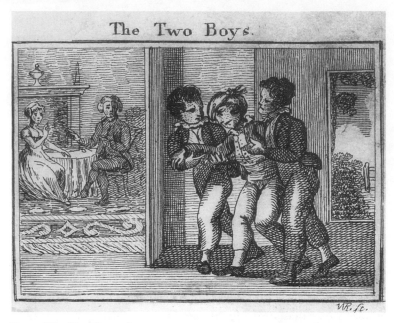

From *The Two Boys*. Courtesy American Antiquarian Society.

well on the way to being ruined. Local farmers reported their losses to Mr. Manship, and late one evening when he was returning to school from a fair, he saw boys in a lane. Hearing one say "it was a nice duck," Manship grabbed the boy's coat. The coat tore and the boy escaped, not, however, without leaving a piece of cloth behind. The next morning, Manship discovered that the piece came from George's coat. When asked if he were the thief, George answered boldly, "I abhor the character; I am no thief; I never took any thing which did not belong to me." "I never," he concluded, "took even an apple from a garden without leave." "You are a shameless, impudent young rogue," his father said and grabbed him. When Manship seized him, a note saying "Remember your appointment to night at nine; do not fail—yours, F. F." fell from George's pocket. When George declined to expose the author of the note, his father concluded that F. F. was one of the thieves.[10]

Immediately he began to beat George. The boy "bore it heroically"; and when his father stopped to rest his arm and asked again if he were a thief, George denied it. "George, George," his father said, "the lie, more than the fault, hurts me." Suddenly he was interrupted by the appearance of Betty Simpson in the grasp of Mr. Porter, a farmer. His hen house had been robbed so often, Porter explained, that he stayed in his barn to catch the thieves. He had not been quick enough to seize the boys, but in running away, one of the boys, he recounted, lost a pocket book, which he then gave to Mr. Manship. Moreover, while chasing the boys, Porter continued, he heard "the screaming of fowls" at Mrs. Simpson's, and after entering her house, found birds which had earlier been stolen from him. Upon examining the pocket book, Manship discovered it belonged to Henry. By mistake Henry had worn George's coat the previous night while the note from Fitz-Adam referred to the plight of a poor widow and her family who had lost their goods in a fire. "We immediately gave them all the money we had in our possession," George later explained, "and agreed to meet in my room this morning, to send them additional relief." Henry's refusal to confess his fault and thereby prevent his brother's punishment disturbed Mr. Manship. At the pleading of Mr. Porter and George, however, he forgave Henry, and only banished him from school, sending him into the country "without seeing your mother, to be deprived of all parental indulgence, for six months." [11]

In many children's books, certainly in those written for girls, Henry would have appeared more admirable than George. Because he was disciplined, he would have reaped financial and moral rewards as an adult. On the other hand, George's lack of control would have turned him into a Timothy Thought-less. However, if education determined a child's future, then thoughtful parents would plan children's educations, both to shape character and determine occupation. Inherent in a child-hood directed toward specific goals was the danger that calcu-lation could become so ingrained in children's lives that they would grow into selfish adults. With attention directed primarily on themselves and on their advancement, they might become unnatural and inhumane. To counteract the tendency of edu-cation to produce narrow, calculating children, some children's books celebrated high spirits. In *First Going to School* (1804) Tom Brown greeted the announcement that he would be sent away to school with a wild burst of enthusiasm. "Huzza, Huzza," he shouted, clapping his hands as he came "running and jumping down his father's court-yard." One of the dangers of high spirits was that they so relaxed a person that he was not careful or calculating enough, and Tom stumbled "over a loose stone, and down he fell with his face on the ground, and cut his nose and chin sadly." As was true of George Manship, Tom's spirits led him astray; this, however, was but a minor failing for on the whole his undisciplined happiness was a sign of good nature. Soon, he bubbled over with enthusiasm instead of tears, describing what he expected from school. After telling Mr. Smyth, who picked him up after his tumble, that he could both read and write, he said, "But there is a great deal more to be learned at school than I learn now; though I can say the pence table quite perfect, and the multiplication table almost." "When I get to school," he continued, "I shall learn so much you will be quite surprised; and then, when I am a man, I shall either be fit to keep a shop, or to be a merchant, or a banker, or a miller, or a farmer, or a captain, or a clergyman, or a gentleman, or a king, which ever trade I like best, Papa says." At school Tom worked and played, and one of his letters home described a trick Tinkler played upon Mr. Trim, the writing usher. In Tinkler's room were five beds; just outside the door was a closet in which Trim slept and studied. One day Tinkler procured a sow that belonged to Mrs. Hibden, the wife of the headmaster. Dressing it in Trim's clothes, he tied a wig and a hat on the sow's head, and fastening the animal to Trim's chair, placed its hoofs on his desk. Next he dressed the sow's ten piglets in caps and nightshirts and put two in each of the beds in the room.[12]

In Tom Brown's high-spirited educational world Tinkler's pranks were not taken seriously. In reviewing *First Going to School*, Sarah Trimmer treated the book lightly, saying "that a little boy of our acquaintance has read it through with pleasure, and therefore we conclude other little boys will do the same; but we hope none of them will think of playing such mischievous tricks as *Tinkler* is said to have done!" Despite Trimmer's genial tolerance of Tinkler, tricks and high spirits were often treated harshly in children's books. High spirits drew children away from proper educational paths and led them into idleness, of which tricks were themselves the visible sign. The boy who played pranks was usually a poor student. Devoted to his studies, the good student rarely indulged in mischief. In *The History of Little Dick* (1793), Richard Small was sent to school because he misbehaved at home. At school Little Dick "made but slow progress in learning as well as in the amendment of his manners; for when the holidays came, he could not spell a word of two syllables." Pleased, however, that he had made some progress, his parents indulged him, loading him with "cakes, play-things, and little books." Dick did not read these or any books when he returned to school; instead he became idle and mischievous. One day when a fair came to town, he purchased a penny's worth of gunpowder and wrapped it in brown paper. Seeing an old woman roasting apples on a piece of tin over a pan of charcoal, he approached her, bought some apples, after which, "pretending to warm his hands, he slyly put the powder into the pan, and then walked off." Shortly afterward, the powder exploded, splitting the pan and throwing the apples into the street. When the woman realized what happened, she chased Dick. Two schoolmates who were in on the prank, however, pulled a cord underneath her feet and she fell to the ground. When the master found out what occurred, he horsewhipped Dick and his friends, made them beg the old woman's pardon, and then pay for "every farthing" of damage they had caused. In *Friendly Advice, on the Management and Education of Children: Addressed to Parents of the Middle and Labouring Classes of Society* (1824), the author warned that "it is, in most cases, owing to idleness, that young people of both sexes are tempted to go into bad company, and to proceed from step to step, till our penitentiaries and prisons are crowded with wretched inhabitants." The playful and idle boy became the bad man. Instead of studying, Dick began to drink and play with town boys who were "seldom or never good for any thing." Eventually he became a highway robber. Fleeing England for the West Indies, he led a mutiny, inciting a crowd to throw the ship's captain overboard and install him as commander. During their journey a storm arose. Paying no attention to a man who warned them to stay on board "and pray to God," the mutineers abandoned ship. The shipwreck did not lead to Dick's reformation and salvation. Resembling Will Grumble, whose pranks led others astray, Dick was the uneducated man at the mercy of uncontrollable elements both within and out-

From Dorothy Kilner's *The Holiday Present*.
Courtesy American Antiquarian Society.

side himself. Instead of being reborn and educating himself on a desolate island, he drowned.[13]

Although most children's books distrusted high spirits and tricks, they emphasized amusement. Blending instruction and amusement, books labored to make learning a "Play and Recreation." In *The Friends* Mr. Freeman helped Billy learn the alphabet by making him furnish homey and playful analogies for each letter. Thus *A* reminded Billy of the roof of the church, broad at the bottom and narrow at the top, while *H* resembled two gentlemen shaking hands. *X* he compared to the turnstile in Farmer Giles's field, and *B* reminded him of "farmer Thomson's great belly." A traveling show had recently passed through the neighborhood; and *I*, Billy said, "stood for the Indian that was shewn in the town." Likewise, *L* stood for "the lion that was shewn" with "the Indian; and a terrible fellow he was too." [14]

Despite the influence of Romanticism, which often bound ignorance to natural truth, educational progress and moral growth usually went hand in hand in children's books. Without an education characters met fates similar to that of Little Dick. Still it was only a short, sensible step from playing children into "a Knowledge of the Letters" to playing them into virtue. In *The Holiday Present* (1787), two boxes containing the paraphernalia of games were delivered to the Jennets' home. The first, the *"naughty child's box,"* contained three rods, a fool's cap, and four silver medals on which were inscribed: "Whoever wears this, is a cross child"; "Whoever wears this, cannot be depended upon when out of sight"; "The wearer of this has told a lie"; and "This medal is a badge of sloth and idleness." In the *"good child's box"* were books, hats, balls, kites, ninepins, marbles, workbags, housewives, dolls, and, as Charles Cheerful put it, "a variety of pretty things, which I do not now recollect." When the Jennets behaved well, they received rewards from the good child's box. One day Miss Deborah, a servant, took Charlotte, Harriet, and "little Tom" for a walk in the field behind the Jennets' house. As soon as Charlotte reached the field, she darted from the path. When Deborah told her to come back, she threw clumps of dirt at her and called Tom and Harriet *"tender chickens* and *foolish goslins."* When the group returned to the house, Mrs. Jennet asked Deborah why she had gone outside in "so very dirty a gown." On discovering that Charlotte had thrown dirt and run wildly about in the field, Mrs. Jennet forced her to wear the fool's cap. In the shape of a sugar loaf, the cap "had two long ears, like asses, hanging from the sides, and was painted red, blue, green, yellow, scarlet, and black." Bits of ribbon hung about it and in the front was "the picture of a naughty child crying." When Charlotte put it on, she screamed so loudly that her mother threatened to tie up her mouth. At dinner Mrs. Jennet told Charlotte she could take the cap off after she apologized to Deborah. Charlotte left the table, but instead of seeking Deborah went upstairs to her room. After a few minutes, she returned and said she had apologized. Having heard Charlotte go upstairs and aware that Deborah was downstairs, Mrs. Jennet knew her daughter lied. To discourage her from repeating the offence, Mrs. Jennet whipped Charlotte "as much as she deserved for being so wicked a girl" and made her wear the liar's medal. She also refused to allow her to speak to her brothers and sisters "for fear she should teach them to be as naughty as herself, saying if she did not make the proper use of her tongue, which was speaking the truth, she should not use it at all."[15]

The combination of play and discipline reformed Charlotte. In this combination was the framework of games. Not only did games offer loose structures in which a child could safely indulge high spirits, but they also could be seen as counteracting the tendency of education to produce calculating children. In school stories what would become important in the nineteenth century was not the lesson taught but the spirit in which the lesson or game was played. Anticipating the emphasis later nineteenth-century children's books would place upon games, some books stressed games. When Alfred Granby came to Dr. Friendly's school in *Aunt Mary's Tales* (1817), he was arrogant and refused to play games. "I dare say," Edward, the most popular boy in school, told him, that "you are come to school for the same purpose that brought us all here: but, perhaps, there may not be any harm, when you are tired with studying Euclid or Virgil, to relieve yourself by a little bodily exercise." Instead of listening and playing, Alfred plotted against Edward, in the process destroying his own character.[16]

Punishment for lying was severe, and Henry's banishment to the country in *The Two Boys* was unusually light. The story of the Earl of Goodwin appeared in several books. When the Earl of Goodwin was accused of being an accessory to the murder of Prince Alfred, Mary Ann Kilner wrote in *The Adventures of a Pincushion*, he seized a piece of bread and calling "God to witness his innocence" stated "if he uttered any thing but the truth, that the next mouthful he eat might choke him"—whereupon "the bread stuck in his throat and he died immediately." As Goodwin's lie was practically blasphemous, so lying was often associated with the fall of man and was seen as the precursor of deadly sin. In *The Adventures of a Pincushion*, the governess of a small school was Mrs. Stanley, typically the widow of a clergyman. Among her pupils was a sort of everychild, Eliza Meekly, who at thirteen was approaching womanhood. One evening after Mrs. Stanley put her to bed, Eliza was so troubled that she confided her worries to her cousin Harriet Una. Like Spenser's Una, Harriet served as her guide and intercessor with, if not the true God, then the true educator. "What have you done, my dear cousin," Harriet asked, "to make yourself so uneasy?" After saying that she did "not like to confess my weakness," Eliza explained that while she was away from school on a visit, Charlotte Airy invited her "to eat some preserved plums, which she said had been made a present of to her Mamma, and which came from *Portugal*." Although the plums "were very sweet and luscious," Eliza refused them at first, explaining that her mother had forbidden her to eat "any thing of that kind." Like the old serpent, however, Charlotte was persuasive and moved Eliza to disobedience. She "laughed at me so much for being so foolish," Eliza recounted, "as to imagine any thing so innocent could hurt me," adding "that she supposed, as I went to *school*, my *mistress*, for so she sneeringly called Mrs. *Stanley*, would *whip* me if I did." "Overcome with her persecutions, and vexed to be treated so much like a baby, and as if I was afraid of punishment," Eliza said, she ate a plum. "Suppose Mrs. *Stanley*," she asked Una, "should ask whether I have eat any thing lately which I ought not; and if she does not put that question, I feel so undeserving of her caresses, that she will see by my looks that I have behaved improperly." [17]

Saying that she was sorry for what Eliza had done, "Miss *Una*" advised her that "the noblest reparation" she could make "would be honestly to inform Mrs. *Stanley* of the crime, and the sincerity of your regret for having been guilty of it." Una's advice was well taken, and Eliza promised to comply the following morning. However, like weak Christian man, she needed an intercessor to plead for her. Too timid to approach Mrs. Stanley, she begged Una to plead her case. In "the mildest terms," Una did so and engaged Mrs. Stanley's "compassion." Afterward Mrs. Stanley greeted Eliza "in the warmest terms" and after praising her frankness and "generous confession" warned her "never to be led into actions which you know are improper, because the company you are with may ridicule your refusal." "It is best never to do any thing which you know to be wrong, though it may appear to be in the smallest instance," she told Eliza, "since the desire of concealing a *trifling* fault, may lead you to hide it by a falsehood, which is one of the *greatest* you can be guilty of." To emphasize her point, she told Eliza the story of Betsey Lloyd. One day Betsey visited her friend Hannah. After they played in the garden, Hannah suggested that they go to a shop and buy gingerbread. At first Betsey demurred, explaining she needed her mother's permission. Hannah ridiculed what she called Betsey's "squeamishness," eventually overcoming "her better resolutions." Having left the garden and its protective hedge of rules in pursuit of sweets, Betsey suffered. The shop was full of boys, one of whom snatched Betsey's pocketbook and ran off declaring "he would see its contents, and know all the girl's secrets." Betsey pursued the boy "until she was a good way from home" and he was joined by schoolmates who "behaved in so wild a manner as to terrify her greatly." At thirteen, the same age as Eliza, Betsey had entered puberty, that time, in Kilner's view, during which rules were essential to protect one from wandering. Alas, Betsey did not learn her lesson, and on returning home, she wandered farther from virtue by lying and compounding her fault. She told her parents that she had gone out with Hannah and Hannah's maid and that a loose horse had so frightened her that she was unable to return home on time. At first this "wicked deceit" made Betsey unhappy, but she "at length grew reconciled as she found herself undetected." Shortly afterward, she went for another illicit walk with Hannah. As she crossed a road, a horse, much like Betsey's own wilfulness or, ultimately, passions, broke "the bridle which confined him" and galloping along the road trampled Betsey and "broke her leg in such a terrible manner, as to occasion her being a cripple ever after." [18]

Disobedience led to lying. In religious books, mortal sin was not far behind. Such books frequently taught that a child's first disobedience was enough to maim not simply character or body but soul. The schoolmistress of *York House* (1820), Mrs. Martin, was also the widow of a pious clergyman. Attending York House were two sisters, Emma and Maria Stirling. At sixteen Emma had learned to control her nature; at thirteen Maria was entering adolescence and like Eliza Meekly found it difficult to resist sweet temptation. Unlike Eliza, who sought Una's intercession with a higher power, Maria mocked Emma when she urged her to take part in devotional exercises. "I really think you will make an excellent *parson*," Maria said; "if *you* chuse to be a *mope*, that is no reason why I should. Religion is very well for old women,

From Mary Ann Kilner's *The Adventures of a Pincushion*.
Courtesy American Antiquarian Society.

who must soon die, but girls have nothing to do with it; give me
a doll and a skipping-rope."

After Maria's refusal, Emma warned that it was necessary "for
us who are still spared, to seek without delay the pardon of our
sins through Jesus, a crucified Saviour, lest we should be suddenly called to appear before God, and the door of mercy be for
ever shut against us." Hearing this speech, Sophia Thompson
told Emma that she went "too far" in calling her "sister's faults,
sins," saying "I cannot think that so harsh a term is applicable
to the foibles of school-girls." Sophia was the voice of the broad
church secularism that pervaded most early children's books,
and Emma rejected her view out of hand. "In the sight of a pure
and holy God, all mankind are guilty, though all have not run
equal lengths in sin; yet," Emma said, "we have the seeds of
every sin in our hearts, and if they do not all spring up and appear in our conduct, it is not because we are naturally better than
others, but because we have not been exposed to equal temptation, or restraining goodness has prevented their growth." Because she prayed, Emma avoided temptation; in contrast, Maria

was unable to resist it. At the bottom of Mrs. Martin's garden was a pear tree. Like Eve, Maria was tempted by the fruit and wanted "to strip one of the branches of its beautiful burden." One day she climbed the garden wall; just as she reached for a pear, the back door of York House opened. Frightened at being discovered, Maria tried to jump from the wall. Unfortunately her foot slipped, and she fell heavily, breaking her leg in two places and suffering a "severe contusion" on her head. For several days she was unconscious. When she awoke, she was terrified. "My sister, where am I? where have I been," she exclaimed; "Emma, I feel that I am dying; but where, oh, where, am I going! O that I had hearkened to the voice of instruction!—pray for me, my sister! Jesus, have mercy!" Mrs. Martin encouraged her "to look to him who heard the prayer of the dying thief." Although Maria rapidly grew weaker, she had energy enough to preach to her schoolmates. "Ah, my dear young friends," she said, "you see me in the fatal consequences of disobedience and folly; let my death prove a salutary lesson, to warn you of the danger of continuing in the path of sin, against the convictions of your judgment and conscience, and contrary to the affectionate advice of parents and teachers." "Had I enough strength," she continued, "I would earnestly entreat you to seek the Lord while he may be found, and to call upon him while he is near. Trust not to the repentance of a death-bed; I have done so, but would *now* give a thousand worlds to enjoy the reflection, that I had when in health desired savingly to know *him* whom in sickness I am constrained to seek, but fear he will not be found of me." The sermon exhausted Maria, and shortly afterward "the vital spark was extinguished," and she died, moaning "Hope—hope—mercy—Jesus!" [19]

Since Maria had not actually lied, hope existed. The confirmed liar had little chance of salvation. "I hope, *Mary*, you always speak the truth?" a teacher asked in *Sunday School Dialogues*; "telling lies is one of the worst sins any one can be guilty of. God is very angry with those who tell lies: they will not go to Heaven when they die." For children from the lower classes who depended upon reputations to obtain employment, lying could destroy this life as well as the afterlife. *The History of Mary Wood* (1800) described the unhappy experiences of a poor girl addicted to lying. One day Mr. Heartwell, the clergyman of a country parish, was sitting on the porch of his parsonage "when he saw a figure rather flying than running down a hill near his house, the swiftness of whose motion made it hard to distinguish *what* she was, much less could he guess *who* she was." When she drew closer, Heartwell recognized Mary Wood, the daughter of Matthew Wood, an honest laborer who died four years previously and for whose wife Heartwell had found a place at the alms house. A crowd followed Mary. Seeing Heartwell, Mary ran to the parsonage and begged him to protect her, saying that she had been wrongly accused of robbery. Heartwell listened, and when the crowd arrived said he would investigate and be responsible for Mary. The crowd explained that "sad doings" had occurred in their village. Squire Banks's gardener and dairymaid had robbed both the squire and Farmer Boucher, for whom Mary worked. Because "she had been telling a mort of lies about them," people suspected Mary of being in league with the thieves. A search of her trunk uncovered six silver teaspoons with the initials of the farmer, E. B., on them. Although Mary "pertested they were none of his'n," she would not reveal where she got them, and since Mrs. Boucher, who was away visiting her father, had recently purchased teaspoons, circumstantial evidence was against Mary. Having been "detected in some falsehoods, that would make against her," Mary lost "all the comfort and confidence of innocence" and fled although she was not guilty.[20]

Mary's past told against her. After the death of Mary's father, Lady Worthy helped her get a place at Mrs. Trueby's. On Mary's second day at work, Mrs. Trueby sent her to dust the best parlor, warning her not to touch the pier glass. Mrs. Trueby's six-year-old son Edward accompanied Mary to the parlor. Mary neglected Mrs. Trueby's instructions, and describing a "balance-master" she had seen to Edward, she attempted to balance the "long broom" on her palm. The broom toppled off and smashed the pier glass. Hearing the crash, Mrs. Trueby hurried to the room and seeing the damage exclaimed, "O Mary! My precious pier glass, the best piece of furniture in my house, and a present from a dear friend who is now no more, quite spoilt! I valued it above ten times its price! Is this your awkwardness,

Mary?" Frightened, Mary lied. "No, indeed, madame," she replied. When Mrs. Trueby asked who broke the glass, she lied again, saying, "A great bird, madame (I don't know whether it was a pigeon) flew in at the window. I tried to drive it out, and it dashed against the glass with its bill and cracked it as you see." Her "invention and assurance" made Edward laugh; and when his mother noticed it, Mary winked at him and said, "Master Edward knows it is true, for he saw it as well as I." "O, fye, Mary," Edward said, "that's too much—I would not have told upon you, but when you say I know it to be true, you make me a liar, as well as yourself, and my mamma says, if I tell lies God Almighty will not love me." "Wicked girl," Mrs. Trueby then said, "would you teach my child to lie? pack up and be gone out of my house." When Edward pleaded for Mary, Mrs. Trueby was unyielding, explaining that she would have forgiven the loss of the glass "but a girl that can so readily invent a lie, and try to draw *you* into it, I cannot possibly suffer to stay a day in my house."[21]

On learning about her daughter's shameful behavior, Mary's mother became ill. The sickness frightened Mary, and she tried to reform. Unfortunately custom proved too strong. Some time later, a gentlewoman who had heard Mary's story took pity on her and decided to give her a place. Before hiring her, however, she asked Mary why Mrs. Trueby dismissed her. When Mary said it was because she broke a pier glass, the woman asked "and was that the only reason?" Again Mary lied and said, "I believe so." "Go," the woman responded sternly; "you will not do for me. I see you are not cured of your vile fault." Eventually, Mary got a place at Farmer Boucher's. Nearby was the home of Mr. Banks, a gentleman who had gone on a tour and had left his gardener and dairymaid in charge of his house. The servants were corrupt. Not only did they make free with their master's property "in every way," they also led Mary astray. Whenever she passed Mr. Banks's house, the gardener gave her fruit and the dairymaid cream for a syllabub. One day when there was a great wash at Farmer Boucher's, they invited Mary to accompany them to a fair, enticing her by saying that a dwarf and a tall woman would be there. The temptation proved too great for Mary, and telling Mrs. Boucher that her mother was ill, Mary asked if she could visit her. Although reluctant to let Mary escape work, Mrs. Boucher allowed her to leave at five that afternoon. That evening Mary's mother came to the farm to visit her. When Mary returned from the fair and learned that her lie was discovered, she wept and promised to reform. After making Mary give her word that she would not see Mr. Banks's servants again, Mrs. Boucher gave her another chance. However, the cream, fruit, and "civil things" which the gardener said to her proved too strong, and Mary secretly renewed acquaintance with the servants.[22]

One day when Farmer Boucher was out and Mrs. Boucher was visiting her father, Mary invited the gardener and the dairymaid for tea. Having already decided to rob his master, the gardener prowled through Boucher's house. Boucher had recently sold grain and had the money in the house to pay rent to his landlord. Aware that the farmer's rent was due and having bought dung from him and seen him put the payment in a bureau in the parlor, the gardener suspected that the rent money was also in the bureau. While Mary busied herself with tea, he examined the fastenings on the parlor window. That night he returned, broke in through the window, and robbed the farmer. When the farmer returned home the evening before the robbery, he asked Mary if anyone had come to the house. Instead of saying that she entertained Banks's servants, Mary lied and said no one had come. Later, during the investigation of the robbery, a ploughboy said he had seen Mr. Banks's gardener looking out the parlor window. This testimony and the spoons found in Mary's trunk convinced people Mary was an accomplice. Mary did not steal the spoons. The dairymaid took them from Mr. Banks's housekeeper Elizabeth Bearcroft and gave them to Mary to hold for her. Mary knew nothing about the robbery, but since she had been sworn to secrecy, she refused to reveal where she got the spoons.

On the return of Mrs. Boucher, who found her teaspoons intact, and on the capture of Banks's servants, the truth came out. Unhappily, it was too late for Mary. Boucher dismissed her, and as a consequence, Mary's mother became "almost distracted" and died. Then Thomas, a young baker who wanted to marry Mary but who had been prevented from doing so by his father, who thought he should marry a wealthy girl, suddenly inherited his father's bakery. A "very honest, sober, agreeable young man," Thomas now rejected Mary. "Had she preserved a better character," he would have married her. "I could not be happy unless I could make a friend of my wife and depend on her truth and faithfulness," he explained; "her pretty face and good humour would be nothing to me, without truth and honesty. Next to a good conscience the best thing is a good character. I bless God I have never forfeited my own; nor will I ever marry a woman that has lost hers." Lying had destroyed Mary's life. After Thomas's rejection, she left the village. Heartwell gave her a letter to a clergyman fifty miles away, and although she got a place, the labor was hard and "hastened on a decline which her sorrows had begun." Mary died "at eighteen years of age," the tale concluded. "May all," the conclusion urged, "who read this story, learn to walk in the strait paths of truth. The way of duty is the way of safety." [23]

In part, Mary's difficulty stemmed from her promise to the dairymaid. Children's books were ambivalent about what the author of *Mary Wood* called "false promises." In refusing to name the person who gave her the spoons, Mary protected a criminal, and, in this case, silence showed that she was unable to distinguish between true and false duty. In Priscilla Wakefield's *Juvenile Anecdotes* (1809) Philip Hervey was best student and the favorite of his master at school. "Because he would seldom be persuaded to join in any of their mischievous pranks" and because he served as school monitor, Philip was not popular with his schoolmates. One summer evening a group of boys decided to rob the master's apple orchard. Just as they were filling their pockets, Philip discovered them. To keep him from telling on them, the boys offered Philip the best fruit in the orchard. Philip refused the bribe, but said if the boys "would promise to behave better for the future," he would "give them his word that he would not betray them." The boys agreed. The next morning Mr. Ashton, the master, discovered the theft. He was particularly upset by the stripping of a "golden pippin tree, the fruit of which he intended to make presents to his friends." He called the school together, and when he questioned the boys, all denied knowledge of theft except Philip who would not lie. "I am conscious of having acted very improperly," Philip explained; "I happened to pass by when the plunderers were stripping your trees, and suffered myself to be bound by an inadvertent promise that I would never betray them." When Ashton said he would punish Philip if he did not expose the thieves, Philip answered that he was "grieved to be under necessity of disobeying your orders; but I have pledged my word, and no punishment shall deter me from keeping it." Begrudgingly Ashton agreed that Philip was right to stick to his word, but he warned him "to be cautious before he made a promise."[24]

For the most part children's books approved of the course Philip took and warned children against becoming "tell-tales." In *Always Happy* Felix's father advised him not to expose his schoolmates' "faults nor cause their punishment; it will be enough for you to guard your own conduct, and not disgrace yourself by being a spy on others." Although she had been treated terribly—taken away from her nurse, locked in a small closet, and fed bread and water for a week, Fanny asked her guardian not to question her about the experience. "My nurse used to tell me," she said in *The New Friend of Youth* (1803), "that *teller's of tales, were as bad as teller's of stories.*" Exceptions to this kind of advice appeared for the most part in books for very young children for the lower classes, as in *Mary Wood*, or in books written primarily for girls.

In books for girls, allegiance to schoolmates or to one's word, when rashly or mistakenly given, was sometimes seen as inferior to duty. Stories which emphasized duty frequently relied upon analogies between a teacher's instructions to her pupils and God's instructions to Adam and Eve. In such stories, the girl who informed upon classmates or threatened to do so was the voice of a rigorous and life-saving morality, not a spy or a tell-tale. In refusing to tolerate disobedience or criminal activity, such heroines protected both gardens and childhood from corruption. Thus in *The Mother's Gift*, Miss Johnson warned schoolmates that she would inform their governess if they disobeyed instructions and ate strawberries. When the other girls said she would then be a "telltale," she responded that she would do what she thought right.[25]

In contrast to this story, which taught that duty obligated the heroine to reveal truth, stories for boys generally stressed that truth came out on its own accord. In stories for girls silence often implied acquiescence or weakness of character; in tales for boys silence implied self-control and strength. Frequently good boys were wrongly accused of crimes; instead, however, of revealing the truth, they suffered punishment, thereby showing that they were able to endure injustice and overcome obstacles comparable to those which they would face as adults. Maria Edgeworth's *Tarlton* (1809) described proper behavior for boys in school. Hardy, the hero of the story, was an admirably strong character. "Beloved" by all the good boys, he did not curry favor and paid no heed when "idle, mischievous, or dishonest boys attempted to plague or ridicule him." In contrast, his friend Loveit wanted to be liked by everyone and "his highest ambition was to be thought the best natured boy in the school." Because he was afraid of offending other boys and being laughed at, he lacked the "courage to say, *no*" and often did "things, which he knew to be wrong." One day after a game of battledore and shuttlecock, Tarlton accidentally threw the shuttlecock over a hedge into a nearby lane. Forbidden to go into the lane, none of the boys volunteered to retrieve the shuttlecock until Tarlton taunted Loveit. Hardy advised Loveit not to go into the lane, but after Tarlton called him "Little Pando" and said he was under the thumb of Hardy, whom he labeled "Parson Prig," Loveit fetched the shuttlecock. This initial disobedience led to worse behavior. From the lane Loveit saw a tree laden with apples, and on returning, described it to Tarlton. That night and for two successive nights, boys crept out of school and stole apples. The tree belonged to an old man who "had promised himself the pleasure of giving his red apples to his grand-children on his birth-day." Not wanting to inform the boys' master, Mr. Trueman, and get them flogged, the man nevertheless knew that the boys had to be stopped. Stealing, the man said, "would surely bring them to the gallows in the end." To prevent the theft, he borrowed the "fiercest mastiff in England," Farmer Kent's Barker, and chained him to the apple tree. Eating forbidden fruit led to worse actions, and although Loveit argued against the act and indeed thought he had dissuaded him, Tarlton decided to poison Barker. For a sixpence Tom, a servant boy, obtained poisoned meat and agreed to give it to the dog. Looking out of the room

From Maria Edgeworth's *Tarlton*.
Courtesy American Antiquarian Society.

he shared with Hardy, Loveit saw Tarlton meet Tom. He was so disturbed that he told Hardy what was occurring. Hardy dressed quickly and chased Tom down the lane. Although Tom threw the meat to Barker, Hardy arrived in time to seize a pitchfork and spear the meat, leaving Barker with only the handkerchief in which the meat had been wrapped.[26]

Returning to school, Hardy was met by Mr. Power, an usher. On Power's discovery of the meat, Hardy warned him that it was poisoned. "You wretch!" Power exclaimed and demanded that Hardy fall upon his knees, confess, name his accomplices, and beg pardon. "Sir," Hardy said, "in a firm, but respectful voice, 'I have no pardon to ask, I have nothing to confess; I am innocent; but if I were not, I would never try to get myself off by betraying my companions.' " Hardy's steadfastness angered Power, and he threatened Hardy, asking "How will you look to morrow, Mr. Innocent" when "the Doctor comes home?" "As I do now, sir," Hardy responded; "ever since I have been at school, I never told a lie, and therefore, sir, I hope you will believe me now. Upon my word and honour, sir, I have done nothing wrong." Power refused to believe Hardy and locked him in a small closet known as the "*Black Hole.*" The next morning Hardy refused to reveal anything about his actions the night before, and Power was preparing to beat him in front of the school when Mr. Trueman and the man entered. After accusing Hardy of being a thief and of trying to poison the dog, Trueman produced the handkerchief. After Hardy denied ownership, Trueman said he would flog all the students beginning with Hardy if the owner of the handkerchief did not claim it. Although Hardy knew it belonged to Tarlton, he remained silent and "looked with a steady eye at the cane." He was spared punishment, however, when Trueman found Tarlton's initials on the handkerchief. Tarlton tried to shift the blame on others, saying that Loveit first mentioned the apples and Tom suggested poisoning the dog. Not simply a telltale but also a coward, Tarlton was dismissed from school, and Hardy "not because you ask it," as Mr. Trueman said, was rewarded by being allowed the gratification of a wish. Generously, he asked that the boys be pardoned, to which, after excluding Tarlton, Mr. Trueman assented.[27]

Hardy's silence reflected not only strength of character but also the sturdy individualism that right education seemed to promise. As prosperity spread during the eighteenth century, dreams became expectations. Almost no success seemed beyond the grasp of the properly educated child. As a result of belief in the malleability of children and the prosperity which made society less rigid, competition grew. Instead of seeing a child as a member of a class or group with whom he would always share common experiences, parents could reasonably expect the educated child to accomplish more than his peers, and advancing through society, achieve individual success. To do this, the child had to avoid Loveit's weakness, and learn to say *no* and to keep his own counsel. In a mobile society in which wild success and dismal failure were everyday occurrences, friendships which linked children to the behavior of others were potentially dangerous, and the successful child had to become self-sufficient, trusting himself and often suspecting others. Although the assured and occasionally lonely individualism that this attitude bred appeared more often in books for boys than in those for girls, it also occurred in books for girls. In Fielding's *Governess*, Mrs. Teachum told her "young Readers" that "Love and Affection" formed the "Happiness of all Societies" and "what we should chiefly encourage and cherish in our Minds." In being affectionate and loving, however, she warned, there was "one Caution to be used, namely, That you are not led into many Inconveniences, and even Faults, by this Love and Affection." This "Disposition" led naturally "to delight in Friendships," she explained; unfortunately, unless one were careful such delight could lead "into all manner of Errors." The person, she said, who tempted "you to fail in your Duty" or justified "you in so doing" was not a "real Friend." "If you cannot have Resolution enough to break from such pretended Friends," she warned, "you will nourish in your Bosom Serpents, that in the End will sting you to Death."[28]

Loveit shared a room with Hardy. If Hardy can be seen not as a character but a trait of character—firmness—then Loveit's confiding in Hardy and relying upon him for direction were signs of development. In drawing upon Hardy, Loveit's weakness disappeared, and if Hardy is viewed as a potential for firmness within Loveit himself, then by the end of the story, Loveit had outgrown the desire to be popular. In the future he would do his duty and rise above weakness and scotch bosom serpents. In some children's books, the desire for love and affection led to telling tales, if not to lying. Unable to resist confidences, weak characters gossiped in order to be popular and as a result undermined not merely their social but also their economic futures. In *First Impressions; or, The History of Emma Nesbit* (1814), Emma was so spoiled by her mother that her father sent her to boarding school. Emma's bedfellow, Miss Morgan, was two years older. Morgan encouraged the younger girl's habit of telling tales in confidence. The most popular girl in school was Caroline Neville, a ward of chancery. Although Caroline was not remarkably clever, she had such "sweetness of disposition" and was such a good "friend of those who were in grief or distress" that students preferred her company to that of Morgan. Cleverer than Caroline, Morgan was jealous and prejudiced Emma against her. One day Emma suffered from a sore throat and slept near the room of Mrs. Patterson, the schoolmistress. While resting, she heard Mrs. Patterson tell a teacher that Caroline's father began work as a chimney sweep. He rapidly bettered himself, and enjoying enormous success, was able to leave Caroline a fortune at his death. Although she heard Mrs. Patterson say that "she hoped no one had the least idea of it" because "Caroline's greatest weakness was her fear of it being known by her schoolfellows," Emma revealed Caroline's secret to Morgan. Later when Caroline took out a dress to wear to a dance, she discovered it was covered with soot. "It is certainly very provoking," Morgan said, "but I dare say, Miss Neville, it is not the first time you have had soot on your clothes, and perhaps some years ago you would not have been so much surprised at it." When the students speculated about who soiled the dress, Morgan, who was guilty, blamed a ghost and then revealed that Caroline's father had been a chimney sweep. "I dare say," she recounted, "her father hearing of the ball, and wishing to see his daughter's beautiful frock, jumped out of his grave, to take a peep at it, and as I conclude, that the ghost would not part with what was through life his constant companion, the soot-bag, I suppose he has, in his admiration and surprise, let it fall on his child's frock." Upset by her bedfellow's behavior, Emma accused her of acting "in a manner at once unkind and unfeeling." Morgan would have none of the rebuke and reminded Emma that she had revealed Caroline's past. "If reproof is the order of the day, I am sure you deserve it much more than I," she said; "you were so contemptibly weak as to mention to me, what you must have been sure I should take advantage of." [29]

Although Emma was repentant, she did not learn a lesson. The child was the mother of the woman, and her weakness undermined not merely Caroline's happiness but her own life. Some time later Emma wanted to attend a concert in Bath "to hear that unrivalled master of the art, Mr. Braham" who had come to sing from London. When she asked her father to buy her a new dress for the concert, he refused. Although he warned her not to tell Emma, Mrs. Nesbit explained to Emma that Mr. Nesbit's bank was temporarily short of funds. Money from abroad was expected, but until it arrived, Mrs. Nesbit said the family would have to watch expenses, adding, "Be careful, I conjure you, Emma, to let no mention of this pass your lips." Emma kept her counsel until the morning of the concert when a schoolmate, Jane Turner, asked if she were going to attend. When Emma said she was not, Jane was surprised and asked, "What in the world is to prevent your going." On Emma's replying that her father would not buy her a dress, Jane accused him of being "most shamefully stingy." Emma loved her father, and unable to hear him wrongly criticized, she explained why he had refused. Immediately Jane left Emma's room and sent a servant with a message to her aunt, urging her to withdraw the money she had in Mr. Nesbit's bank. The withdrawal started a run on the bank and by late afternoon it failed. Mr. Nesbit was ruined, and blaming herself, Emma's mother "fell into a state of despondency, from which nothing could rouse her, and expired soon after in the arms of her husband." [30]

Children's books criticized living a lie. The most obvious outward sign of such a life was aristocratic behavior. For some critics, the best, and thereby the most dangerous, description of luxurious life was found in Lord Chesterfield's *Letters to His Son*. At the end of the eighteenth century selections from Chesterfield's writings appeared in many conduct books. In *The Accomplished Youth: containing A Familiar View of the True Principles of Morality and Politeness* (1811), for example, selections from Blair, Raleigh, the Marchioness de Lambert, and Chesterfield furnished the contents of short essays on subjects such as piety, true glory, choice of friends, cleanliness, decency, and temperance in pleasure. In 1774 Francis Newbery published a selection from the letters for children. In 1786, Elizabeth Newbery published "A New Edition," entitled *Lord Chesterfield's Maxims: or, A New Plan of Education, on the Principles of Virtue and Politeness. In which the exceptionable Parts of that Noble Lord's Letters to his Son are carefully rejected, and such only are preserved as cannot fail to form The Man of Honour, The Man of Virtue, and The Accomplished Gentleman.*[31]

Many such books were published for children. Miscellancies, they contained advice on proper conduct and good manners and appealed to the middle classes. Occasionally the collections betrayed an uneasiness with teaching manners and worldly conduct and pretended to be more than they were. In the dedication to his *Words of the Wise* (1768), John Potter declared, "Wisdom Virtue, and Morality, were once the Inhabitants of this lower World: But as Vice, Ignorance, and Immorality, prevail'd amongst Mankind, in proportion to their Riches and Luxury, they were obliged to withdraw and seek a place of rest among the Souls of the Blessed." Under headings such as man, life, conversation, god, death, and heaven, brief essays followed containing the advice of the conventional conduct book but written in a florid, biblical style. Because conduct books seemed to stress accommodation with this world, even to celebrate it, religious critics were often uncomfortable with the genre. Since his letters were popular and furnished matter for many conduct books, these critics often attacked Lord Chesterfield. For many people he represented the world, the flesh, and the devil, all the deceptions that seduced children away from what really mattered. In truth, critics of conduct books were on solid ground. In Elizabeth Newbery's *Maxims*, for example, seventeen pages of text were devoted to company, fifteen to knowledge of the world, nine to good breeding, and eight to pleasing. In contrast, religion filled one and a half pages, virtue two and a half, humanity a third, modesty a half, and learning one and a half.[32]

In 1776 the *Gospel Magazine* published "Christianity Reversed: or, A New Office of Initiation, for all Youths of the Superior Class. Being a Summary of Lord Chesterfield's Creed." The creed began,

> I believe, that this world is the object of my hopes and morals; and that the little prettinesses of life will answer all the ends of existence. I believe, that we are to succeed in all things, by the *graces* of civility and attention; that there is no sin, but against good manners; and that all religion and virtue consist in outward appearance. I believe, that all women are children, and all men fools; except a few cunning people who see through the rest, and make their use of them. I believe, that hypocrisy, fornication, and adultery, are within the lines of morality: that a woman may be honourable when she has lost her virtue. This, and whatever else is necessary to obtain my own ends, and bring me into repute, I resolve to follow; and to avoid all moral offences: such as scratching my head before company, spitting upon the floor, and omitting to pick up a Lady's fan. And in this persuasion I will persevere without any regard to the resurrection of the body or the life everlasting. *Amen.*[33]

With varying degrees of fervor, critics of children's literature repeated the *Gospel Magazine*'s condemnation of Chesterfield, arguing that his ideas undermined virtue and taught superficial and inessential manners. In discussing the *Letters* in the *Guardian of Education*, Sarah Trimmer declared it "a very dangerous book, unfit for the perusal of youth, as has been exemplified, we fear, by the fatal experience of many, who, while they have been studying in it the *science of the graces*, or, in other words, a system of *artificial manners, devoid of religious or moral principle,* have made shipwreck of their sincerity and virtue." There was "no hope of educating young people to a love of integrity in any family," Maria Edgeworth wrote, where "the Chesterfieldian system" was adopted. One of the villains of *The Infidel Father* was Lord Glanville, whose manners, Jane West wrote, "were formed in the school of Chesterfield, that is to say, they were corrected by the opinion of the world, and restrained by prudential and interested motives." Such a man could not provide children with a proper education, and after being seduced, his daughter stabbed herself before him, rebuking him as she died, crying, "You have cut me off from all hope in this world; and MARK! if there be an hereafter, my soul will be required of you, whose precepts have misled me; and my blood be upon you for ever!" Some few days later Glanville himself died in "unspeakable misery," misery, however, that was just a prelude to what he would suffer "in the day of final retribution."[34]

In Maria Budden's *Valdimar; or, the Career of Falsehood* (1820), living the Chesterfieldian life led to lying and finally to misery. Valdimar Augustus Frederic Walsingham was the only, and spoiled, son of Sir Frederic Walsingham, the owner of Purwood. Living at Purwood with the Walsinghams was Valdimar's orphaned cousin Allan. Allan's father died when the boy was an infant; happily, however, his mother worked hard to educate him. Allan was seven when she died, just as "he became sensible of her value, but not before she had imprinted on his mind one momentous principle—the love of truth." Like many orphans, Allan was fortunate enough to be neglected, if not mistreated. In contrast to Valdimar who was "fed to loathing with delicacies and sweetmeats," Allan's uncle gave him only simple food. Since he was not the heir to Purwood, comparatively little attention was paid to Allan's education. When Valdimar entered Eton at ten, Allan remained at Purwood to be taught by a local curate, who "took more pains with the morals than the manners of his pupil."[35]

At home Valdimar learned to lie. After hearing his parents order servants to lie, telling callers that the master and mistress of the house were away from home when they were actually present, Valdimar concluded "that rich people may tell lies whenever lies are more convenient than truth, but the poor only when the rich command them." At four Valdimar was "quite a little gentleman," for his mother had taken "immense pains to make him such," teaching him the worldly creed of Christianity Reversed. "He was the perfect master of all the seemings and counterfeitings, that are necessary to courtly demeanour," Budden wrote; "he did not answer rudely, because it would *sound* so vulgar. He did not eat heartily because it would *seem* so odd. He did not speak honestly because it would *appear* so strange. The semblance of all cardinal virtues were his; eyes, voice, and limbs, were all governed by the rules of taste and ton. His heart had nothing to do in the affair." One morning Valdimar handled his bow and arrows carelessly and shattered panes in his mother's conservatory. On being asked not to betray him, Allan responded forthrightly, "I will never betray you." When Mrs. Walsingham discovered the damage, she asked Valdimar if he were responsible. "I! no, indeed, mother," he answered "with an unblushing cheek." On the gardener's saying that either he or Allan must have broken the windows because they were the only people in the garden when the damage was done, Mrs. Walsingham asked Allan if he were responsible. Although he said he had not broken the panes, Allan appeared "less steady" than Valdimar because he "trembled for his cousin." Allan's appearance convicted him, and Mr. Walsingham beat him. After Allan had been beaten "long and severely," the gardener reappeared, bringing Valdimar's bow and arrows. When Mr. Walsingham asked him why he did not reveal that Valdimar was "the culprit," Allan responded, "Then, uncle, at last you believe I spoke the truth," adding "that is enough, I do not mind the beating." [36]

Sir Frederic was ashamed, and he asked Allan what compensation he could make for his "rash violence." Allan was silent until Sir Frederic began to beat Valdimar; then leaping in front of Valdimar and taking the blow meant for his cousin he said to his uncle, "You offered me a compensation for the beating I have received. I claim your offer—forgive Valdimar." Allan's request was granted; unfortunately Valdimar needed punishment then and later. Not receiving it, he grew into a bad man. After Valdimar left Eton, his father bought him a commission in the army. Eton and manners had done all they could for Valdimar. "Divinely handsome," he "danced well, dressed well, rode well, managed the prancing steeds of his curricle with inimitable grace and skill, spoke elegantly, moved gracefully, bowed like a Vestris, and adulated like a Chesterfield." While the exterior had been groomed, the interior man had been allowed to run wild, and he was a gambler and seducer. In contrast, Allan had built a reputation for honesty and had gone to work for Mr. Lambton, a solicitor who took him on without a premium. Subsequently only Allan's assumption of his cousin's debts kept Valdimar out of jail. On the day of his marriage to Lady Mary

Beaufort, Valdimar ran off with Fanny Beverley, the daughter of a curate, a girl with whom he had dallied for some time. Valdimar's treachery to Lady Mary was a sign of what was to follow. Not long afterward he became a forger, and eventually he was killed in a duel. On the death of Sir Frederic, Allan inherited Purwood, becoming Sir Allan and marrying Lady Mary Beaufort. "Falsehood," a minister said to Allan, "has gradually hurled Valdimar from title, wealth, existence, fame! Truth has elevated you from obscurity and penury, to fortune, honours, reputation!"[37]

A "useful education," Kitty Bland's brother said in *The Brother's Gift* (1786), was "the basis of the chief happiness and enjoyment of this life." Unfortunately, many subjects taught in boarding school were "chiefly ornamental" and instead of preparing girls for life sent "them into the world fit objects to be deceived and undone." In teaching the ornamental appurtenances of aristocratic leisure, schools turned out girls prepared to live lies. Instead of learning to work, students learned to be gracefully idle; instead of doing good, they talked well. Not only did idleness numb the understanding, Kitty's brother said, but it corrupted the heart, for it was "inconsistent with a state of ease and indolence to have the strong, but fine affections of love, pity, compassion, sorrow, sympathy, and the like frequently awakened and excited in the breast." Like Hannah More's distinction between sentiment and principle, concerns resembling those of Kitty's brother appeared in many children's books. Words without deeds, declarations without action, typified the false and unnatural behavior of aristocrats. In *Correspondence between a Mother and her Daughter at School*, Laura's mother sent her to school because, she said, "our own insulated neighbourhood does not afford us the means of giving you some advantages we wish you to possess." The school had an honest, regular Georgian appearance and accordingly taught the useful rather than the ornamental. Almost as if it existed in an unfallen world— as in some sense it did since students were not encouraged to covet—the school was in a village. Its "red-brick house" stood "in a garden, a little way back from the road, with an immense row of tall poplars before it, looking like so many sentinals." Despite the natural barriers, it was inevitable that evil would enter the Edenic garden, tempt the girls, and disrupt Green-grove House. Two sisters who "had been at a high school in London" suddenly appeared. "Very gay, dashing girls," Laura wrote, they looked "down with contempt upon every thing, and every body here."[38]

Shortly after their arrival, the sisters suggested that all the girls donate money and they form "*The Juvenile Ladies' Branch Bible Association.*" During a discussion of the association, "Grace" spoke, saying "there is a pretty little girl who calls here some-times with watercresses: I saw her this morning, as I was crossing the hall, and asked her if she could read." When the little girl replied that she could read, Grace asked if she were able to read the Bible. "O, yes," the girl answered, adding that although "she was a very good scholar" neither she nor her mother owned a Bible. "Shall we give her one, then?" Grace said to the group, and turning to the older sister, asked if she would share the ex-pense with her. The difference between words and deeds was great, and the sister answered, "Perhaps, I may; though I don't know why *I* should, in particular: indeed, at present I have very little to spare; besides we are just now talking of something quite different." "If our object is to give poor people Bibles," Grace responded, "it is, you know, exactly the same thing: but if we are only wishing for the fun, or the credit of having a *Juvenile Ladies' Branch Bible Association*, it is, certainly, as you say, *quite different.*"[39]

Although the sisters accused Grace "of a want of zeal about the subscription" to the society, the next time the girl called with watercresses Grace gave her a Bible. In *Memoirs of a Peg-Top* (1788), Mr. Heedmore, a shoemaker, lectured his son Charles on honesty. "Those who are so wicked as to *lie*," Heedmore said, "will be guilty (at least are to be suspected) of any crime, since to forfeit your word, is to break every tie of honour; it is like the hemp with which we sew shoes, *Charles;* if that fails, they will come up in pieces, you know, and be rotten, and good for nothing." In early children's books, liars became good-for-nothings while those who lived lies accomplished nothing, and like the class to which they belonged, were destined to vanish from society.[40]

Appendix

*   *   *   *   *

Emblems in Early

Children's Books

eligiosity mitigated criticism of *Robinson Crusoe*. Although the short editions written for children did not contain as much religious matter as lengthier versions, they did show, as Sarah Trimmer put it, "what ingenuity and industry can effect, under the divine blessing." Moreover, the reader familiar with religious allegory and emblem would have recognized traditional Christian material. Despite emphasis upon worldly success, many children's books—allegorical and not allegorical—appeared structured around emblematic scenes similar to those found in *The Pilgrim's Progress* and Francis Quarles's *Emblems Divine and Moral* (1777). Among the traditional emblems which commonly appeared in the narratives of early children's books were the shipwreck, the maze, the fight between schoolboys, and the garden containing for-

bidden fruit. Besides providing lumber for central instructive scenes, emblems furnished material for a range of educational lessons. The matter of two related emblems, the looking glass or vanity mirror and the perspective glass or telescope, for example, often appeared in children's books.[1]

The thirty-ninth emblem in John Bunyan's *Divine Emblems: or, Temporal Things Spiritualized. Fitted for the Use of Boys and Girls* (1794) depicted a woman primping before a mirror. Accompanying the woodcut was the poem "Upon a Looking-glass." Bunyan wrote:

> In this, see thou thy beauty, hast thou any;
> Or thy defects, should they be few or many.
> Thou may'st (too) here thy spots and freckles see,
> Hast thou but eyes, and what their numbers be.

The spots were inner, not outer. Seeing only the surface of things, the woman was spiritually blind. "Without eyes" opened by Christianity, she was seduced by luxury and could not foresee her "eternal fate." Bunyan wrote:

> Many that seem to look here, blind men be.
> This is the reason, they so often read
> Their judgment there, and do it nothing dread.

Francis Quarles's vanity mirror resembled Bunyan's looking glass. "Believe her not," Quarles urged, "her glass diffuses / False portraitures." The mirror abused "her mis-inform'd beholder's eye" and instead of a "true reflection" scattered "Deceitful beams."

Like the mirror that made the observer "fairer, goodlier, greater," the prism deceived and focused attention on "present toys" instead of "future joys." In a discussion between Flesh and Spirit in book three of *Emblems Divine and Moral*, Quarles used the prism and the telescope to elaborate upon vanity and seeing. Noticing the telescope at her "sister's eye," Flesh asked Spirit what she saw. When Spirit replied that she was looking at "Grim death," Flesh asked, "And is this all? Doth thy prospective please / Th'abused fancy with no shapes but these?" Spirit then described another sight: Judgment Day. While "the angel-guarded Son" sat on his "high tribunal," the battlements of heaven sweltered in flames. Far below, Spirit said, was a "brim-stone sea of boiling fire." There fiends "with knotted whips of flaming wire" tortured "pour souls" that gnawed "their flame-tormented tongues for pain." Into these purple waves "queasy-stomach'd graves" vomited the dead, who cursed "all wombs for bearing, and all paps for nursing." Thinking the sight horrible, Flesh invited Spirit to put aside the telescope and look into her prism. There she would see, Flesh said in lyrically seductive language,

> The world in colours; colours that distain
> The cheeks of Proteus, or the silken train
> Of Flora's nymphs; such various sorts of hue,
> As sun-confronting Iris never knew.

"Ah, fool," Spirit replied, "how strongly are thy thoughts be-fool'd, alas! / To doat on goods that perish with thy glass."[2]

At the beginning of the eighteenth century, most books published for children were godly books and used not only Quarles's emblems but a similar language. In *A Looking-Glass for Children. Being a Narrative of God's gracious Dealings with some little Children* (1708), Abraham Chear asked, "What are the Toyes, of Wanton Boyes, / To an Immortal Spirit?" He wrote:

> If naughty Boys, allure with Toys,
> to sin, or lies to tell;
> Then tell them plain, you tempt in vain,
> such wayes go down to Hell.

In the poem, "Written to a young Virgin," after looking "in a Glass" and thinking "how sweetly God did form me," the narrator moaned, " 'Tis pitty, such a pretty Maid, / as I, should go to Hell." Chear's book celebrated the holy deaths of young Christians. To escape Hell the young virgin had not merely to reject vanity but life itself. By century's end the notion of the mirror as an instructive device remained, but the ends and language had changed. Instead of reminding children of their mortality, mirrors taught morality. One of the most popular children's books at the end of the century was Arnaud Berquin's *A Looking-Glass for the Mind*, a collection of instructive stories which led children to reflect upon worldly honor rather than heaven and hell. "As a useful and instructive *Pocket* LOOKING-GLASS," the preface of an edition of 1794 stated, "we recommend it to the Inspection of every Youth, whether Miss or Master; it is a MIRROR that will not flatter them, nor lead them into Error; it displays the Follies and improper Pursuits of the youthful Breast, points out the dangerous Paths they sometimes tread and clears the Way to the *Temple of Honour and Fame.*"[3]

In *The Telescope; or, Moral Views for Children* (1804), a wise old man let Ellen and Henry look through his telescope. Like Spirit, the old man explained what the children saw. Although the sights were instructive and often cautionary, they proffered advice for this world and did not contain graphic pictures of suffering and damnation. Focusing on the Hill of Learning, for example, the children saw a road climbing to the top while a boy wearing the Cap of Folly stood lost at the bottom. In Harriet English's *Faithful Mirror* (1799), a religious education brought happiness to this life. Consisting of a series of views, the book was divided into two sections: "The Mirror's Pleasing Reflection" and "The Contrast." In the former section at the birth of their daughter, Julia's parents addressed "their joint prayers to a throne of grace, with hearts filled with gratitude, and praise." They prayed that she would "be endowed with all goodness: and with prosperity in this world" according to "the will of their heavenly Father." In "The Contrast" although Helen's parents loved her, they did not pray at her birth. "Poor babe!" English wrote, "no pious prayers are made for thee. Can this perishing world satisfy an immortal soul? Alas! thou wilt find it cannot." Returning to the mirror sometime later, English observed that Julia's "parents' prayers have been heard." Modest, humble, and fair, Julia was "a blessing to her family, and a blessing to the world." Although Helen's face was fair and her form delicate, her mind was not "beauteous." She was "a prey to passion, a prey to folly." Later English saw that Julia was now "the joyful mother," "happy in the performance of all her duties." Helen, unfortunately, had become "the slave of fashion." Although she, too, was "a wedded dame," she had no "domestick joys" and sought "pleasure in the midnight dance, the rout, the play, the masquerade."[4]

Magically instructive mirrors and telescopes commonly appeared in collections of rarities. Among the curiosities which Mr. Set'em-right showed children in *The Prettiest Book* were a twelve-foot-long telescope, made by Mr. Faith-and-Hope, through which children could glimpse "a noble city" in comparison to which the Enchanted Castle was but "a fool," and a looking glass invented by Mr. Flatter-none which reflected the inner rather than outer person. Among the items sold in *The Lilliputian Auction* was "a curious Looking-Glass," which, Charly Chatter explained, "will be of use to any little perverse Lilliputian, since it shews what a disagreeable figure any person makes, when in a passion, or shewing unnecessary Airs." Master Mulish, Charly recounted, once owned it. One day after beating his brother "heartily," Mulish looked into the "faithful Glass." He appeared "so extremely ugly" that he frightened himself; immediately he ran "to his Brother and begged his pardon," after which he returned to the glass and "found he had recovered his original prettiness." On another occasion, "seeing a beggar Woman before the Door, he flew to her like lightning, and gave her a shilling, which was all the Money he had. As soon as he looked into this glass, he found himself as beautiful as an Angel." When Charly offered the glass for sale, Master Froward declared that he did not want it, saying, "I have no occasion for it, for I have no faults to be told of; and if I had, I should not like to be told of them." "Indeed, Master *Froward*," Master Affable answered, "you have great occasion for it; so I'll buy it myself, and make you a present of it."[5]

Among the curiosities displayed at *The Exhibition of Tom Thumb* was "the *intellectual perspective-glass*," made by Mr. Long-Thought. "This truly wonderful optick-glass," Tom explained, "has the property of making every object which is viewed through it, appear in such a form, as is most suitable to its natural qualities or probable effects." When examined, through the glass "a basket of unripe apples or gooseberries" changed "into a swarm of worms and other devouring reptiles" while "a bowl of punch, or a bottle of wine" appeared "to be full of snakes and adders." Like Interpreter explaining the significance of a painting to Christian, the perspective glass "explained" a series of pictures to children. In a painting by Mr. Josiah Thriftyman, the principal figure was a young prodigal who seemed "highly delighted with the expensive follies and gratifications to which he has eagerly resigned himself." Seated in a public garden, he was surrounded by a "crowd of harlots, pimps, musicians, bullies, and sharpers," all of whom were "eager to court his favour, and ready to assist him in his foolish amusements." When viewed through Mr. Long-Thought's glass, the prodigal changed into a beggar "bedewing his face with a plentiful shower of tears, and stamping on the ground, and wringing his hands like a mad-man." Nearby were "a surly bailiff and his followers" who had just arrested him and were "dragging him to a gloomy prison." In the corners of the picture stood "the late companions and ministers of his folly," all of whom ridiculed him.[6]

Despite widespread criticism of its not having, as Baroness d'Almane said, "a moral tendency," the fairy tale grew in popularity during the eighteenth century. Faced with the fact of the fairy tale's hardy resistance to criticism, educators and writers did what they had done with allegory and the eastern story: adapted the magical paraphernalia of the tales to their own instructive ends. In Ellenor Fenn's *Fairy Spectator* (c. 1790), Miss Sprightly was dreaming that a fairy was about to give her "two of the prettiest looking-glasses that ever were seen" when Miss Friendly woke her, warning her it was time to get up. Later, after Sprightly described the dream to Mrs. Teachwell, her governess, Mrs. Teachwell said she would write dialogues in which the fairy appeared. Sprightly was pleased, she said, because the fairy "would teach me to be good." "I love you for your earnest wish to be good," Mrs. Teachwell answered, "but tell me, is not every action, word, and thought known?" "To whom, Madame?" Sprightly asked. "Consider!" Mrs. Teachwell responded.[7]

After making sure that Sprightly knew the difference between the spiritual world and the world of imaginary spirits, Mrs. Teachwell began her account. Lady Child, she said, had "fitted up" a closet of instructive books and toys for her daughter, Miss Child. Unfortunately, Lady Child died when her daughter was five years old, and Miss Child's education was taken over by a governess, interested only in the "outward person." Consequently, "the poor girl's mind and temper were neglected; so that she grew proud, selfish, peevish, and vain." One day when Miss Child sat in her closet looking over feathers and artificial flowers "in order to make choice of such as should be most becoming to her complexion," a beautiful fairy appeared. Saying "I am the guardian of your mind," the fairy gave the little girl two "ENCHANTED GLASSES." Like the pictures in English's *Faithful Mirror*, the glasses showed contrasting reflections. "*One*," the fairy explained, "shows you as you *are*, the other as you *might and should be.*" In giving the glasses to Miss Child, the fairy recounted their histories, saying they had cured Miss Pettish of peevishness and Miss Lavish of prodigality. With the glasses, the fairy also gave Miss Child a book in which she could keep account of her moral progress. "Look in *this*," the fairy said of the glasses, "nay, never start; you must first see your faults, before you can mend them." "Record in this book," she continued, "the report of the glasses; on the one leaf *what you are;* on the opposite, *what you should be.*" [8]

Mirrors were also used for moral purposes in the eastern story. In *The Enchanted Mirror, a Moorish Romance* (1814), Leonora, one of two sisters, was "the most delightful creature in form and countenance that ever was beheld by mortal eyes." Unhappily, "her mind was at variance with her outward appearance. For she was so perverse, peevish, capricious, obstinate, and extremely ill-tempered and violent, that she usually went by the name of *Vixena*, which in the Moorish language signifies a perverse creature, from which our word *vixen*, is derived." In contrast, the other sister, Isabella, was homely. Excluded by her looks from a corroding fashionable life, she "took great pleasure in reading and improving her mind" and "paid great attention to instructions of her masters." As her mind developed so did her character, so much so that she was known as Euphrasia, or Well-Beloved. One day Leonora insulted Abu Ferez, the one-hundred-and-ten-year-old Knight of the Black Plumage. Almost immediately she found herself in "THE SALOON OF THE ENCHANTED MIRROR," where her figure was "reflected ten thousand times." Instead, though, of being pleased Leonora "shrieked with horror," for her appearance had changed. "Her nose appeared flattened, her skin of a deep yellow, as if she was jaundiced, her eyes little and red, one side of her mouth drawn down to the bottom of her chin, and her whole face was distorted; instead of the charming ringlets which fell down her bosom, her head was covered with white wool, and a serpent wreathed round her neck, and darting its forked tongue, hissed with unspeakable fury."

From the saloon Leonora was transported to a wild forest where the giantess Urganda forced her into service. Warned not to contradict Urganda, Leonora said nothing when the meal of cold ham, chicken, and canary wine that Urganda offered her consisted of black bread, onions, and muddy water. Leonora almost objected when the pink and silver robe that Urganda offered her turned out to be an apron and a brown stuff gown. Before she spoke, however, she overheard a conversation. " 'And so you are a black beetle for life, because you were too proud to wear a stuff gown, and a check apron; I do not pity you.' 'Do not approach me with my folly, but look at home,' pertly replied a black beetle; 'are not you become a cockchaffer, because you said you preferred green tea to bohea.' " Much as the souls of bad children were imprisoned in animals in *Vice in its Proper Shape*, so Urganda changed haughty people into contemptible creatures. Frightened that she too might become one of Urganda's toads or bats, Leonora endured a succession of humiliations. In the process her pride was curbed and "habitual mildness" became part of her character. Because she suffered, she grew capable of pity and felt sorry for people whom Urganda transformed. As Leonora's character improved, the images in the Enchanted Mirror became less frightening. Finally when the mirror reflected her inner beauty, Leonora was freed from servitude and again became "the Princess of Cordova." Wiser and better, she now resembled her sister Isabella, and she lived happily ever after, marrying Abu Ferez, who after being boiled in a cauldron, turned into a handsome, desirable young man.[9]

Although it clearly remained the stuff of moral instruction, emblematic material lost much of its doctrinaire Christianity in the company of fairies and giantesses. This separation from religion brought two results. On one hand, emblems gained new instructive power in furnishing matter for children's books. On the other, dissociation from the traditional and the familiar made them and the narratives in which they appeared liable to criticism. Inherent in emblematic material, as in all allegory, was the appeal to the imagination, always a suspect moral guide. In depending upon a fantasy not associated with the religiously familiar, stories containing marvelous telescopes and mirrors could be seen, like fairy tales, as leading the imagination astray. Not only would readers be so attracted by magical devices that they would miss lessons conveyed but they would be led to worlds seductively and unhealthily different from those in which they would spend their lives. There could be "no comparison," the *Monthly Review* claimed, between "the moral utility" of "fable, built on the marvellous, and of those which originate in true pictures of life and manners." [10]

Unlike stories which relied upon the marvelous aspect of emblems, domestic moral tales, which became popular in the late eighteenth century, eschewed the fantastic and described, if not ordinary events, at least the furnishings of middle-class life. A large number of these stories were "mirror" tales, depicting "The Mirror's Pleasing Reflection" and "The Contrast." As Miss Child's glasses or Spirit's telescope revealed the ends of good and bad behavior, so the stories followed the fortunes of good and bad characters. Like *The Enchanted Mirror*, they often described the lives of two sisters, one of whom was beautiful but bad while the other was homely but good. In *The Sugar Plumb* (1787), a poor farmer had two daughters. "A very great beauty," Betsey unfortunately was "very affected, and proud." "She only loved her own dear Self, was hardhearted to the poor, and behaved unmannerly to every one, and would not do any kind of work, for fear of spoiling her fine white hands." In contrast, Laura "had been very handsome before the small-pox; But this disorder had robbed her of her beauty, without giving her much concern, as she put no great value on such a fading flower. She was loved by all her neighbours for she endeavoured to oblige every body, and frequently deprived herself of bread to give to the poor." As good education and virtue invariably brought success, so the good reflection in these domestic "mirror tales" was often rewarded with means and marriage. One day while the sisters were milking cows, "a rich gentleman" passed by on the road. Betsey's beauty was so great that he fell in love and began to court her. Much like the child, however, who read this story and learned that physical beauty was inferior to moral beauty, the gentleman soon discovered Betsey's nature, and he rejected her and married Laura.[11]

Countless variations upon this formula appeared in children's books. In almost all, however, good was rewarded and evil, if not punished, was so chastised that it learned better. Occasionally even something close to magic was included. In *Moral and Instructive Tales for the Improvement of Young Ladies* (1797) appeared the story of two sisters, Arabella and Fanny Delville. "At certain seasons of the year," Arabella "was entirely disfigured by an eruption which had all the appearance of a leprosy." Knowing that beauty would not pave a way for her, Arabella cultivated her mind. In contrast, Fanny, who was lovely, paid little attention to education and became vain and cruel. One day when a poor old woman carrying a heavy load fell in a meadow, she laughed. After Arabella went to the woman's aid and then talked to her, Fanny said scornfully, "I wonder at your meanness, to stand chattering in that manner with such low bred people." In children's books, good deeds were a manifestation of right education and led to happiness. The old woman gave Arabella a bottle containing a medicine that would cure her complexion. Sickening "*at the sight of her sister's increasing charms,*" Fanny stole the bottle. Before throwing it away, though, she applied some of the medicine to her face in hopes of becoming even more beautiful. "But what was her horror and astonishment," Dorothy Kilner wrote, "to see those features, which nature had rendered beautiful, covered over with the most dismal hue! so changed that any one must have believed she had been seven years an inhabitant of the torrid zone." "Too late" Fanny "repented that she had neglected to cultivate those mental charms which lend attraction even to the poor homely face," and for the remainder of her life she was "an object of disgust."[12]

Domestic moral tales were often cluttered with the ordinary, and celebrated simplicity and the natural at the expense of luxury and vanity. In *The Adventures of a Pincushion* (1788), the "Pleasing Reflection" was Hannah Mindful, the daughter of a small farmer. At fourteen Hannah, the oldest of six children, was "a healthy looking country girl." "Her complexion," Mary Ann Kilner wrote, "was burnt by the sun, and her hands hardened by laborious toil; she was not ornamented by dress, though her person was at all times made agreeable by neatness: She had never been taught those graces, which so forcibly recommend the possessor to general observation; but a constant cheerfulness, and a desire of obliging, which was never interrupted by petulance, made her beloved by every one who knew her." "The contrast," Sally, who was a year older than Hannah, "had been a half boarder at a great school near *London*." There she grew vain and luxurious. When she became an orphan, her Uncle Mindful welcomed her to his family. Sadly, she was incapable of appreciating simplicity, and like the different images in Miss Child's glasses, her behavior and that of Hannah showed "what we are, and what we ought to be." [13]

Instead of helping Hannah in the morning with chores, Sally "would disdainfully turn around to sleep." The simple clothes Hannah wore upset Sally, and conversation between Hannah and her resembled a contemporary and secularized version of that between Quarles's Flesh and Spirit. Seduced by the "world in colours," Sally could not appreciate the natural, not only in dress but within herself and others. "O! Hannah," she said, describing her schoolmates' clothes, "had you seen the caps, and feathers, and muslin, and gauze frocks, which they used to wear on a dancing day, and how smart they looked in their silk shoes, or else red morocco ones, you would not wonder that I do not like these great black leather things. Indeed, Hannah, I could cry, whenever I see you and your sisters clothed in such coarse gowns, with your black worsted stockings, and that check handkerchief on your neck, and your round cloth caps, with that piece of linen for a ribbon." After hearing Flesh praise the prism, Spirit responded, "Ah, fool! that doat'st in vain, on present toys / And disrespect'st those true, those future joys." Although her response was not religious, Hannah's reply to Sally was similar in tone. "O, fie, *Sally*!" she said, "that is quite ungrateful for the good things which you are blessed with." Sally responded arrogantly, exclaiming, "What good things?" "Do you call this dowlas shift, this coarse apron, this linsey wolsey gown, *good things*? Or do you call the brown bread we eat, or the hard dumplings you was making just now, *good things*? And, pray, this old worm eaten bed without any curtains to it, and this little window which is too small to admit one's head out, and what a little hole there is, quite crammed full of honeysuckles; or this propped up chest of drawers, or that good for nothing chair with a great hole in the bottom, which you know, *Bet* nearly fell through yesterday, when she got upon it to reach the box which holds her *Sunday* straw hat; do you call these *good things*? because if you do, I am sorry you know no better."

With its simple, wholesome food and useful basic furnishings and with honeysuckle filling the window, Hannah's world was, if not an Eden, certainly a natural garden. Misled by vanity, Sally was not home in the garden and did not listen to Hannah when she, like Miss Child's helpful mirror, urged her to appreciate her surroundings. "I think our bread is as good as any body need wish for," Hannah said, "and I am sure the dumplings you so scornfully mention, will be very well tasted and wholesome. As to the furniture, if it is old, I will answer for its being clean, *Sally*; and my father says he can nail a piece of board over that chair, which will last as many years as the back does." "And as to our clothes, I am sure they are whole and tight," she continued; "they are coarse to be sure, but they are as good as our neighbours, and many a one would be thankful to have such to put on." [14]

Sally ignored Hannah's good sense. Consequently she made a ridiculous, almost contemptible, appearance at the neighborhood "Saloon" of mirrors, Oakly Hall. To celebrate his daughter's eighteenth birthday, Squire Goodall invited his tenants and their families to an entertainment at Oakly Hall. Hannah and her two sisters appeared "as neat as rustick simplicity could adorn them." Each wore a nosegay of flowers, a light brown stuff gown, a white apron, a handkerchief, and a straw hat. Hannah decorated her hat with green ribbons while her sisters decorated theirs with pink. Not satisfied to wear the garnet-colored stuff gown she had been given, Sally waited until the rest of the family left for Oakly Hall, then put on a silk coat which she wore at school. Hannah's waggish brother Jack helped Sally prepare for the party. Although the coat did not fit, Sally did not know it because Jack hid the mirror. When she put on a hat "which exhibited the most tawdry collection of old gauze, bits of ribbon, and slatternly tassels, that can be imagined," Jack praised it, and when Sally was not looking stuck pieces of straw in it. On a ribbon which he pinned to Sally's shoulder, he tied two sheep's feet and so rigged them that Sally would not notice them until he pulled the ribbon and they tumbled down her back and bounced loudly on the floor. Like the woman in front of Quarles's mirror, Sally thought she was "fairer, goodlier, greater" than she was. "The laugh which her appearance occasioned" at Oakly Hall undeceived her, and chagrined she ran away.[15] In *Cobwebs to Catch Flies* (1783), Ellenor Fenn urged parents "if the human mind be a *rasa tabula*,—you to whom it is entrusted, should be cautious what is written upon it." In making use of the matter of traditional emblems, writers were both cautious and experimental and in the process produced shelves of stories.[16]

Notes

*   *   *   *

Many good studies have been and are now being made of children's literature. Those that have helped me in writing this book, however, have been historical and bibliographical. Essential for anyone interested in the historical development of early children's books in English is F. J. Harvey Darton, *Children's Books in England*, third edition, revised by Brian Alderson (Cambridge: Cambridge University Press, 1982). The best concise history of early children's books is Mary V. Jackson's *Engines of Instruction, Mischief, and Magic* (Lincoln: University of Nebraska Press, 1989). Jill E. Grey's learned account of the early school story in her facsimile edition of Fielding's *The Governess* (London: Oxford University Press, 1968) provides a helpful list of school stories published before *Tom Brown's School Days* (1857). For a discussion of Mary Sherwood and nineteenth-century evangelical writers, see M. Nancy Cutt, *Mrs. Sherwood and Her Books for Children* (London: Oxford University Press, 1974) and *Ministering Angels* (Wormley, Eng.: Five Owls Press, 1979). Particularly useful to me were the standard bibliographies of early children's books: Sydney Roscoe, *John Newbery and His Successors, 1740–1814* (Wormley, Eng.: Five Owls Press, 1973); Marjorie Moon, *John Harris's Books for Youth, 1801–1843* (Cambridge: Printed for the Compiler in association with Five Owls Press, 1976); Sydney Roscoe and R. A. Brimmell, *James Lumsden & Son of Glasgow* (Middlesex: Private Libraries Association, 1981); and d'Alte A. Welch, *A Bibliography of American Children's Books, Printed Prior to 1821* (Worcester, Mass.: American Antiquarian Society and Barre Publishers, 1972).

PREFACE

1. Geoffrey Summerfield, *Fantasy and Reason* (Athens: University of Georgia Press, 1985), xi.

195

2. *Nurse Truelove's Christmas-Box* (London: Carnan and Newbery, c. 1770), 22. *Nurse Truelove's Christmas Box*, 2d Worcester ed. (Worcester, Mass.: Isaiah Thomas, 1789), 22.

3. *The Juvenile Story-Teller* (London: James Imray, 1805), 58–63.

1 . ALLEGORY AND EASTERN TALE

1. Mary A. Burges, *The Progress of the Pilgrim Good-Intent, in Jacobinical Times* (London: John Hatchard, 1800), viii. For the conservative reaction in Britain to the French Revolution see my *The Moral Tradition in English Fiction, 1785–1850* (Hanover, N.H.: University Press of New England, 1976). Roger Sharrock, ed., *John Bunyan: Grace Abounding to the Chief of Sinners and The Pilgrim's Progress* (London: Oxford University Press, 1966). Charly Chatter, *The Lilliputian Auction. To Which All little Masters and Misses are Invited* (Philadelphia: Jacob Johnson, 1802), 25–27. *The Twelfth-Day Gift* (London: J. Newbery, 1767), 3–4. *The Important Pocket Book, or the Valentine's Ledger* (London: J. Newbery, c. 1765).

2. Henry MacKenzie, *The Lounger*, 20 (18 June 1785), 80. Stephen Jones, *The History of Tommy Playlove and Jacky Lovebook* (London: E. Newbery, 1793). *The History of Little King Pippin* (Glasgow: J. Lumsden and Son, 1814).

3. John Clowes, *The Caterpillars and the Gooseberry Bush* (Salem, Mass.: Thomas C. Cushing, 1802), 4, 7, 20. *A New Hieroglyphic Bible* (Boston: W. Norman, 1796), ii. *Guardian of Education*, 1 (1802), 381–82.

4. *The Selector: Being a New and Chaste Collection of Visions, Tales, and Allegories* (London: E. Newbery, 1797), 189–92.

5. *The Selector*, 192–97.

6. *Vice in its Proper Shape* (Worcester, Mass.: Isaiah Thomas, 1789), viii, 13–14, 23–27. James L. Axtell, ed., *The Educational Writings of John Locke* (Cambridge: Cambridge University Press, 1968), 114.

7. *The Friends* (Hartford: John Babcock, 1801), 3–7, 17.

8. *Vice in its Proper Shape*, 35–36, 39. Richard Johnson, *Juvenile Rambles through the Paths of Nature* (London: E. Newbery, 1786), 124, 126, 128.

9. *The Adventures of Master Headstrong, and Miss Patient in Their Journey towards the Land of Happiness* (London: J. Harris, 1802), 6, 18–20, 25, 35, 87.

10. For Locke on play and recreation, see chapter three in my *John Locke and Children's Books in Eighteenth-Century England* (Knoxville: University of Tennessee Press, 1981).

11. *The History of Master Jackey and Miss Harriot* (Worcester, Mass.: Isaiah Thomas, 1787), 5, 10, 14–18, 20–27.

12. Sharrock, 182, 302. Chatter, 5–6, 29–30.

13. *The Exhibition of Tom Thumb* (Worcester, Mass.: Isaiah Thomas, 1787), 5–6, 9–11, 34–36.

14. Giles Jones, *The Lilliputian Masquerade, Occasioned by the Conclusion of Peace between Those Potent Nations, The Lilliputian and the Tommythumbians* (Worcester, Mass.: Isaiah Thomas, 1787), 5–9, 15–16, 27, 30–34, 36–37.

15. George Burder, *Early Piety* (New Haven: Sidney's Press, 1806), 7, 9, 13–16, 22.

16. Burder, 34–39, 45, 50–52. For a learned and provocative discussion of Locke's relationship to Methodism and Romanticism, see Richard E. Brantley, *Locke, Wesley, and the Method of English Romanticism* (Gainesville: University of Florida Press, 1984).

17. Mary Sherwood, *The Infant's Progress* (Wellington, Shropshire: F. Houlson and Son, 1821), iv.

18. Sherwood, *The Infant's Progress*, 4–5, 7, 23.

19. Sherwood, *The Infant's Progress*, 35, 37–38, 93–94.

20. Sherwood, *The Infant's Progress*, 112–15.

21. For the influence of the evangelicals, see Ford K. Brown, *Fathers of the Victorians* (Cambridge: Cambridge University Press, 1961).

22. *Modern Arabia Displayed, in Four Tales* (London: J. Harris, 1811), iii. Mme. de Genlis, *Adelaide and Theodore; or Letters on Education* (London: C. Bathurst, 1783), 1, 37, 38.

23. *Monthly Review*, 11 (1793), 153–54.

24. *The Selector*, 160. *Guardian of Education*, 2 (1803), 498.

25. *Hamlain; or, the Hermit of the Beach* (London: E. Newbery, 1799). *Guardian of Education*, 1 (1802), 312, 314–15.

26. Eliza Andrews, *The Manuscripts of Virtudeo* (London: Hatchard, 1801), 115. *The Governess; or, Evening Amusements at a Boarding School* (London: E. Newbery, 1800), 157–59.

27. *The Governess*, 158–61.

28. Edward A. Kendall, *The Adventures of Musul* (Windsor, Vt.: Thomas and Merrifield, 1808), 8, 50, 89, 94–95.

29. Lucy Peacock, *The Adventures of the Six Princesses of Babylon* (London: J. Buckland, 1785), xxvi–xxxi.

30. A Young Lady, *Constance and Caroline* (London: J. Harris and Son, 1823), vi. *Guardian of Education*, 4 (1805), 173. Don Stephano Bunyano, *The Prettiest Book* (London: J. Coote, 1770), 15, 25–27.

31. Bunyano, 19–20, 23–25.

32. Sharrock, 175–76, 182, 302. Bunyano, 33, 43, 52, 60–61.

33. Bunyano, 6–8, 65–68. Sherwood, *The Infant's Progress*, 113.

34. *Guardian of Education*, 2 (1803), 488–89. Clowes, 20. Sherwood, *The Infant's Progress*, iv. *Evangelical Magazine*, 14 (1806), 491.

1. Elizabeth Sandham, *The School-Fellows: A Moral Tale* (London: J. Souter, 1818), vi. Ellenor Fenn, *School Dialogues for Boys* (London: John Marshall, 1783), 1: ix. Sarah Fielding, *The Governess* (London: A. Millar, 1749). Richard Johnson, *The Little Female Orators* (London: T. Carnan, 1770). O. M., *The Village School* (Wellington, Shropshire: F. Houlston and Son, 1817).

2. Roger Sharrock, ed., *John Bunyan: Grace Abounding to the Chief of Sinners and The Pilgrim's Progress* (London: Oxford University Press, 1966), 221. Fenn, *School Dialogues*, 1: 50. Rhoda Wishwell, *The Pleasures of Benevolence* (London: J. Harris, 1809), 36.

3. Mary Pilkington, *Mentorial Tales* (London: J. Harris, 1802), 35. Mary Ann Kilner, *A Course of Lectures for Sunday Evenings* (London: John Marshall, 1783), 1: 18–19.

4. Dorothy Kilner, *The Rotchfords; or, the Friendly Counsellor* (London: John Marshall, 1783), 1: 18. Ellenor Fenn, *School Occurrences: Supposed to have arisen among a Set of Young Ladies under the Tuition of Mrs. Teachwell* (London: John Marshall, 1782), 38–39.

5. Hannah More, *Strictures on the Modern System of Female Education* (London: T. Cadell, Jun., 1799), 1: 12, 14–15. Mrs. and Jane Taylor, *Correspondence between a Mother and her Daughter at School* (London: Taylor and Hessey, 1817), 107. Richard Johnson, *Moral Sketches* (Dover, Del.: William Black, 1802), 32. Fenn, *School Dialogues*, 2: 76–77.

6. *Tales of the Academy* (London: Cowie, 1820), 1: 9, 13–18, 65.

7. Mary Pilkington, *Biography for Boys* (Philadelphia: Johnson and Warner, 1809), 65.

8. More, *Strictures*, 1: 56–57. Mary Wollstonecraft, *A Vindication of the Rights of Woman* (London: J. Johnson, 1792), 5. A Lady, *New and Elegant Amusements for the Ladies of Great Britain* (London: S. Crowder, 1772), 3.

9. Jane West, *Letters to a Young Lady* (London: Longman, Hurst, etc., 1806), 1: 139.

10. Richard Johnson, *The History of Jacky Idle and Dicky Diligent* (Philadelphia: Adams, 1806), 8–11, 23, 26, 28–30, 44, 49, 54.

11. West, *Letters to a Young Lady*, 1: 58, 121. Mrs. and Jane Taylor, 140–41.

12. Fielding, 1–2.

13. More, *Strictures*, 1: 149–50. Miss M. Woodland, *Bear and Forbear* (London: Tabart and Co., 1809), 1. Priscilla Wakefield, *Reflections on the Present Condition of the Female Sex* (London: Darton and Harvey, 1798), 34. Mary Pilkington, *The Disgraceful Effects of Falsehood, and the Fruits of Early Indulgence* (London: J. Harris, 1807), 96–102.

14. Dorothy Kilner, *Anecdotes of a Boarding-School* (London: John Marshall, 1795), 2: 52–64.

15. Mrs. and Jane Taylor, 12–13. Maria Edgeworth, *The Parent's Assistant; or, Stories for Children* (London: J. Johnson, 1800), 3: 4–6, 30, 41–43.

16. West, *Letters to a Young Lady*, 1: 145. More, *Strictures*, 1: 62. *The Mother's Gift: or, a Present for all Little Children* (Worcester, Mass.: Isaiah Thomas, 1787), 2: 48, 66–67.

17. Elizabeth Somerville, *The History of Little Charles and his Friend Frank Wilful* (Litchfield, Conn.: Hosmer and Goodwin, 1808), 26. Anna and John Aikin, *Evenings at Home; or, the Juvenile Budget Opened* (Philadelphia: T. Dobson, 1797), 2: 145–47.

18. *The Friends* (Hartford: John Babcock, 1801), 18–24.

19. Wakefield, *Reflections*, 9. More, *Strictures*, 2: 24.

20. G. Walker, *The Adventures of Timothy Thoughtless: or, the Misfortunes of a Little Boy who ran away from Boarding-School* (London: G. Walker, 1813), 5–6, 9, 16–17, 22–24, 36–38, 47–49.

21. Lucy Watkins, *Sophy; or, the Punishment of Idleness and Disobedience* (Philadelphia: Wm. Charles, 1819), 12.

22. Ernest de Selincourt, ed., corrected by Stephen Gill, *Wordsworth: The Prelude, 1805* (London: Oxford University Press, 1970), 73, 77, 79. Fielding, 1. Wollstonecraft, 246.

23. Priscilla Wakefield, *Juvenile Anecdotes, Founded on Facts* (Philadelphia: Johnson and Warner, 1809), 110. *Boy with a Bundle, and The Ragged Old Woman* (Windham, Conn.: Samuel Webb, 1819), 14. *Wishwell*, 36.

24. Mary Sherwood, *The History of Little Henry and His Bearer* (New York: J. C. Totten, 1819), 8–9.

25. Sherwood, *Little Henry*, 10–13, 14, 16, 18, 24–25.

26. Sherwood, *Little Henry*, 31, 46–47.

27. A. M., *The Way to be Happy* (Glasgow: J. Lumsden and Son, 1819), 35–40. Sharrock, 146. Fenn, *School Dialogues*, 1: ix.

3 · ROBINSON CRUSOE

1. A Lady, *The Little Scholar's Mirror* (London: J. Harris, 1812), 131–39.

2. *Guardian of Education*, 3 (1804), 298. Maria and Richard Lovell Edgeworth, *Practical Education* (Boston: T. B. Wait, 1815), 1: 291–93.

3. *The History of Little King Pippin*, 7–8. Edgeworth, *Practical Education*, 292.

4. Priscilla Wakefield, *Reflections on the Present Condition of the Female Sex* (London: Darton and Harvey, 1798), 63, 142–48. J. Donald Crowley, ed., *Daniel Defoe: The Life and Strange Surprizing Adventures of Robinson Crusoe* (London: Oxford University Press, 1972), 3–4, 38–40.

5. For a discussion of early American editions of *Robinson Crusoe*, see Clarence S. Brigham, "Bibliography of American Editions of *Robinson Crusoe* to 1830," *Proceedings of the American Antiquarian Society*, 67, pt. 2 (October 1957), 137–83.

6. *The Wonderful Life and Surprising Adventures of that Renowned Hero, Robinson Crusoe* (Boston: N. Coverly, 1794), 32. *Travels of Robinson Crusoe* (Worcester, Mass.: Isaiah Thomas, 1786), 6–7, 23–27.

7. Ellenor Fenn, *School Occurrences: Supposed to have arisen among a Set of Young Ladies under the Tuition of Mrs. Teachwell* (London: John Marshall, 1782), 89–92.

8. Dorothy Kilner, *The Holiday Present* (Worcester, Mass.: Isaiah Thomas, 1787), 57–60.

9. *An Alphabet in Prose, Containing Some Important Lessons in Life, For the Use and Edification of all Great and Small Children in New England To Which is Added Tom Noddy and his Sister Sue, A Lilliputian Story* (Worcester, Mass.: Isaiah Thomas, 1798), 24–26.

10. Richard Johnson, *The Adventures of a Silver Penny* (London: E. Newbery, c. 1786), 56–58. Joachim Campe, *The New Robinson Crusoe* (Boston: Thomas and Andrews, 1790), 11.

11. Mary Wollstonecraft, *A Vindication of the Rights of Woman* (London: J. Johnson, 1792), 115–16. *A Birth Day Present; or, a New Year's Gift* (Boston: Caleb Bingham, 1803), 56. *The Book of Games* (Philadelphia: Johnson and Warner, 1811), 27. *The Child's Friend, or Careful Guardian* (London: J. MacKenzie, c. 1790), 16–17. *The Brother's Gift* (Worcester, Mass.: Isaiah Thomas, 1786), 28. Sarah Trimmer, *An Essay on Christian Education* (London: F. C. and J. Rivington, 1812), 53. Campe, 12. Jane West, *Letters to a Young Lady* (London: Longman, Hurst, etc., 1806), 1: 139.

12. Campe, 128. *The Little Islanders* (Philadelphia: Johnson and Warner, 1809), 11, 16, 36.

13. Richard Johnson, *The Blossoms of Morality* (Philadelphia: William W. Woodward, 1795), 78, 81–88.

14. Jane West, *Letters Addressed to a Young Man* (London: Longman, 1801), 1: 20–21. Mary Pilkington, *The Shipwreck; or, Misfortune the Inspirer of Virtuous Sentiments* (London: William Darton, Jun., 1819), 8, 39. Anna and John Aikin, *Evenings at Home; or, the Juvenile Budget Opened* (Philadelphia: T. Dobson, 1797), 6: 309, 312–13.

15. William Sullivan, *The History of Mr. Rightway and his Pupils* (London: William Darton, Jun., 1816), 3, 46–47, 51, 81.

16. Jean Jacques Rousseau, *Emilius and Sophia: Or, a New System of Education* (London: R. Griffiths, 1762–63), 1: 1–2, 16; 2: 59–61.

17. Rousseau, 1: 115. West, *Letters Addressed to a Young Man*, 3: 385–86. Campe, iv, 45.

18. Rousseau, 1: 99–100, 135. Thomas Day, *The Children's Miscellany* (Boston: Spotswood, 1796), 3–8, 13, 36–37.

19. Jane West, *The Advantages of Education; or, the History of Maria Williams* (London: William Lane, 1803), 34; *Letters to a Young Lady*, 1: 139; *The Infidel Father* (London: A. Strachan, 1802), 1: 23–24.

20. West, *The Infidel Father*, 1: 64–69, 82–83.

21. *Tales of the Academy* (London: Cowie, 1820), 1: 137–43, 146, 152, 198–201.

4. THE FOUNDLING

1. Hannah More, *Thoughts on the Importance of the Manners of the Great to General Society*, 4th ed. (London: T. Cadell, 1788), 16–17. Sarah Trimmer, *An Essay on Christian Education* (London: F. C. and J. Rivington, 1812), 67. Mrs. Cockle, *The Juvenile Journal; or, Tales of Truth* (London: J. Harris, 1807), 1. *The Juvenile Story-Teller* (London: James Imray, 1805), 23–24, 27–28.

2. Richard Johnson, *The Juvenile Biographer* (Worcester, Mass.: Isaiah Thomas, 1787), 29–32. Mrs. Rice, *The Nabob* (London: J. Harris, 1807), 3–4.

3. Richard Johnson, *The Foundling; or, the History of Lucius Stanhope* (Boston: Folsom, 1798), 6, 11–12.

4. Johnson, *The Foundling*, 11, 12, 24, 27.

5. Mary Pilkington, *Henry; or, the Foundling* (Philadelphia: James Thackara, 1801), 4–6, 13–15.

6. Pilkington, *Henry*, 16, 41–42, 45–46.

7. Pilkington, *Henry*, 63–64.

8. Barbara Hofland, *Matilda, or the Barbadoes Girl* (Philadelphia: M. Carey and Son, 1817), 8–9, 11, 14. Mary Pilkington, *Tales of the Hermitage; Written for the Instruction and Amusement of the Rising Generation* (Philadelphia: James Thackara, 1800), 13, 16.

9. Pilkington, *Tales of the Hermitage*, 24, 30.

10. Richard Johnson, *The History of Jacky Idle and Dicky Diligent* (Philadelphia: Adams, 1806), 5–6. Barbara Hofland, *The Son of a Genius* (New York: Eastburn, Kirk, and Co., 1814), 12–13.

11. Hofland, *Matilda*, 85. Mrs. C. Mathews, *Anecdotes of the Clairville Family* (York, Eng.: T. Wilson and R. Spence, 1802), 5–6, 61–63, 67–68.

12. Elizabeth Somerville, *Charlotte, or the Pleasing Companion* (New York: T. B. Jansen, 1803), 49, 51–52.

13. Margaret Ives Hurry, *The Faithful Contrast; or, Virtue and Vice accurately delineated* (London: J. Harris, 1804), 1–4.

14. Hurry, 8–9, 14, 20–21.

15. Hurry, 25–26, 29, 33, 36–38.

16. *The History of Tommy Titmouse. A Little Boy, Who became a Great Man by minding his Learning, doing as he was bid, and being good-*

natured and obliging to every Body. Together with the Adventures of the Old Man of the Woods, and other Stories equally pleasing and instructive (Boston: John W. Folsom, 1798), title page, 15–18, 23, 50–52.

17. *Tom Thumb's Folio, for Little Giants* (Boston: Thomas and John Fleet, c. 1780), 2–4. *The Lilliputian History* (London: W. Tringham, c. 1795), 2–3, 5, 10.

18. *Memoir of Jane Evans* (Concord, N.H.: Shepard and Bannister, 1825), 4, 10, 27. Hurry, 36.

19. *History of Henry Fairchild and Charles Trueman* (Philadelphia: Sunday and Adult School Union, 1819), 4, 10, 15–17.

20. *Memoirs of the Lives of Hannah Hill, George Chalkley, and Catharine Burling* (New York: Samuel Wood, 1815), 4. George Hendley, *A Memorial for Children* (New Haven: Sidney's Press, 1806), 6, 19, 66. Rebekah P. Pinkham, *A Narrative of the Life of Miss Lucy Cole* (Boston: James Loring, 1830), 55.

5 . *P A M E L A*

1. Aaron Hill, *The Works of the Late Aaron Hill* (London: Printed for the benefit of the family, 1753), 2: 286, 290. Alexander Thomson, *Essay on Novels; A Poetic Epistle. Addressed to an Ancient and to a Modern Bishop* (Edinburgh: P. Hill, 1793), vi, 4. *Eclectic Review*, 1 (1805), 127. *Christian Observer*, 4 (1805), 45. Thomas Munro, *The Olla Podrida*, 15 (June 23, 1787), 88. Priscilla Wakefield, *Reflections on the Present Condition of the Female Sex* (London: Darton and Harvey, 1798), 148–49.

2. Jonas Hanway, *Virtue in Humble Life: containing Reflections on the reciprocal duties of the wealthy and indigent, the master and servant* (London: J. Dodsley, 1774), 1: vii, xxxvi.

3. Samuel Richardson, *Pamela; or, Virtue Rewarded* (London: Samuel Richardson, 1742), 4: 152.

4. Wakefield, *Reflections*, 58, 61–62. *The Annual Register; or a View of the History, Politics, and Literature of the Year 1759* (London: R. and J. Dodsley, 1760), 424–25. Hannah More, *Strictures on the Modern System of Female Education* (London: T. Cadell, Jun., 1799), 1: 62; *Essays on Various Subjects, Principally designed for Young Ladies* (London: J. Wilkie, 1777), 18–19, 131–32.

5. Samuel Richardson, introduction by William Sale, Jr., *Pamela* (New York: W. W. Norton, 1958), 18. Hannah More, *Thoughts on the Importance of the Manners of the Great to General Society*, 4th ed. (London: T. Cadell, 1788), 116–17. Richardson, *The History of Pamela* (Worcester, Mass.: Isaiah Thomas, 1794), 164–65.

6. Richardson (Norton edition), 324. *The Mother's Gift: or, a Present for all Little Children* (Worcester, Mass.: Isaiah Thomas, 1787), 2: 6–8.

7. *The Mother's Gift*, 2: 14–15, 26.

8. Dorothy Kilner, *Anecdotes of a Boarding-School* (London: John Marshall, 1795), 1: 54–57.

9. Dorothy Kilner, *Anecdotes*, 1: 72–73, 97.

10. Hannah More, *The Two Wealthy Farmers; or, the History of Mr. Bragwell*, in *Cheap Repository Tracts* (London: John Marshall, 1795), part 1: 8, 11, 18–19. *Christian Observer*, 4 (1805), 45.

11. Solomon Sobersides, *A Pretty New-Year's Gift* (Worcester, Mass.: Isaiah Thomas, 1786), 6–10.

12. Charles and Mary Lamb, *Mrs. Leicester's School* (Georgetown, D.C.: Cooper for Milligan, 1811), 13–15.

13. West, *Letters to a Young Lady*, 2: 101–2. *The Infant Preacher* (Newburyport, Mass.: Charles Whipple, 1818), 6, 17, 21–24.

14. Legh Richmond, *The Young Cottager* (London: J. Hatchard, 1815), 6–7, 12–13, 17–18, 34–35, 53.

15. Richmond, 1.

16. Hannah More, *The History of Hester Wilmot* in *Cheap Repository Tracts* (Boston: E. Lincoln, 1803), 2: 365–68, 373–74.

17. More, *Hester Wilmot*, 380–81.

18. More, *Hester Wilmot*, 384–85.

19. More, *Hester Wilmot*, 388–90.

20. *The Lilliputian Magazine* (London: T. Carnan at Mr. Newbery's, 1752), 21–26.

21. Richard Johnson, *The Adventures of a Silver Penny* (London: E. Newbery, c. 1790), 45–48.

22. *The History of Little Goody Two-Shoes* (London: John Newbery, 1765), 21, 23–24, 28, 38, 137–38.

23. *The Renowned History of Primrose Prettyface* (London: John Marshall, c. 1780), 7, 16, 21, 25, 36–37.

24. *Guardian of Education*, 1 (1802), 436. James Lackington, *Memoirs of the first Forty-five Years of the Life of James Lackington*, a new edition (London: James Lackington, 1792), 386–87.

25. Mary Sherwood, *The History of Susan Gray; as related by a Clergyman*, a new edition (Wisbech, Eng.: J. White, 1815), title page. *Guardian of Education*, 1 (1802), 267–68.

26. Prudentia Homespun [Jane West], *The Advantages of Education, or, The History of Maria Williams, a Tale for Misses and their Mammas* (London: William Lane, 1793), 1: preface, 3.

27. West, *Advantages*, 1: 19, 35–36.

28. West, *Advantages*, 1: 132, 171–72.

29. West, *Advantages*, 1: 206–7, 228.

30. West, *Advantages*, 1: 235–36.

31. West, *Advantages*, 2: 21, 67, 169–70, 176.

32. Hanway, 1: xxxvi, 408. Richardson, *The History of Pamela* (Thomas edition), 166–68.

6. SERVANTS AND INFERIORS

1. James L. Axtell, ed., *The Educational Writings of John Locke* (Cambridge: Cambridge University Press, 1968), 114, 227–28.

2. Stephen Jones, *The History of Tommy Playlove and Jacky Lovebook* (London: E. Newbery, 1793), 17, 20–21.

3. Jones, 28, 56–67.

4. Jones, 74–77, 84–87.

5. Mary Sherwood, *The History of the Fairchild Family* (London: J. Hatchard, 1818), 57–58.

6. Hannah More, *Essays on Various Subjects, Principally designed for Young Ladies* (London: J. Wilkie, 1777), 95–96. *A Gift for Children* (Norwich, Eng.: Sterry and Co., 1796), no pagination.

7. Axtell, 228. Mary Pilkington, *A Reward for Attentive Studies* (London: J. and E. Wallis, c. 1800), 7–9.

8. Anna and John Aikin, *Evenings at Home; or, the Juvenile Budget Opened* (Philadelphia: T. Dobson, 1797), 5: 172–78.

9. Maria Edgeworth, *Moral Tales for Young People* (Philadelphia: Johnson and Warner, 1810), 2: 4, 28, 34–35.

10. Edgeworth, *Moral Tales*, 2: 35, 38, 40.

11. Axtell, 228. *The History of Miss Kitty Pride* (Worcester, Mass.: Isaiah Thomas, 1799), 5–11.

12. *Kitty Pride*, 11–18.

13. Jane West, *Letters to a Young Lady* (London: Longman, Hurst, etc., 1806), 1: 291–92.

14. Sarah Trimmer, *Sunday School Dialogues; Being an Abridgement of a Work by M. P.* [Dorothy Kilner] (London: John Marshall, 1784), 19–23.

15. Hannah More, *Patient Joe: or the Newcastle Collier*, in *Cheap Repository Tracts* (Boston: E. Lincoln, 1802), 1: 256–58.

16. Dorothy Kilner, *The Life and Perambulation of a Mouse* (London: John Marshall, 1783), 2: 9, 12–15, 22.

17. Samuel Jackson Pratt, *The Paternal Present* (New York: Robert Moore, 1804), 91–107.

18. Sarah Trimmer, *Sunday School Dialogues*, 23; *The Sunday-School Catechist* (London: T. Longman, 1788), 147.

19. Sarah Trimmer, *The Servant's Friend* (London: T. Longman, 1787), 10.

20. Trimmer, *The Servant's Friend*, 16–18.

21. Trimmer, *The Servant's Friend*, 17–19.

22. West, *Letters to a Young Lady*, 3: 299, 301. Hannah More, *Thoughts on the Importance of the Manners of the Great to General Society*, 4th ed. (London: T. Cadell, 1788), 116–17.

23. Maria and Richard Lovell Edgeworth, *Practical Education* (Boston: T. B. Wait, 1815), 1: 110–13. *The Deceitfulness of Pleasure; or,*

Some Account of My Lady Blithe in *Cheap Repository Tracts* (London: Hatchard, 1798), 4–6.

24. *The Deceitfulness of Pleasure*, 11, 13–15.

25. Jean Jacques Rousseau, *Emilius and Sophia: Or, a New System of Education* (London: R. Griffiths, 1762–63), 1: 140–41. Mary Wollstonecraft, *A Vindication of the Rights of Woman* (London: J. Johnson, 1792), 329. Axtell, 154, 164, 187, 228. *A New Gift for Children* (Boston: Fowle and Draper, 1762), 7–8.

26. Axtell, 171. *The Mother's Gift: or, a Present for all Little Children* (Worcester, Mass.: Isaiah Thomas, 1787), 1: 33–34.

27. Rousseau, 3: 200. Wollstonecraft, 30. Thomas Day, *The History of Sandford and Merton* (London: J. Stockdale, 1783), 1: 1–3; (1789), 3: 295.

28. Arnaud Berquin, *Biography for Boys, or Interesting Stories for Children* (New Haven: Sidney's Press, 1808), 47–51.

29. Berquin, 56–59.

7 . L I A R S   A N D   T E L L - T A L E S

1. James L. Axtell, ed., *The Educational Writings of John Locke* (Cambridge: Cambridge University Press, 1968), 114, 239, 241–42, 244.

2. Dorothy Kilner, *Letters from a Mother to her Children* (London: John Marshall, c. 1780), 1: 156. Mary Pilkington, *The Disgraceful Effects of Falsehood and the Fruits of Early Indulgence* (London: J. Harris, 1807), vi. *The Fairing* (Worcester, Mass.: Isaiah Thomas, 1788), 34.

3. Maria Budden, *Always Happy* (New York: William B. Gilley, 1816), 46, 48. William MacKenzie, *The Academy* (London: J. Harris, 1808), 116.

4. MacKenzie, 66–68, 77.

5. *Martin and James; or, the Reward of Integrity* (Philadelphia: H. and P. Rice, 1794), 5–7, 9.

6. *Martin and James*, 22–23, 32, 35.

7. *Martin and James*, 37, 43–46.

8. *Martin and James*, 48–49, 58–59.

9. *The Two Boys; or, The Reward of Truth* (Philadelphia: Bailey for Johnson and Warner, 1810), 5–8.

10. *The Two Boys*, 11–12, 19–21, 23, 26.

11. *The Two Boys*, 27, 30, 32, 35–36.

12. Dorothy Kilner, *First Going to School; or the Story of Tom Brown and His Sisters* (London: Tabart and Co., 1804), 3, 10–11.

13. *Guardian of Education*, 4 (1805), 412. Little John, *The History of Little Dick* (Philadelphia: Bailey, 1793), 13–16, 28, 57. *Friendly Advice, on the Management and Education of Children* (London: John Hatchard and Son, 1824), 37–38.

14. Axtell, 255. *The Friends* (Hartford: John Babcock, 1801), 8–10.

15. Axtell, 256. *The Holiday Present* (Worcester, Mass.: Isaiah Thomas, 1787), 82–84, 86, 93–99.

16. Mary Hughes, *Aunt Mary's Tales for the Entertainment and Improvement of Little Boys* (New York: D. Bliss, 1817), 4.

17. Mary Ann Kilner, *The Adventures of a Pincushion* (Worcester, Mass.: Isaiah Thomas, 1788), 30, 41–42.

18. Mary Ann Kilner, *Pincushion*, 42–49.

19. Anna Kent, *York House* (London: Francis Westley, 1820), 19, 22, 28, 180–85.

20. Sarah Trimmer, *Sunday School Dialogues; Being an Abridgement of a Work by M. P.* [Dorothy Kilner] (London: John Marshall, 1784), 52. *The History of Mary Wood* in *Cheap Repository Tracts* (Philadelphia: B. and J. Johnson, 1800), 3, 7–8, 10.

21. *Mary Wood*, 11–14.

22. *Mary Wood*, 15–19.

23. *Mary Wood*, 27–33.

24. *Mary Wood*, 33. Priscilla Wakefield, *Juvenile Anecdotes Founded on Facts* (Philadelphia: Johnson and Warner, 1809), 143–47.

25. Budden, *Always Happy*, 46–47. *The New Friend of Youth* (New Haven: Sidney's Press, 1803), 16. Axtell, 241. *The Mother's Gift: or, a Present for all Little Children* (Worcester, Mass.: Isaiah Thomas, 1787), 2: 14–15.

26. Maria Edgeworth, *Tarlton* in *The Parent's Assistant* (Georgetown, D. C.: Joseph Milligan, 1809), 1: 51–52, 55, 64–65.

27. Edgeworth, *Tarlton*, 76–78, 83, 85.

28. Sarah Fielding, *The Governess* (London: A. Millar, 1749), vii, xiii–xiv.

29. *First Impressions; or, The History of Emma Nesbit* (London: J. Harris, 1814), 50, 55, 59–61, 66–67.

30. *First Impressions*, 93, 96–101, 118.

31. *Letters Written by the Right Honourable Philip Dormer Stanhope, Earl of Chesterfield to his Son* (London: J. Dodsley, 1774), 2 vols. *The Accomplished Youth* (London: B. Crosby and Co., 1811). *Lord Chesterfield's Maxims* (London: E. Newbery, 1786), "a new edition."

32. John Potter, *The Words of the Wise* (London: Francis Newbery, 1768), v.

33. *The Gospel Magazine, or Treasury of Divine Knowledge*, 3 (1776), 487–88.

34. *Guardian of Education*, 2 (1803), 425. Maria and Richard Lovell Edgeworth, *Practical Education* (Boston: T. B. Wait, 1815), 1: 172. Jane West, *The Infidel Father* (London: A. Strachan, 1802), 1: 144–45; 3: 305, 307, 311.

35. Maria Budden, *Valdimar; or, the Career of Falsehood* (London: J. Harris and Son, 1820), 4, 8, 79.

36. Budden, *Valdimar*, 13, 17, 31–35.

37. Budden, *Valdimar*, 34–35, 201, 327.

38. *The Brother's Gift* (Worcester, Mass.: Isaiah Thomas, 1786), 5–6, 23–24. Mrs. and Jane Taylor, *Correspondence between a Mother and her Daughter at School* (London: Taylor and Hessey, 1817), 2, 6–7, 82.

39. Mrs. and Jane Taylor, 92–93.

40. Mrs. and Jane Taylor, 93. Mary Ann Kilner, *Memoirs of a Peg-Top* (Worcester, Mass.: Isaiah Thomas, 1788), 76.

A P P E N D I X : *Emblems in Early Children's Books*

1. *Guardian of Education*, 3 (1804), 298. For my approach I am indebted to Barry Qualls. His *The Spiritual Pilgrims of Victorian Fiction* (Cambridge: Cambridge University Press, 1982) is splendid and should be of interest to all concerned about the relationship between Christianity and literature.

2. John Bunyan, *Divine Emblems: or, Temporal Things Spiritualized. Fitted for the Use of Boys and Girls* (New York: James Carey, 1794), 68. Francis Quarles, *Emblems Divine and Moral* (London: H. Trapp, 1777), 71, 142–43. Those interested in emblem books for children in the eighteenth century should consult John Huddlestone Wynne, *Choice Em blems, Natural, Historical, Fabulous, Moral, and Divine, for the Improvement and Pastime of Youth* (Philadelphia: Joseph Crukshank, 1790). Wynne's book was very popular in the eighteenth century; it did not, however, contain emblems of the telescope or vanity mirror.

3. Abraham Chear, *A Looking-Glass for Children. Being a Narrative of God's gracious Dealings with some little Children*, 4th ed. (London: J. Marshall in Gracechurch-street, 1708), 27, 30–31, 42. Arnaud Berquin, *The Looking-Glass for the Mind*, comp. Richard Johnson (Providence, R. I.: Carter and Wilkinson, 1794), preface.

4. Margaret Roberts, *The Telescope; or, Moral Views for Children* (London: Darton and Harvey, 1804). Harriet English, *The Faithful Mirror* (London: E. Newbery, 1799), 15–16, 18, 30–31, 33, 45–47.

5. Don Stephano Bunyano, *The Prettiest Book* (London: J. Coote, 1770), 52, 55. Charly Chatter, *The Lilliputian Auction. To Which All Little Masters and Misses are Invited* (Philadelphia: Jacob Johnson, 1802), 9–12.

6. *The Exhibition of Tom Thumb* (Worcester, Mass.: Isaiah Thomas, 1787), 12–14, 21–24.

7. Mme. de Genlis, *Adelaide and Theodore; or Letters on Education* (London: C. Bathurst, 1783), 1: 57–58. Ellenor Fenn, *The Fairy Spectator; or, the Invisible Monitor* (London: John Marshall, c. 1790), 7, 10.

8. Fenn, 16, 21–27, 31, 38–39.

9. *The Enchanted Mirror, a Moorish Romance* (Hartford: B. and J. Russell, Jr., 1814), 3–4, 6, 33, 54–55.

10. *Monthly Review*, 11 (1793), 153–54.

11. *The Sugar Plumb; or, Sweet Amusement for Leisure Hours: Being an Entertaining and Instructive Collection of Stories* (Worcester, Mass.: Isaiah Thomas, 1787), 79–80.

12. Dorothy Kilner, *Moral and Instructive Tales for the Improvement of Young Ladies* (Leominster, Mass.: Charles Prentiss, 1797), 112, 117–18, 120–23.

13. Mary Ann Kilner, *The Adventures of a Pincushion* (Worcester, Mass.: Isaiah Thomas, 1788), 80, 88. Fenn, *Fairy Spectator*, 21.

14. Mary Ann Kilner, *Pincushion*, 80–85. Quarles, 142–43.

15. Mary Ann Kilner, *Pincushion*, 92, 95, 97. Quarles, 71.

16. Ellenor Fenn, *Cobwebs to Catch Flies* (London: John Marshall, 1783), 1: ix.

Index

*   *   *   *

References to illustrations are in
italic type.

Locke, John, vii, 1, 73, 78, 100,
134; on early education, 5, 9,
50, 52, 53, 60, 61; on
children's delight in change,
9, 17; and publishers, 9, 14; on
amusement and instruction,
14, 158–60; criticism of, in
Infant's Progress, 18–19; and
collections of stories, 17; on
servants, 125, 144; on
truth, 148

M.,A.: *Way to be Happy*, 56–57
M.,O.: *Village School*, 32
MacKenzie, Henry: *The
Lounger*, 2
MacKenzie, William: *Academy*,
149–50
Martin and James, 150–52
Mathews, C.: *Anecdotes of the
Clairville Family*, 89–90
Memoir of Jane Evans, 95
*Memoirs of the Lives of Hannah
Hill*, 96
Modern Arabia Displayed, 21
Monthly Review, 21–22, 190
More, Hannah, viii, 34, 81, 101,
102, 128, 180; and female
virtues, 41–42, 48; on luxury,
45; *Two Wealthy Farmers*,
105–6; *History of Hester
Wilmot*, 111–14; *Patient Joe*,
135; *Thoughts on the
Importance of the Manners of
the Great*, 141–42;
Deceitfulness of Pleasure, 142–
43; *History of Mary Wood*,
164–68, 169
Mother's Gift, 45, 102–4, *103*,
144–45, 169–70
Munro, Thomas, 99

Newbery, Elizabeth, 99, 176
Newbery, Francis, 176
Newbery, John, 2, 17, 114

Newbery and Carnan, ix, 99, 119
New Friend of Youth, 169
New Gift for Children, 144
New Hieroglyphic Bible, 3
*Nurse Truelove's
Christmas-Box*, ix

Only child: dangers of, 82

Pamela, ix; criticism of, 98–99;
as fable, 99–100; and society,
100–102; and education, 100–
106, 120; and prayer, 102–3,
104–5; and godly books, 111
Peacock, Lucy: *Adventures of the
Six Princesses*, 25–27
Pilkington, Mary: *Mentorial
Tales*, 33; *Biography for Boys*,
37, *38–39*; *Disgraceful Effects
of Falsehood*, 43, 149;
Shipwreck, 71; *Henry; or, the
Foundling*, 85–87; *Tales of the
Hermitage*, 87–88, 120;
*Reward for Attentive
Studies*, 129
Pinkham, Rebekah: *Narrative of
the Life of Miss Lucy Cole*,
96–97
Potter, John: *Words of the
Wise*, 176
Pratt, Samuel: *Paternal Present*,
137–38

Qualls, Barry, 207 (n.1)
Quarles, Francis: *Emblems
Divine and Moral*, 182–84,
192, 194

*Renowned History of Primrose
Prettyface*, 117–19, 124
Rice, Mrs.: *Nabob*, 82–83
Richardson, Samuel. See
Pamela

Richmond, Legh: *Young
Cottager*, 110–11
Roberts, Margaret:
Telescope, 185
Robinson Crusoe, ix, *63*, 82, 90,
99, 128, 182; industry in, 58–
59, 60–64, 68–69, 70–76;
dangers of, 59–60; as
Christian, 60; as Locke's
infant, 60; and Bettering
Society, 60–61; Wakefield on,
61–62; and rambling, 64, 65,
68; sequels, 64; and
disobedience, 65–66, 67–68;
and idleness, 68–69; loss to
gain, 70–73; Rousseau on, 73–
74; impracticality of,
78–80
Romanticism, 158; of child, 106–
8; and religious child,
109–14
Rousseau, Jean, 75, 77–79, 143–
44, 145; *Emilius and Sophia*,
73–74, 76, 77

Sandham, Elizabeth:
School-Fellows, 31
School stories, ix; and allegory
and eastern tale in *Prettiest
Book*, 27–29, 31; little world
of, 31–32, 57; firmness in, 32,
34, 41, 54, 172–75; duty to self
in, 32–33; popularity and
ridicule in, 33–34; difference
for boys and girls, 34–35, 41–
45, 48, 169–70, 173; fighting
in, 35–37, 41–42, 43–45, 48,
130–32, 139–41, 182; and
aristocracy, 35–37, 43, 47–48;
luxury and luxurious behavior
in, 40–41, 45, 46–47; and
passive virtues, 41–45; and
rural life, 46; and lower and
middle classes, 35–36, 47–48,
130–32; and educational

progress, 48–54; on
disobedience, 48–53; and
imagination and character,
52–56; dishonesty in, 153–55;
and high spirits, 155–58; and
idleness, 157; games and
knowledge in, 158–60; and
telltales and lying, 168–73;
and friendships, 173–75
Selector, 3–4, 22
Separation of man from animal,
5–7, 43–44
Servants, ix; Locke on, 125, 144;
cruelty toward, 126–28;
kindness toward, 128–29, 130–
32; and social mobility,
132–41; in school, 139–41;
influence of luxury on, 141–
43; Rousseau on, 143–44;
danger of, 144–47
Sherwood, Mary, 27, 29, 95;
Infant's Progress, 18–21, 34;
Little Henry, 54–56; *History of
Susan Gray*, 119–20; *History of
the Fairchild Family*, 127–28
Sobersides, Solomon: *Pretty
New-Year's Gift*, 106–7
Somerville, Elizabeth: *History of
Little Charles*, 46; *Charlotte*,
90
Sturm, Christoph: *Reflections on
the Works of God*, 61
Sugar Plumb, 190–91
Sullivan, William: *History of
Mr. Rightway*, 72–73
Summerfield, Geoffrey, viii
Sunday School Movement, 134

Tales of the Academy, 35–37, 49,
78–80, 86
Taylor, Mrs. and Jane:
*Correspondence between a
Mother and her Daughter*, 34,
42–44, 180–81
Thomas, Isaiah, ix, 64–65, 78

Thomson, Alexander: *Essay on Novels*, 98
Tom Jones, 83–85
Tom Thumb's Folio, 94
Trimmer, Sarah, viii, 59, 81, 119–20, 156, 182; *Guardian of Education*, 3, 22–23, 27, 29, 118–19, 177; on allegory, 3, 22–23, 29; *Family Magazine*, 61; *Essay on Christian Education*, 69; *Sunday School Dialogues*, 134–35, 138, 164; *Sunday School Catechist*, 138; *Servant's Friend*, 139–41; *Two Farmers*, 139–41
Truth: Locke on, 148; and lying, 148–50, 164; rewards of honesty, 150–52; and dishonesty at school, 153–55; punishment of lying, 160–62; and disobedience, 162–64; and lower classes, 164–68; and promises and telltales, 168–73; and aristocratic life and Chesterfield, 175–80
Twelfth-Day Gift, 2, 17
Two Boys, 153–55, *154*, 160

Vice in Its Proper Shape, 5, 7, 10, 189

Wakefield, Priscilla, 48, 54, 67, 100–101; *Reflections on the Present Condition of the Female Sex*, 43, 61–64, 99; *Juvenile Anecdotes*, 53–54, 168–69
Walker, G.: *Adventures of Timothy Thoughtless*, 48–51, 56, 74, 92, 157
Watkins, Lucy: *Sophy*, 51
West, Jane, 141; *Letters to a Young Lady*, 40, 41, 45, 69; *Letters Addressed to a Young Man*, 71, 74, 76; *Advantages of Education*, 76, 120–24; on false expectations, 120; *Infidel Father*, 76–77, 177–78; on fashionable education, 134
Wishwell, Rhoda: *Pleasures of Benevolence*, 32
Wollstonecraft, Mary, 40, 52, 68, 144, 145
Woodland, M.: *Bear and Forbear*, 42–43
Wordsworth, William, viii, 52, 73, 74, 109
Wynne, John, 207 (n. 2)

Young Lady, A.: *Constance and Caroline*, 26–27